THE
CREATIVE THEOLOGY
OF P. T. FORSYTH

THE
CREATIVE
THEOLOGY
OF P. T. FORSYTH

Selections from his works

edited by
SAMUEL J. MIKOLASKI

WILLIAM B. EERDMANS PUBLISHING COMPANY
GRAND RAPIDS, MICHIGAN

CONTENTS

Introduction   7

   I: P. T. Forsyth: The Man and His Faith   9

  II: The Theological Task   15

 III: Revelation   30

  IV: God   55

   V: Christ   71

  VI: Creation   91

 VII: The Work of Christ   121

VIII: The Christian Life   161

  IX: The Church   191

   X: Eternal Life   245

      Bibliography   262

INTRODUCTION

The revival of interest in the writings of Peter Taylor Forsyth (1848-1921) is a significant feature of contemporary theology. He is best known for his passionate concern with the theology of the Atonement, and with vital Christian experience in contrast to formal religion. But he wrote equally well on Religious Authority, History and Revelation, the Church, the Sacraments, the Person of Christ, Art, and other subjects.

These selections from his writings will serve to introduce the reader to Forsyth's major ideas and works. The bibliography includes the books from which the selections are drawn. For biographical data on Forsyth, note may be taken of my essays "The Theology of P. T. Forsyth," and "P. T. Forsyth on the Atonement" (*Evangelical Quarterly*, XXXVI, Nos. 1 and 2, 1964) ; and the chapter entitled "P. T. Forsyth," in *Creative Minds in Contemporary Theology* (ed. P. E. Hughes [Eerdmans, 1966]). All readers of Forsyth are indebted to his daughter, Jessie Forsyth Andrews, for the memoir of her father published in the second edition of *The Work of Christ*, pp. vii-xxviii.

The influence of Forsyth has been great, not only within the Free Church movement, but also beyond it, including Continental and American theology. That his views are parallel to those of other nineteenth-century evangelicals, especially R. W. Dale and James Denney, is no occasion for surprise, though they developed their views largely independently of his. Contemporary independent parallels may also be noted, including the work of Leonard Hodgson, late Regius Professor of Divinity in the University of Oxford. The late Canon J. K. Mozley has freely acknowledged his indebtedness to Forsyth. Professor Emil Brunner of Zürich not infrequently alludes to Forsyth. As I have indicated elsewhere, there appears to be an important, early influence of Forsyth on the young Dr. Brunner while the latter was in England (1913-14). The effect of this upon subsequent "Crisis Theology" in Europe has yet to be investigated more fully.

His style of writing will trouble some, but those who take care to probe his meaning will be rewarded richly. The sheer intellectual vigor of the man is astounding. With this is coupled a contagious devotion to Jesus Christ as his Redeemer and Lord.

I: P. T. FORSYTH: THE MAN
AND HIS FAITH

Might I venture here to speak of myself, and of more than thirty years given to progressive thought in connection, for the most part, with a pulpit and the care of souls. Will you forgive me? I am addressing young men who have the ministry before them, as most of mine is behind, strewn indeed with mistakes, yet led up of the Spirit.

There was a time when I was interested in the first degree with purely scientific criticism. Bred among academic scholarship of the classics and philosophy, I carried these habits to the Bible, and I found in the subject a new fascination, in proportion as the stakes were so much higher. But, fortunately for me, I was not condemned to the mere scholar's cloistered life. I could not treat the matter as an academic quest. I was kept close to practical conditions. I was in a relation of life, duty, and responsibility for others. I could not contemplate conclusions without asking how they would affect these people, and my word to them, in doubt, death, grief, or repentance. I could not call on them to accept my verdict on points that came so near their souls. That is not our conception of the ministry. And they were people in the press and care of life. They could not give their minds to such critical questions. If they had had the time, they had not the training. I saw amateurs making the attempt either in the pew or in the pulpit. And the result was a warning. Yet there were Christian matters which men must decide for themselves, trained or not. Therefore, these matters could not be the things which were at issue in historic criticism taken alone. Moreover, I looked beyond my immediate charge, and viewed the state of mind and faith in the Church at large — especially in those sections of it nearest myself. And I became convinced that they were in no spiritual condition to have forced on them those questions on which scholars so delighted and differed. They were not entrenched in that reality of experience and that certainty of salvation which are the position of safety and command in all critical matters. It also pleased God by the revelation of His holiness and grace, which the great theologians taught me to find in the Bible, to bring home to me my sin in a way that submerged all the school questions in weight, urgency, and poignancy. I was turned from a Christian to a believer, from a lover of love to an object of grace. And so, whereas I first thought that what the Churches needed was enlightened instruction and liberal theology, I came to be sure that what they needed was evangelization, in something more than the conventional sense of that word. "What we need is not the dechurching of Christianity, but the Christianizing of the Church." For the sake of critical freedom, in the long run that is so. Religion without an experimental foundation in grace readily feels panic in the presence of criticism, and is apt to do wild and unjust things in its terror. The Churches are not, in the main, in the spiritual condition of certainty which enables them to be composed and fair to critical methods. They either expect too much from them, and then turn upon them in disappointed anger when it is not forthcoming. Or they expect so little from them that they despise them as only ignorance can. They run either to rationalism or to obscurantism. There was something to be done, I felt, before they could freely handle the work of the scholars on the central positions.

And that something was to revive the faith of the Churches in what made them Churches; to turn them from the ill-found sentiment which had sapped faith; to reopen their eyes to the meaning of their own salvation; to rectify their Christian charity by more concern for Christian truth; to banish the amiable religiosity which had taken possession of them in the name of Christian love; and to restore some sense not only of love's severity, but of the unsparing moral mordancy in the Cross and its judgment, which means salvation to the uttermost; to recreate an experience of redemption, both profound and poignant, which should enable them to deal reasonably, without extravagance and without panic, with the scholars' results as these came in. What was needed before we discussed the evidence for the resurrection, was a revival of the sense of God's judgment-grace in the Cross, a renewal of the sense of holiness, and so of sin, as the Cross set forth the one, and exposed the other in its light. We needed to restore their Christian footing to many in the Churches who were far within the zone which criticism occupies. In a word, it seemed to me that what the critical movement called for was not a mere palliation of orthodoxy, in the shape of liberal views, but a new positivity of gospel. It was not a new comprehensiveness, but a new concentration, a new evangelization, that was demanded by the situation.

But the defective theological education of the ministry seemed to put a great obstacle in the way of such a revival as I have described. For, incredible as it may seem to many, and even alarming, theology was (for reasons on which it would be ungracious for me to enter) not only distrusted, but hated by many of the stewards of the Θεοῦλόγος. And I have longed and prayed to see the man arise to alter all this, with an equal knowledge of his sin, his Saviour, and his subject, to do the work that had to be done in rearing men with a real, thorough, humble and joyous belief in their own message, and to do it on a scale to compel the attention, and even the concern, of our Churches.

Meantime my own course seemed prescribed. It was, in the space of life, strength, and work which was yet mine, to labor as one who waited for that messianic hope, and to try to persuade those who would hear to join me in preparation

for so great a gift of God. I withdrew my prime attention
from much of the scholar's work and gave it to those theological interests, imbibed first from Maurice, and then more
mightily through Ritschl, which come nearer to life than
science, sentiment, or ethic ever can do. I immersed myself
in the logic of Hegel, and corrected it by the theology of
Paul, and its continuity in the Reformation, because I was
all the time being corrected and humiliated by the Holy
Spirit. My faith in critical methods is unchanged. My acceptance of many of the new results is as it was. This applies to
the criticism of traditional dogma no less than of Scripture.
But the need of the hour, among the only circles I can reach,
is not that. The time for it will come, but not yet. It is a slow
matter. For what is needed is no mere change of view, but a
change and a deepening in the type of personal religion,
amounting in cases to a new conversion. There is that amiss
with the Churches which free criticism can never cure, and
no breadth or freshness of view amend. There is a lack of
depth and height, an attenuation of experience, a slackness
of grasp, a displacement of the center, a false realism, a dis-
location of perspective, amid which the things that make
Christianity permanently Christian are in danger of fading
from power, if not from view. In a word, I was driven to a
change of front though not of footing — to the preacher's and
the pastor's treatment of the situation, which is also the New
Testament view, and which is very different from the scholar's. The savant may or must frame results and utter them
regardless of their public effect, but the preacher may not.
The order of truth he deals with has its own methods, his
office has its own pedagogic, and his duty its own conscience.
In most cases the best contribution the preacher can make
at present to the new theology is to deepen and clear the old
faith, and to rescue it from a kind of religion which is only
religion and hardly Christian faith. What has often passed as
the new theology is no more, sometimes, than a theology of
fatigue, or a theology of the press, or a theology of views, or
a theology of revolt. Or it is an accommodation theology, a
theology accommodated only to the actual interests of the

cultured hour.[1] The effort made is to substitute for the old faith something more human in its origin, more humane in its temper, and more halting in its creed, something more genial and more rational and more shallow. It is that rather than the effort to deepen the old theology by a sympathetic reinterpretation, which pierces farther into its content of revelation, and speaks the old faith in a new tongue. The tongue is new enough, but it is not certain that it speaks the old thing, or develops its position from a profounder acquaintance with the holiness of the love of God within the Cross. It analyzes the Bible, but it does not reconstruct from the Bible, but from what is known as the Christian principle, which is mainly human nature re-edited and bowdlerized.

I am sure no new theology can really be theology, whatever its novelty, unless it express and develop the old faith which made those theologies that are now old the mightiest things of the age when they were new. Well do I know how little a theology in itself can do, and how the mighty doer is the living faith. But I know well also that that faith is not the real thing unless it compels and loves an adequate theology; and if it cannot produce it, it dies. I know well also how seldom it is really objections to an outworn system that keep men from Christ, and retard the gospel. I am sure that, if we had a theology brought entirely up to date in regard to current thought, we should not then have the great condition for the kingdom of God. It is the wills of men, and not their

---

[1] While I was writing this I read the address of an estimable preacher of up-to-date theology who was demanding that the theologians should come down and accept a theology imposed by three things — physical science, historical study (especially as to the origin of the Bible), and comparative religion. Well, these results are pretty familiar to most of us by now, and very sterile. But you will hardly believe that there was not a word about the study of the gospel, our application to the contents of Christ's revelation of God, the implications of His idea of God, or the principles of His work. No, that would have put the preacher beside the theologians. He would have had to ask questions about what was meant by God's most holy love in Christ, questions which no science of nature, history or religion can answer. Our spiritual shyness of God's holiness has more than something to do with the ordinary reaction against theology.

views, that are the great obstacle to the gospel, and the things most intractable. The power to deal with those wills is the power of the gospel as the eternal act of the will and heart of God. And the power of the gospel as a preached thing is shaped in a message which has had from the first a theological language of its own creation as its most adequate vehicle. To discard that language entirely is to maim the utterance of the gospel. To substitute a vocabulary of mere humane sympathies or notions for the great phrases and thoughts which are theology compressed into diamonds is like the attempt to improve a great historic language, which is a nation's record, treasure and trust, by reducing it to Saxon monosyllables, and these to phonetics. I cannot conceive a Christianity to hold the future without words like grace, sin, judgment, repentance, incarnation, atonement, redemption, justification, sacrifice, faith and eternal life. No words of less volume than these can do justice to the meaning of God, however easy their access to the minds of modern men. It needs such words to act on the scale of God and of the race. And the preacher who sets to discard them or, what is more common, to eviscerate them, is imperilling the great Church for a passing effect with the small. For a living and modern theology our chief need is a living and positive faith, moving in those great categories, and full of confident power to absorb and organize the sound thought of the time. To rouse and feed this faith is the great work of the preacher. And thus the service the preacher does to theology is at least no less than the service theology does to him. A mere theology may strain and stiffen the preacher. But the preacher who is a true steward of the Christian Word makes a living theology inevitable, which, because it lives, demands new form and fitness for each succeeding time.

(*From* Positive Preaching and the Modern Mind, *pp. 192-198.*)

II: THE THEOLOGICAL TASK

HETERODOXY AND ORTHODOXY

I tried once in an article in the *Hibbert Journal* (January 1910) to indicate the difference between heterodoxy and heresy. I suggested that the former had a place permanent and precious in a Church of theological progress, while the other not only had no such place, but was made heresy by the fact that it destroyed the Church idea, that is, the social idea, and disconnected Christianity from a society. And as the Church was made by the Word of the New Testament gospel, which remains its authoritative element, the Church-destroying thing was that which destroyed that Word, by stripping it of its unique quality, its historic finality, its absolute redemption, and by reducing it to be but the upper level of the other religions of the world, or the general religiosity of the race. It reduced Christianity to be one among many religions, *prima inter pares,* though one that did more justice than the others did to certain spiritual instincts which they were all trying to express or meet. It made any form of religion but a tentative expression of something *in* man, something real however latent, instead of an authoritative revelation of something *to* man, final however progressive. To that article I might venture to refer some who may wish to raise questions here. I pointed out that there was a large and valuable range within the Church for a heterodoxy which yet maintained the evangelical continuity, and which declared the reality of a historic and moral redemption of the race in the Cross of Christ. Such a heterodoxy is still one with the Church in that solidarity of apostolic tradition which centers in the absolute Word and not in its successive prophets, in a historic point and not a historic line. Fixed there, a great Church, like a great oak, may be flexible everywhere else, and stronger against storms than a stiff tower. But to be loose there is not to be flexible but vagrant. It is to have no root, no revelation, anywhere, in the strict, true, and final sense of that word. And no liberty is legitimate which does not spring from, or consent with, the liberty that historically gave the Church its being — the evangelical liberty of the guilty soul in its experienced salvation by the grace of a holy God in the Cross of Jesus Christ, now risen and reigning in the glory He had before all worlds.

I would here approach the matter from another point of view.

Criticism has of late passed into a new phase which really makes its results a new religion rather than a new stage, a new ship rather than the old docked and scraped. And it would send the Church out with no hold of anything, with only a progressive sympathy. We are presented with the religious-historical method. This is not an extension of the old method, but the creation of a new. And it is really less critical than dogmatic in its inspiration. The older criticism was, often at least, compatible with the recognition of a unique and final revelation in the Gospel of Jesus Christ. It left possible a liberal theology. It had room for the recognition of a final intervention of God at a point of history. It stripped away, indeed, a good deal that belonged to that historic moment, by its free handling of the Bible which carried the gospel. Primitive Christianity was found to have been much colored by the influences, and bound by the limits, of that age, that land, and the lands around. Pure revelation was muffled in many of the hulls of the popular religion amid which it rose. Inspiration was a challenge to current religion, and not its incandescence. But criticism did not feel that it must treat the trappings as the horse, or the current as the picture. It thought that it was possible and necessary to clear Christianity both of contemporary alloy and later accretions, and yet to preserve the distinctive, real, and final revelation of God in Christ. The secondary elements, the merely historic, could be detached, and the primary, the superhistoric, the evangelical, be all the more free and effective. There was a core of absolute revelation not traceable to, and not explicable through, any other influence than the actual and unique visitation of God redeeming in His Son. This was the foundation of the Church and the charter of its pulpit; and all its progress in theology or elsewhere was the expansion of this.

But criticism has entered a new and more dogmatic phase. The starting-point is not the objective gospel of the Church but the subjective religion of Humanity. The general principles which form the precipitate of ideas in all religions are now held to account for Christianity also; which is but another and a finer mythology of them, accidentally attached to a certain Jewish rabbi of whom little may be really known. Christ is a mythology built around Jesus, as a pearl upon grit; and religion did more to produce Christ than any Christ did to produce religion. The Church was not a creation by God's unique act in Christ, but a social product from certain redemptive ideas that seized the world with an epidemic force quite peculiar to those lands or days. Christianity is thus levelled down in authority, even while its refinement in idea is recognized. It loses in power as it gains in poetry; as in the modern representations of Macbeth, all the terror and sublimity of a deed brief but endless is lost in the effort to clothe it with intimacy and beauty. It is called more spiritual than the rest, but it is not therefore more real, not more sure as a revelation of God, or as a special act of His, to say nothing of a final, and one crucial for our fate. There is nothing wherewith to prove the spirits whether they be of God. It is but relatively different from other faiths.

It is less original and independent at its heart than we were taught. We can at most speak only of the independence of religion, not of the independence of Christianity at all. And any authority of the Church is not only archaic but odious in an age of fraternal sympathy and individual liberty. All spiritual events are entirely and equally subject to the general laws of historical evolution. Historical science forbids us to allow any real branch of the evolutionary method in the most significant personality. All that happens in the spiritual region must be explained immanently, i.e., from the nature of spiritual Humanity. And Christ Himself can only be received insofar as He conformed more fully to the laws of that nature elsewhere shown. His spiritual knowledge He reached along the same lines as other men. Christ is explained by history, not history by Christ. The Church made Him more than He the Church. He is the product of the Church more than its provider to this day. There is no history of redemption apart from the ascending history of the race developed with God's aid. Christ is more an expression of whatever revelation there may be in Humanity than of any revelation to it. The reality or the possibility of a constant revelation in everything we establish on other grounds, if we can, and then go on to find its classic instance in Christ. Not only are miracles banished from revelation, but the miracle of revelation as redemption is abolished. It does not invade us and new create us. It only fulfils us and gives us effect. It does not regenerate. And the Church rests upon no initial miracle of the resurrection, and upon no standing miracle of the Spirit. It cannot speak down to the old creation from the new.

That is the latest phase of historical and critical science applied to the origin of Christianity. Its treatment has gone far beyond the secondary elements of faith; it has plucked the source of Christianity out of its native heaven and made it natural to earth. But in doing so it has surely proclaimed another religion and dissolved the apostolic Church. It is not a valuable heterodoxy, but a fatal heresy. It has surely stepped over the line of freedom in any true Church, by dissolving the Church into a mere continuous vitality, stripped of the central, positive, and creative Word which keeps its vitality up, and reinforces it constantly by the Holy Spirit.

And to press the right of such a position in the teaching of an evangelical Church is to provoke a bitterness that was vanishing from mere theological difference. For heresy in itself does not now make trouble, except when it appears as treason. Attacks from without must be quite differently viewed than betrayal within.

(*From* The Principle of Authority, *pp. 219-223*.)

RELIGION AND THEOLOGY

Christianity at least cannot live without a theology which sets forth such a revelation. It is impossible there to separate religion from theology, man from God's purpose, faith from grace. It can only be attempted at the cost of one of them. The object of Christian faith is a theological God, or else He is not Holy Love. It is impossible to separate the questions, "Whom do you trust?" and "What do you believe about Him?" For the latter only means, "For what do you trust Him?" We only trust Him in a theological function — as our Saviour; not simply as our Father — that is not Christianity — but as the Father of the Eternal Son and sole Redeemer. .

The word theology is here used with some care, and with particular reference to its historical base. It is the intelligible content, the inevitable statement (spreading out to the elaborate exposition), of the act and person given in a historic revelation. If we discard that historic base, and still pursue the scientific interest, the matter of religion may be treated in two ways. Either it is taken in hand by a rationalism in which it is trimmed down to the laws indigenous to formal thought; or it is given over to a theosophy in which the matter itself is provided by an intuitive knowledge somewhat intractable to logical control. So that while rationalism ceases to be Christian, theosophy ceases to be scientific. There is no doubt that the latter — an intuitive idealism — is the favorite resort of the hour. It seems to offer a generous escape from hard rationalism on the one hand and from hard orthodoxy on the other. And it does it in a way in which the individual seems to himself able at once to indulge his individuality of standard, to escape from external authority, and to preserve a mysticism of atmosphere and a stamp of reason.

Of course, the word theosophy is not here used in the current sense which suggests India. It means any idealist creed whose subject matter is provided by present intuition, genial or intellectual, rather than historic revelation, and which refuses the limitations of the mere understanding in the freedom of the speculative reason. It claims for its ideas a reality which belongs to no mere abstraction or projection of thought but to Being as thought. But it does not escape the arbitrariness of imagination. Both rationalism and theosophy, logic and intution, are too inward to be other than arbitrary. They do not release us from the ban of our subjectivity. We do not escape to a real object who approaches and seizes us, loves and saves. And they agree in their impotence for social purposes. They belong to single thinkers (like all culture), or to groups and schools at most. They do not create a Church; nor can they keep one alive. But theology, on the other hand, is the statement, simple or scientific, of a living revelation given at a historic point, creating its own society, and persisting in a continuous social experience. It is not the science of the Christian experience, which would be no more than a Christian psychology, or a phenomenology of the Christian spirit. But it is the science of such a historic and self-communicated God as is given only in the region of our experience in receiving Him, and especially in the region of a Church's collective experience. It is superhistoric in the field of history, and superegoist in the field of our own experience. And its content is God's supreme act and deed of self-bestowal toward mankind in a racial Redeemer through a universal Church. In a theosophy (like Hegel's system) what we use is the intuition of thought by thought, in theology it is the intuition of a person by faith. In the one we have an ideal monism, thought discovering itself everywhere; in the other we have a moral dualism, in which a person finds another person by

way of salvation and not mere discovery. In the one case
it is the intuition of truth in a mind, in the other the intuition of personality in a community.

Without some theology based on a historic revelation
Christianity cannot even be spoken of, and cannot live. And
it must grow to be a theology on a scale corresponding to
the centrality of the revelation, i.e., corresponding to its
finality.[1] For a revelation central to the *whole* of human
history, past or future, must be final. And, if Christianity
represents the final revelation, then the Christian theology
flowing from it must be universal. That is to say, not merely
empirically universal, but ideally — universal in its nature,
and not simply in the extent of its recognition. It must be
adequate and adjustable to the whole knowledge, action,
and destiny of the race. It must at least have the aspect, not
indeed of final form, but of final greatness and command.
And the Church will always be inferior in a thinking world
till it acquire and handle such an adequate creed with a
dogmatism mightier, sharper, and sweeter than the world's
own.

(Ibid., *pp. 211-214.*)

THEOLOGICAL METHOD

There is one misunderstanding I should like to avert.
When I speak of a reduction of belief I do not mean an
attenuation of belief. I do not mean to discredit an ample
theology. I do not think of consigning the greater part of
faith's area to the region of agnosticism, and compelling
the mind to be satisfied with a few general principles. By
the reduction of belief I mean reducing the amount of our
claim upon the belief of the public, shortening the articles
of association, so to say. I do not mean that every truth of
theology should be capable of verification by experience —
the preexistence of Christ is not. Theological truth is far
wider than experience. But I do mean that we should not

---

[1] I have in my mind the frequent distinction between a prime theology
which is the plain and fundamental *statement* of the revelation, and a
secondary which is the swelling *exposition* of this central truth in terms
of the Church's growth in experience and culture. It is the latter I have
chiefly in view here.

base the Church's appeal to the public upon truths which are outside experience — meaning Christian experience. In asking people to concentrate more upon what we offer we cease asking them to attend to what they have not means of understanding. We ask them to go in upon their moral experience with more earnestness and resolution. We would remove their interest from things they are incompetent to solve, and kindle it on matters that appeal to their own soul, conscience, and destiny. So that what we offer is not so much a new system of theology as a new pronunciation of theology. It is theology uttered with a change of accent. The stress is differently distributed. The emphasis falls on other parts of the great Word. We certainly would escape from the monotone of a whole system of equal value and obligation in all parts. And we would dwell with but minor force upon some truths which are not so much saving truths as their corollaries. If I took an example of what I mean, I would say that we ought to restore to Christ's atoning Cross much of the popular interest so easily arrested by His birth and its manner. We should lean but lightly on the virgin birth, which does not make a moral appeal to us, but too often appeals to a ready interest either in a baby or a miracle; and we should bear far more heavily on the center of all moral action and regeneration in the Cross, which the popular mind so readily shuns because there the world is crucified unto us and we unto the world. And a like transfer of emphasis should take place from the truth of Christ's preexistence, which is outside the range of our experience, to that of His risen and royal life, wherein we ourselves are made partakers of His resurrection and vouchers of His real presence. So that in the order of importance we should go to the world first of all with the atoning Cross, which is the Alpha and Omega of grace; second, with the resurrection of Christ, which is the emergence into experience of the new life won for us on the Cross; third with the life, character, teaching, and miracles of Christ; fourth with the preexistence of Christ, which is a corollary of His eternal life, and only after such things with the virgin birth, which may or may not be demanded by the rest. It is not a case of denying any of these points or even challenging them. They may all be accepted, but let it be in their true perspective, the perspective of faith. And they are offered to the public, and belief is claimed, in the degree of their relevancy to a vital Christian experience of the one Christian doctrine of grace. For when we carry reduction to its length we condense upon that one principle and power of grace which has in it the promise of the potency of all the soul's life and all Christian truth.

(*From* Positive Preaching and the Modern Mind, *pp. 86-88.*)

The living Christ who died has destroyed my guilt, and brought me God. That is not the action of the resurrection but of the Cross. I believe that the divine power in Him which wells up in my faith, rather than the irrepressible vitality of His divine "nature," is the power by which Christ rose. But it is still more the power by which He gained His finished victory on the Cross. Without the primary theology of the Cross the resurrection of Christ would have no more value than a reanimation. The most present and real fact of our Christian faith is the fact accessible to faith alone. It is the fact that Christ has brought us God and destroyed our guilt. You do not yet know the inner Christ who are but His lovers or friends. You need to have been His patients and to owe Him your life. That is Christianity. A Church without that experience at its center is not Christianity. What makes a Church Christian is not the historic fact of His death, but the theological, spiritual, experimental fact that His death meant that, and did that, and ever does it. Where there is no such experience it is hard, if not impossible, to convince anybody that His death was more than the close of His life, or the sealing of His witness with His martyr blood. But as a present fact that evangelical action of Christ's death is far more real, and therefore more effective, with us than the death of any Jewish martyr at Roman hands 2,000 years ago. Therefore dogmatic conviction of this kind may have a great effect on criticism, but criticism has only a minor effect upon it. We may be led to recast some of our ideas as to the historical conditions amid which the great life and death transpired. We may modify much in our views as to Christ's omniscience, and similar things affected by His emptying of Himself. He accepted some of the limitations of human ignorance. He consented not to know, with a nescience divinely wise. The story is all recorded in a book, and therefore literary criticism has its rights. Christ worked through history, and in the concretest relation to the history of His race and age; and, in so far as you have history, historic criticism has its rights. Christ lived a real, and therefore a growing, human life, as a historic personality. Therefore, being in psychological conditions, He is amenable so far to psychological criticism. But allowing for all such things, the question remains dogmatic, Was He, is He, what Christian faith essentially believes? Did these convictions, of His and of the Church, correspond to reality? Was He, is He, in God what He thought He was, and what He was held to be? When the first Church worshipped Him with God's name, and set Him on God's throne, were they a new race of idolaters? Was his influence so poor in quality that it could not protect them from that? He thought Himself redeemer; did He really redeem? Did God redeem in Him? Was God the real actor in His saving action? These are the questions; and in all such questions, criticism is *ultra vires*. These things are settled in another and higher court, and criticism must work under that settlement. The soundest criticism is the criticism by a believing Church, daily living on the grace of the Cross and the venture of faith.

It is quite true that these truths become dogmas which, in their statement, are fair matter for criticism. The theology of the Church is not a closed product of the Holy Spirit, any more than the Bible is a closed product of verbal inspiration. A process of criticism, adjustment, and correction has always been going on. Theology, on the whole, has been constantly modernized. But it all proceeds on the basis of a reality above logic and beyond criticism, the reality of experienced redemption in the Cross, of faith's knowledge, and the Church's communion with Christ. It is thus something within dogma itself that is the great corrective of dogma. Christian truth in a Church carries in itself the conditions, and the resources, of its own self-preservation through self-correction. The Church's dogmatic faith is the great corrective of the Church's dogmatic thought. The religious life in a risen and royal Redeemer is always ahead of the religious thought about the nature and method of redemption. The old faith is always making theology new. The true critic of Christian history is its primary theology. You expected me perhaps to say the true critic of a Christian theology is its history. But that is now a commonplace. I meant something less obvious. It is a theological Christ we have centrally to do with — an atoning Christ. And it is only a theological Christ that we need take immense pains to preserve for the future. It is that piece of experienced theology, an atoning, reconciling, redeeming Christ, that has made all the rest of theology. And it must therefore be its living test. With historical criticism, simply as a branch of exact science, pursued by the scholars, and taught in the schools, you have as preachers only a minor concern. You may take it up as you might any other science, only as your nearest pursuit. But you do not wait on it for your message. You must deliver that message while the critics are still at war. Christ is there and urgent, whatever is happening to the story of Christ. A knowledge of criticism may help you to disengage the kernel from the husk, to save the time so often lost in the defense of outposts, to discard obsolete weapons and superfluous baggage, and to concentrate on the things that really matter for eternal life and godliness — like the reconciliation of the Cross. All true science teaches us also its own limits, and so destroys its own tyranny. But the real criticism with which we have to do, from which all our religion starts when we take the whole Christian field into account, is not our criticism of Christ, but Christ's criticism of us, His saving judgment of us. The higher criticism casts us on the highest. There is a secondary theology of corollaries from faith, and there is a primary of faith's essence. To handle this great and primary theology the first condition is the new man. Our most judicious thing is to treat Christ as our judge, to know Him as we are first known of Him, and to search Him as those who are searched to the marrow by His subtle Spirit.

(Ibid., pp. 189-192.)

THEOLOGY AND EXPERIENCE

Appeals are made to us not to omit in all our activity to cultivate the spirit of devotion. Appeals of the kind are useless. Devotion which is cultivated to preserve our balance is not devotion. The only devotion worth having is that which is made inevitable by the nature of faith as itself the fontal devotion, an act of obedience far more than a state of experience, a submission to a real objective with a native right and power to rule us from the center.

In like manner we are familiar with pulpit appeals for more love, more trust, more sympathy, more of the whole gamut of Christian ethic and piety. We are told what Christianity means. It is not presented to us as Christ. I know we are told it is Christ, and we are to imitate Him. But imitation is not obedience. It is rather independence. And even while we are told that Christianity is Christ, the method of the preaching does not correspond to that phrase. "Believe, believe," is the whole tone of many a fruitless preacher. It is bound to be fruitless. It is asking, urging people to lift themselves by their own waistband. It is ignoring the fact that both faith and repentance and all Christian experiences are supernatural things, are the gift of God. Let us cease imploring or commanding people in a forcible, feeble way to believe and to love. These things are not at our volition. Let us offer men not appeals but gifts. Let us come with the gift of a real gospel. Look to the gospel and it will see to the experiences. Don't beg men to believe in Christ; put before men a Christ that they cannot help believe. It is not so easy. It is easy enough to utter appeals with more or less ardor — I will not say passion. It is easy, though not so easy, to impress men with the spell or fervor of our own enthusiasm, or even our own real experience. But it is not so easy to take home the gift of God to ourselves in Christ that we may carry it to others with its native and exclusive power to stir the love, the trust, the penitence which we try to flog up in vain. To preach Christ is not to declare our experience of Christ only or chiefly. It is so to study Christ and His gospel, so to wind ourselves into His slow, yielding secret, that from a problem He becomes a power to us, and we become not only His witnesses, but His sacraments. Propagandists have faith as an ardor, and prophets have it as an insight. But the apostles have it as personal obedience to a personal revelation of a gospel. And there are more propagandists and prophets than apostles. Little of your preaching lacks religiosity, but some of it does lack religion, which loses the inspiration of the man in the revelation of the message. It has every other grace, but lacks faith.

I fear I am forgetting the text set me by the power here, which I have not only to experience, but to obey. I am speaking about preaching when I am charged to speak about theology. Well, to tell the truth, I find it hard to speak of theology to an audience like this, and in twenty minutes. Strict theology is a matter of lectures more than of addresses. And no lecture is of any use under an hour. But I have not really lost my bearings. When I say that the type of faith which was engrossed with subjective experience is making way for a type which centers in objective obedience, I am saying, in other words, this — that in religion experience comes to the ground if it be not sustained by a theology. I mean more than historic facts. I mean facts which are theological even more than historic. You can have a godly soul without much theology, but you cannot for long have a godly Church. It will become a feeble Church, and then a worldly Church; it will not have grit enough to resist the externalism of the world, its clear definitions and its positive ways. The inner man which really copes with the world is not merely the pious sympathetic man, but the man permeated with the power of an objective gospel and its facts and truths. It is our objective base that the formidable critics assail; and we shall never secure our case against them by escaping into the subjective piety of a Christian consciousness. It must be clear that by theology I do not mean something distilled from experience, but something presented, revealed to experience as its source, however condensed or implicit. The theology of experience is one thing — that is Schleiermacher; it is the theology which explicates the Christian consciousness. But the experience of theology is another thing, and it is the experience which explicates the Christian gospel. And the great movement which arose out of Schleiermacher to correct Schleiermacher, the movement associated with the principle of Ritschl (and going far beyond this system), is the movement to an objective gospel carrying a theology that does not arise in experience, but only makes its appeal to experience.

. . . .

What we need is a theology that creates an obedient experience rather than experience that creates an interpretive theology. What is created from Christian experience is theologoumena rather than theology. Of course I understand by any experience which is used as the basis of theology the positively Christian experience of the regenerate man, and not mere experience of the world, or of life, or of the humanist pieties and ideals. But even the positively Christian experience of a quite new life cannot be the basis either of a gospel or of a theology. What can be such a basis is Christ's experience and that of those in first and direct contact with His person and work. The value of our experience as a base, or even as a test, is small; it is too narrow, it is too variable, it is too impure. The fundamental thing is not experience, but the *a priori* element in experience; the thing of which we have experience; the datum revealed in it and to it; the thing which produces our experience, the object of our faith. Faith is the great thing; and faith is not an experience in the sense of a mood, but as response to a revelation. It is there in great measure to save us from our experiences as subjective states, and to enable us to do without them on occasion, as our Lord did in the world-saving moment of the dereliction on the cross. Besides, some of the greatest convictions of our faith are beyond the range of our possible experience. What can experience tell us of the preexistence of Christ? What can it tell us of the final victory of Christianity in history, and the consummation of all things in the coming kingdom of God? Can any experience assure us that

all things work together for good to love except an experimental faith in the love that has reconciled all things to Himself, and constantly sees in Christ a reconciliation hidden to
us? The reconciliation of faith and experience exists but in
the object of our faith — the Reconciler. What we need is,
not to see a reconciliation by Christ, but to experience
heartily Christ as the reconciliation. Again, is Christianity
the highest we have come to? Experience says Yes; comparative religion says Yes; the historic-religious method says
Yes. But is it the highest we can come to? Is it a final revelation? Is it absolute? To that question what can experience
say? But is there any doubt that New Testament Christianity
claims to be final and absolute? It does not contemplate the
possibility of another and more adequate gospel. Such was
the experience of Christ, and, through Him, of the apostles.
But was Christ's experience here a mere part (though the
highest part) of human experience Godward? The Christian
contention has been that Christ's experience was not man's
so much as God's in man. He is a revelation in terms of
human experience, but not a revelation of the resources of
human experience. We go back to history not only to
correct the Christian experience, but to found it, and to give
it something to crystallize on. And we have this in the historic Christ, who is now neither debris left by the pyrrhonist
critics on the one hand nor a mere part of history on the
other, but an eternal reality in history. Christ corresponds
in history to the *a priori* element given in individual experience. He is above the relativity of comparative methods.
These and such things belong to our faith and not our experience, to the grand venture and not to the verification.
Faith, indeed, is experimental or nothing. But we have
surely got beyond the error which confuses faith with
experience. A faith merely experimental becomes merely
empirical, and at last dies of secularity.

(From "The Place of Spiritual Experience in the Making of Theology,"
pp. 71-76.)

III: REVELATION

THE DIVINE ACTION IN HISTORY

In Christ God does not simply announce Himself, and He cannot be preached by a mere announcement. He gives no mere revelation about Himself. The revelation *about* God is the bane common both to orthodoxy and to rationalism. Both are the victims of that intellectualism. What we need, what God has given, what preaching has to convey, is Himself. It is sacramental work. His revelation is His actual coming and doing. He is there *in* Christ, not *through* Christ. Revelation is self-communication; and it is self-communication which is not the mere offer of Himself but the actual bestowal of Himself, His effectual occupation of Man-soul and not His mere claim of it, not the soul's opportunity but the soul's seizure by an act of conquest. God is the matter of His own revelation; and, therefore, He only succeeds if he wins, not the soul's assent, but the soul itself. If it was Himself He gave, it is man's self He must have. And He is not really revealed to man, for all His outgoing, till He receive that answer, till He redeem, and return upon Himself with man's soul for a prey. Revelation must take effect in restored communion. God is not really opened to me till He opens me to Him.

All this is only possible if revelation and preaching be much more than declaration. Revelation must be an act. Reality is action. *Im Anfang war die That.* Christ spoke far less of love than he practiced it. He did not publish a new idea of the Father — rather He was the first true Son. Christ as God's revelation is God's act; and our conveyance of Christ in preaching is Christ's act. Otherwise, God's love would be a mere lenient word, or a mere affection on His part, lacking in moral energy and in power to give effect to itself. God then would not fully identify Himself with the human case. He feels for men, and speaks to them, but He does nothing. He sends, but He does not come. This sending, no doubt, is a great thing, but it is not a gospel that inspires preaching in the high and powerful sense, in a sense commensurate either with tragic humanity or a triumphant Church. And the philanthropy based on this, prolific as it may be for a time, has not a future, for lack of staying power. The divinest love which could not put its whole self into a saving act might but wring its hands on the shore, or wade a little in, as many do, who mean the very best, but who can only tickle the evil of a world with which they cannot grapple. When we preachers ask about the revelation of God's love what we ask for is its deed.

Remember above all things that the love we have to do with is holy love. And holiness is the eternal moral power which must do, and do, till it see itself everywhere. That is its only satisfaction and atonement, not the pound of flesh but entire absolute response in its own active kind. And that is what we have in Christ as our head.

(*From* Positive Preaching and the Modern Mind, *pp. 239-240.*)

Thus we can never settle the question of a final moral authority (which is the last authority of all) except in the region where will meets will and faith takes home God's act of grace. It is quite insoluble in the region where cosmic process takes the place of moral action, or in the region where conscience responds but to an ideal, or reason accepts truth.

It is not with truth we have to do but reality. And reality is
a moral thing, a matter of a person, and his will, and his
act. Life in its reality is a great act and choice, and not a
long process. And therefore, the authority is not a standard,
as a truth, or an architecture of truths, might be. It is a living
law. And a living law, not in the sense of a historic institution, acting as the custodian of truth, and the trustee of its
development. It is a living, holy, historic God and Saviour
witnessed, preached, and truly conveyed, by the whole
Church, but dispensed by none. It is a living and holy God
in much more than presence (which were mere mysticism).
It is God in power, in moral power, in historic and sempiter-
nal action. It is a God real in a historic act, which is perpetual in its energy, achieved at one point but throbbing at
every other, a timeless act, parallel with every human action,
and mutually involuted with it (if one may so say), but
involved in the way of struggle and conquest rather than
mere permeation — an eternal Cross rather than a universal
Spirit. It is this act that is prolonged as the arduous emergence through history of that kingdom of God, which, for all
its immanence, is much more a gift to history than its
product. The last authority is God in His supreme, saving
act of grace to mankind in Christ's Cross, which is the power
of God addressed to what is at once the power and the
weakness in us, our will, conscience, and total moral self.
Our last authority is something we can only obey by sub-
jugation, reconciliation, and worship, and not by mere
assent. It is that saving act of God which makes all our best
moral action possible. It is an invasion of us, however inward, it is not an emergence from us; nor is it merely the
stroke upon our hard shell which releases our innate divinity.
It is an invasion, creative more than tonic, redeeming
rather than releasing, putting into the Soul a new mainspring and not disentangling the old which had caught.

                                        (Ibid., *pp. 42-43*.)

   In positive revelation we have to do with two things.
The one fact has two constituents. We have, first, the history
or the manifestation, and we have, second, the inspiration

or the interpretation of the history. We have, first, God entering the world, and we have, second, this entry of God entering man. We have the fact, and we have the word of the fact. The fact we have in Christ; but the word of it, the meaning of it, we have in believers and apostles moved by Christ. And especially in the apostles, whose insight becomes itself a fact, in turn, working upon believers from faith to faith. So that we have three things — first the incarnate fact, then, the word or interpretation of it by apostles, and, thereby, the fact again, but the fact enshrined in the soul of the believing Church. To use philosophical terms, we have the thesis, planting itself out in an antithesis, and then reclaiming, recovering itself in a synthesis. We have, first, the fact incarnate, then the fact interpreted, and then the fact enthroned. But we must have the word as well as the fact, if the fact is to do anything with men. The word is an essential part of the fact, or, let us say, an essential function of it. It is the act reacting on itself. It is the vast, eternal action of Christ reverberating in the consciousness of His apostles. It went out as power and returns as light, doubling back luminously upon itself, as it were, to search its old track by this inspiration. Only in such a sense is the incarnation prolonged in the Church. The total revelation needs the inspiration as well as the manifestation, the thought no less than the thing, "The fact without the word is dumb; and the word without the fact is empty."

Now it is only with the interpretation of the fact that inspiration has to do, and not with the fact itself; for we do not speak of Christ the fact as an inspired man. Nor has it directly to do with the establishment of the fact as a fact. Inspiration has not to do with information but with insight. It has to do entirely with the theology of the matter, and not with its historicity. What a pagan or mantic notion of inspiration they must have who use it to discredit theology, who in the name of truth discredit interpretation by afflatus. The facts in the Bible were established by the usual means, as in Luke's case (Luke 1:1). But the meaning of the fact — that is the field of inspiration. The fact of the Cross, for instance, is established by the ordinary historic evidence;

but it was no ordinary means that enabled Paul to see its interior — the atonement, the centrality, and the finality of it for Christ's work. The idea of propitiation, for instance, was in Judaism and its ritual. That is something of which we have the due historic evidence. The inspiration of the apostle was not in discovering the idea; it was in seeing its real truth and consummation to be in the fact and act of Christ. The idea had at last become historically and finally effective in Christ. The fact of the Cross was seen to mean that consummation. Yet the insight was the result of that fact's own peculiar nature, working on Paul's peculiar nature, through the Lord the Spirit. So that the New Testament writings are really a part of that fact; just as the Old Testament is an essential part of Israel's history, and not merely a description, nor only a product of it. The apostles read God's will in the fact of Christ; but it was from a height of faith to which that fact had raised them. Christ by His work made them saints, and by the inspiration of His Spirit He made them theologians. The inspiration of the Redeemer gave them that understanding. They saw the deep things in Christ under the moral coercion of the fact and its nature, under its creative and illuminative action on them. It reorganized their whole conceptual world by giving it a new vital center, and therefore a new reading. They saw a new world because a new king was on its throne. And it was a vital and creative center. There was new vision, not simply a new point of view, because the eyes that saw it were the eyes of new men.

(*From* The Person and Place of Jesus Christ, *pp. 159-161.*)

The kingdom of God in Christ is the key of all history, and the Church has the power of that key. It was the revelation which made both that first made a comprehensive view of history possible. The first to construct a philosophy of history was St. Paul, by his theology of universal redemption. The only final unity of man is objective in God's purpose of grace, not subjective in the touch of nature, which makes us often more kin than kind. Had that redemption by grace been but mystic illumination, and had

the coming of Christ been but light, there would have been
no such vision of universal history, and no such institution
as a Church to correspond. For the inner light is but
atomic; it lights each several soul; and its breadth is but
multitudinous, it is not organic. It is cosmopolitan, it is
not Catholic. But the revelation in Christ was action much
more than light. It was redemption, not illumination. It
was power, and social power, it was not mere presence. It
was therefore a matter of history, where men do act, and
not of thought, where they do not. It intended not a new
sect but a new Humanity, which was to put out on the
stream and not preach from the shore. In so doing it was
bound to make mistakes, but not such mistakes as if it did not.

Two great mistakes have certainly been made about
revelation. First it has been treated as if its element were
truth and not action. It has been offered as something to
hold instead of something to obey. It has been thought to
be a notional theology (or still worse a theosophy) instead
of a moral energy of God. It has regarded Christ as the
great theophany instead of the great — I wish the word
theurgy had not been stolen for mean uses, it is what I
want here. And the second mistake about revelation has
been to treat it as the divine arcanum of a Church instead
of the moral key to the whole of history, and the regeneration of the whole of Humanity. No wonder people do not
care about redemption or regeneration when they have been
made to regard such words as the technical terms for certain
processes that were the secret of certain spiritual syndicates.
How are we ever to reclaim words like these for their true
Christian use? There are many thinking men who are driven
to believe that *the* interest of Humanity is the historic
and moral interest; how are we to convince them that the
supreme interest of that conscience is that it should be
redeemed? That is a question we cannot stop to discuss
here. But this may be said. So long as the Cross is regarded
as a device for the benefit of a few instead of the moral crisis
of the race, so long will its advocates seem but sectaries
without moral purchase on the race. So long as the kingdom of God is regarded as but the extension of a private

company's operations (as many view missions), so long also will it be an ineffectual thing. It will be regarded as one of many rival enterprises, all pushing to the front, instead of the suzerain and overlord of them all. And it will be left to its luck in the struggle. But it is not the extension of a private enterprise promoted to increase the shareholders of a joint-stock religion. It is the dominant power and final goal of history, if there be a God, if He has most to do with history, if His holy morality is the nature of things, if His Son is not simply the Head of the Church but the King of Humanity, if His Cross is the turning-point of moral being. We can only get mankind to attend to the kingdom of God if we can make it appear for what it is — the inmost core, the ruling principle, the moral ultimate, the spiritual dominant, the new creation, and the final purpose of Humanity. And the theology of the Church must be adjusted thereto, the message of the Church must be so delivered, the nature of the Church must be so defined. The regeneration it preaches is *the* moral issue of the world. Only thus can we change the German view of Humanity, as manure for the intensive culture of favored races, to the Christian view of it as a family of nations to be loved, gospelled, and saved. The real organizing principle of the race is what it is in Christ — the life of the kingdom of God. The coming of the kingdom is the growing organization of spiritual Humanity under the Church's moral gospel and King of holy love. It is the moralizing of every affection, thought, and enterprise by the *Holy* Spirit — which, if it do reside in the Church, yet goes to business daily in the national world.

(*From* The Church and the Sacraments, *pp. 101-103.*)

THE BIBLE

Bible preaching then means that we adjust our preaching to the people's disuse of the Bible. We have to regain their interest in it. It is, therefore, not the preaching of doctrine with proof passages. It is not preaching which does the Bible the lip homage of taking a text. Nor is it simply preaching historic facts on the one hand, or personal experience on the other. But it is the preaching of those facts and

gifts of grace which are experimentally verifiable and creative
of experience. It is only on points so verifiable that the Bible
can be doctrinally used by the laity. A fact like the virgin
birth is not at all on the same footing as the resurrection
of Christ, who is met as the risen Lord by His disciples to
this day. Christianity is not the religion of a book, though
it is a book religion. Nor is it the religion of a Church,
though it is a Church religion. But it is the religion of a
gospel and a grace. These are the facts that make the
Church. Doctrine as doctrine is a precious and indispensable
possession of the Church, but it was not such doctrine that
made the Church. Neither ideas nor truths do that, but only
persons and powers. Nor does such doctrine make the great
changes of the Church. The Reformation was not a reformation of theology, but of faith. It is remarkable how little of
the theology it changed in its first stage. It was the renewed
action, not of truth, but of grace. It was the greatest of
evangelical revivals. That is why it rediscovered the Bible.
It was not the Bible that lighted up grace for Luther, but
grace to his needy soul lighted up the Bible. Biblical preaching preaches the gospel and uses the Bible, it does not preach
the Bible and use the gospel.

For the gospel the Bible must be used. The minister
must so live in it that he wears it easily. One reason why
people are repelled from it is that the preachers cannot
carry it with easy mastery. They are in Goliath's armor.
Now the ideal ministry must be a bibliocracy. It must know
its Bible better than any other book. Most Christians hardly
know their Bible at first hand at all. They treat it with
respect, no doubt. They keep a great Bible in the house;
but it is on a little table, not very steady, in the parlor
window, and it has stiff clasps. It is in the room least used; it
carries a vase of once pretty flowers; and it gets in the way
of the rich lace curtains. Which is all an allegory. Some
preachers know it only in the way of business, as a sermon
quarry. But the true ministry must live on it. We must
speak to the Church not from experience alone, but still
more from the Word. We must speak from within the
silent sanctuary of Scripture. We do not realize always how

eager people are to hear preaching which makes the Bible
wonderful by speaking from its very interior, as men do who
live in it and wonder themselves. I do not believe in verbal
inspiration. I am with the critics, in principle. But the true
minister ought to find the words and phrases of the Bible so
full of spiritual food and felicity that he has some difficulty
in not believing in verbal inspiration. The Bible is the
one Enchiridion of the preacher still, the one manual of
eternal life, the one page that glows as all life grows dark,
and the one book whose wealth rebukes us more the older
we grow because we knew and loved it so late.

(*From* Positive Preaching and the Modern Mind, *pp. 25-26.*)

There are some who recognize in Christ's death no action
beyond what it had, and has increasingly, upon mankind.
It did not act on God but only from Him. Those who
so think may be particularly asked what provision Christ
made that a work with that sole object should be secured
to act on history, and should not go to waste. He wrote
nothing Himself. If He had it could not well have included
the effect of His death — unless He had done with a post-
humous pen what my plea is He did by His apostles. He
did not even give instructions for a written account which
should be a constant source for the effect on us intended
by His life. Nor did He take any precautions against per-
versions in its tradition. Yet it is hard to think that a mind
capable of so great a design on posterity should neglect to
secure that His deed and its significance should reach them
in some authentic way. He surely could not put Himself into
so great an enterprise, and then leave it adrift on history,
liable to the accidents of time or the idiosyncracy of His
followers. He could not be indifferent whether an effective
record and interpretation of His work should survive or not.
He would then have shown Himself unable to rear the deed
He brought forth. It would have been stillborn unless the
close of it in some way secured its action on the posterity
which we are told was its sole destination, on those whom
alone it was to affect or benefit. But that completion of His
work He did secure if He inspired its transmission and

interpretation in the Bible. If He died to make a Church, that Church should continue to be made by some permanent thing from Himself, either by a continuous apostolate supernaturally secured in the *charisma veritatis,* as Rome claims, or by a book which should be the real successor of the apostles, with a real authority on the vital matters of truth and faith. But, we discard the supernatural pope for the supernatural book. And so we come back, enriched by all we have learned from repudiating a verbal inspiration and accepting an inspiration of men and souls, to a better way of understanding the authority that there is in the inspiration of a book, a canon. We move from an institutional authority to a biblical; and then from biblicism we advance to Evangelism. But it is an Evangelism bound up with a book because bound up with history. The Bible is a historic book in a sense far other than the Koran. There is more in the matter than personal inspiration, just as there is more in the corporate Church than a group of sacred souls. Were personal inspiration all, the end might have been reached by one great hierophant. But we have a group of them, with a central message in common, however complementary its various aspects are, however contradictory even some of its minor apsects might be. And this because, for all the pronounced personality of each apostle, he was yet the representative of a whole Church, an eternal Saviour, and a universal salvation. The interpretation of the manifold work of Christ should be a corporate matter. The salvation of the whole Church could not be duly interpreted by one man in it; one man could not even make a liturgy for a Church; any such man would be too nearly its saviour or its intercessor. Therefore in apostles, chosen at His will, the sole Saviour became the sole interpreter, so far as the elements were concerned which made Him Saviour. He was the real author of the New Testament (if the image might be pardoned), with the apostles, as it were, but His staff, though with a very free hand. He rounded off His great work by inspiring an authoritative account of it, in records which are not mere documents, but are themselves acts within His integral and historic act of salvation. They are spiritual sources and not historic memoranda — sacraments even more than sources. And they have an authority of their own greater than is due to mere proximity — however we may be guided by the critics, as subalterns of the same spirit, in adjusting the fabric or cleansing its face.

There are two classes of historical document. There are those that simply report a transaction as a narrative of it might do, either in a book or a newspaper. And there are documents which are documents in the case, which, like treaties, focus the action, form an integral part of the deed itself, and carry not only the consent which made the act, but the signature which sends it forth, and perhaps codicils of authoritative explanation. The New Testament writings (taken of course out of the ban of verbal inspiration, or of an equal inspiration in every part) belong to the second class. They are part of the whole transaction, integral to the great deed. And we do not get the whole Christ or His work without them.

The same Christ, the same Spirit as acted in the redeeming deed acted also in the interpretation; and with a like novelty, a like originality, a like miraculous, creative, and final power — with a like absolute originality, but in a different form. The New Testament, we have seen, is an integral part of a binary revelation, which consists of the manifestation and the inspiration or interpretation which the manifestation itself creates, and creates both from its historic base and from its home in the unseen. The difference of this inspiration from every other lies in the unique nature of the personal fact, in the generic difference from every other deed of the deed whose spirit was in both — both in the fact and in the interpretation — the deed of the Cross.

(*From* The Person and Place of Jesus Christ, *pp. 170-173.*)

As to the authority of the Bible, especially on a matter like the Godhead of Christ, we may note this. The mere historical aspect of the Bible is a matter of learned inquiry. Its evidence for a mere historical fact must stand at what it is historically worth. The difficulty only begins with facts which are more than merely historical, whose value lies not in their occurrence, but in their nature, meaning, and effect. It is not the crucifixion that matters but the Cross. So it is not reanimation but resurrection. And here the authority of the Bible speaks not to the critical faculty that handles evidence but to the soul that makes response. The biblical witness of salvation in Christ is felt immediately to have authority by every soul pining for redemption. It is not so much food for the rationally healthy, but it is medicine for the sick, and life for the dead. All the highest interpretation of the Bible comes from that principle of grace. Even historical criticism, which is a real part of theology, should be pursued on that basis. It should be a work of the Church much more than of the schools. And from the Church must come the final correction and appraisement of the criticism of the schools. It is only knowledge with a soul of faith that grasps the full scope of revelationary history. For it is the history of a revelation we have to do with in Christianity, it is not a revelation of history. Mere history does not need to be revealed; it can look after itself by its own scientific methods.

The authority in the Bible is more than the authority of the Bible; and it is the historic and present Christ as Saviour. The gospel and not the book is the true region of inspiration or infallibility — the discovery of the one gospel in Christ and His Cross. That is the sphere of inspiration. That is where inspiration is infallible. Inspired men have been wrong on points and in modes or argument — just as, even with Christ living in them, they sinned in life. They have not always been right by the event. But they were right in the interpretation of the gospel in Christ as the final work of a holy God for the race. They were not infallible, but they were penetrating and they were final, final as to the nature of the gospel, of Christ, and of the Church. The true region of biblical authority is therefore saving certainty in man's central and final part — his conscience before God. And all its parts are authoritative in the degree and perspective of their relation to that final salvation. What distinguishes the Bible from other books is not appreciable by those that seek no revelation, no spiritual footing, no other world amid this, and no security in the other world. It is only intelligible in its core to those who are being saved in some positive way. It is to what the Reformers called justifying faith that the Bible appears most unique and authoritative — to faith in a justifying God. And it has been said that the canon is authoritative so far as this, at least, that we have no writings outside it that could eject one of those within.

It is by the Bible that Christ chiefly works on history. All the Church's preaching and work is based on it, on what we only know through it. As no man could succeed the apostles in their unique position and work, but their book became their true successor, so no book can replace this. The apostles are gone but the book remains, to prolong their supernatural vision, and exercise their authority in the Church. In so far as the Church prolongs the manifestation and is Christ's body, the Bible prolongs the inspiration and is Christ's word. The writers were and are the only authentic interpreters of Christ. They said so, under the immediate shadow of Christ's action on them, whether His historic or His heavenly action. They never contemplate being superseded on the great witness till Christ came. If they are wrong in that, where are they right? And where are we to turn? To a critical construction of what they said — they including the evangelists? But does that not make the critics, the constructors, to be the true apostolate? And if it come to construction (as I have already said) I prefer the apostolic to to the critical, if we must be forced on a choice. If the Bible is not inspired but only documentary we are at the critic's mercy. For what does it give us apart from its inspiration? Nothing of Christ's, but only of the apostles. In so far as it is a record it is not so much a record or document of Christ but of the apostolic view and message of Christ in His salvation. But it is really a document for apostolic inspiration, for the apostolic reading of history, rather than for history as such. It documents not so much the history of the revelation as the revelation in the history, a certain construction of the purpose and meaning of the divine coming and the divine action. If this apostolic view of things be without inspiration,

then about Christ and His meaning we must simply guess
according to our needs and sympathies. But if it be authoritative anywhere it is on the place, person, and work of Christ,
and not merely on the facts, sequences, or pragmatisms of His
biography. In its substance it is a part of the revelation; its
penumbra; and it is as authoritative *in its way* as the manifestation whose vibration it is. It is of eternal moment to
the soul whether it take or leave the Christ that this book
as a whole preaches to the world. For it does not give us
the data for a Christ but Christ's own interpretation of
Himself.

(Ibid., *pp. 178-181.*)

THE WORD AND THE SPIRIT

We have therefore in the New Testament, at the very
beginning of the Church, the two elements of the Word and
the Spirit, evangelism and spiritualism, the historic and the
pneumatic. Both were quite necessary for the missionary
action of the Church, as we see from Peter's evangelical
interpretation of the tongues in Acts 2. And when John
16:13 says of the Spirit, "He shall not speak of Himself, but
whatsoever He shall hear that shall He speak," we have the
same inseparable connection expressed in the form of a
justification of the fourth Gospel in relation to the Synoptics.
The ministry of the Spirit was not to supersede the historic
salvation, and yet it was to do more than merely transmit
it. It was to be at once its continuity, its amplification, and
its individualization — all three. The Holy Spirit was never
to be detached from the fontal Word. Nothing is more certain
than this in the New Testament. Any manual of New Testament theology will illustrate textually the fact that Word and
Spirit are, if not identical, yet inseparable aspects of one
power and one action. Things done in one place by the
Word — things like conversion or regeneration — are done
in another by the Spirit.

We can further mark the process by which the Church
was led, from speaking of the unique thing in Christ as the
Spirit which moved the prophets, to recognizing it as distinct
from that by a difference more than gradual. It was not mere-

ly the same Spirit acting in another way — it was now something more intimately divine, the Holy Spirit. The Spirit *visited* the prophets, they *had* the Spirit; but Christ, the living Word, *was identified* with Him, with not only the power but the holiness of God. When Paul in Romans 1:4 says that Christ rose by the spirit of holiness, the meaning of holiness there is not merely ethical. For in the Old Testament the Holy Spirit of God is more than that, and means the majesty and sublimity and Godhead of a God that transcends even the ethical world. The spirit of holiness which rose in Christ was the supernatural element which placed Him in the eternal majesty of God, and set Him as far above prophets or kings as these were above nature. We are here dealing not with the spirit of the Creator uniquely pervading the creation, nor only with the unique presence of God in human history, selecting a nation or inspiring its prophets, or living in a Son, but with His unique and individual action in the Church of the Son's regenerates — with the Holy Spirit. The Holy Spirit is associated in the most close and exclusive way with the act of the Son, the action of the Word, and the existence of a Church of new souls. It is given by Christ as His greatest gift; therefore it was the fruit of His greatest act and consummation. It has its source in the Cross, and its first action in the resurrection and its Word. Its prime action therefore is in its nature miraculous; it is not to ethicize, not to sanctify, but first to regenerate, by organizing men into Christ's new creation. So that it is not one of Christ's gifts, as the gospel is not, but the complete and effective gift of Christ Himself, as the Saviour of the world brought home to the individual in the communion of God and the community of a Church. So that, also, we cannot continue to speak of the Spirit as *it,* but must go on to speak of *Him,* as He enters more deeply the personal life.

The Holy Spirit is thus inseparable from this work of Christ and from the word of it in the apostolic preaching which is crystallized in the Bible. It is certainly not, in the New Testament, the Christlike spirit, meaning thereby a particular type of religious subjectivity, a specific frame of mind. In the New Testament the Holy Spirit, the Lord the Spirit, is an objective power, working, before all sanctification, a new creation, and effecting it from the focal point of the Cross and resurrection, and the thing done there once for all. It is not the spirit of discipleship but of regeneration by that Word. The suggestion is not approaching an ideal but crossing a Rubicon. And it creates not a fraternity but a Church. God's action in the Spirit is thus not an independent action alongside the Word, or following it and crowning it. It is not as if a first act of God gave historical information in the general Word, and a second fructified it for particular experience. We have not two causalities. Such an idea cuts the certainty from faith in the Word. It lands us in an idea of absolute predestination, apart from the gospel, on the one hand, or in a false and unhistoric mysticism on the other. There is an inner and organic connection between the Word and the Spirit. It is not partnership, it is wedlock; not cooperation but polarity. For the purposes of salvation the Spirit acts reciprocally in, with, and through the Word, as in the natural realm God does through nature. The Holy Spirit does not effect a direct contact of God as the spiritual power with man's inner nature, as if it switched on the inner light. That makes the work of Christ either superfluous or no different in kind from the work of all other men in rousing and kindling nature. And it could not then be the supreme and distinguishing act of God's love, as it is so constantly called in the New Testament (John 3:16; Romans 8:32). Revelation would then be but illumination, and not redemption; it would flood us and submerge, rather than lift and save. The response would be but visionist and not moral, it would be but insight not committal, knowledge not action, piety not faith, states and feelings and not will, turning on a truth we perceive rather than a reality we enter. The Word is the organ of the Holy Spirit for the purposes of salvation into holiness. And yet not in the sense that the Spirit inspired the Word and then left it to act for itself, as the Deists used to think God made the world, and retired from it, and left it to run. The Holy Spirit which inspired the universal Word is not only immanent in it always as the Creator Spirit is in universal nature, but also present to the soul every time the Word comes home. The ministry of the Word is the chief agency of the Holy Ghost, and the chief function of the Church; whose business is not simply publication of a truth but confession of an experience — the experience of the indwelling Spirit as its life. It is the Holy Spirit that makes the Word to be revelation; it is the Word that makes revelation historic and concrete. It is historic not only in the sense of being actual, but in the sense of being concrete with history, solidary with the organic whole of historic affairs, and not merely pointed for illuminate individuals, or diffused in mystic Humanity. The action of the Spirit through the historic Word is integral to God's whole action on the race. There is no action of God on man which is out of relation to His central, final, and saving action in Christ by the power of the Holy Ghost. Light from God comes indeed to man without the historic mediation of Christ. But it is all from the God and Father of Christ. And in Christ alone is the power of God unto the race's salvation, and so to its final illumination.

(*From* Faith, Freedom, and the Future, *pp. 11-16*.)

Sermons preached by a lover and venerator of Jesus can impress us for long; but they do not regenerate till the Word is taken out of the preacher's lips and spoken by a present Spirit, through whom he is far more than Christ's lover, lyrist, or hierophant. The Christian preacher is not a hierophant but an apostle. The Spirit then acts *directly* through the *medium* of the Word — which way of putting it must be true because it is a paradox, and such exasperating paradoxes are the native language of the Spirit to faith, which the plain and natural man cannot receive. For religion is natural and simple, but faith is not. The sun acts *directly* and most powerfully upon us through the *medium* of a lens; it could not thus act through a book. And so, it has been said, the Bible is more than a book, "a storied window richly dight," and it partakes of something which gives it rather the effect of a spiritual lens. It is this present individualizing action of the Spirit that gives the Bible its unique place after all the discounts allowed to criticism, and makes it canonical for us in respect of the gospel. It is this that makes it equally the book of every age and stage. We are enlarged by Shakespeare, but on the Bible we live. Shakespeare is in our study, but the Bible is by our deathbed.

The true inspiration of the Bible thus comes home only to regenerate men. The inspiration of genius is one thing, and it can make an indelible impression upon us; but the inspiration of the Holy Ghost is a thing quite other; and when that finds us it does not simply leave us different, it leaves us changed. Here is a μετάβασις εἰς ἄλλο γένος. We are loved with the same love with which the Father loves the Son, we are incorporated into the inner life of God. We are loved not as His children but as members of His Son. By Him God is not impressed on us so much as we are engrafted into God. And we might express the gain and the loss in current preaching by saying that it was more confidential in its note with men than intimate in its communion with God.

(Ibid., *pp. 33-35*.)

REVELATION, CHRIST, AND CERTAINTY

In the true sense of the word revelation it must be final. If we possess a criterion of revelation it is the criterion that becomes the revelation. Revelation can only be judged by revelation. Christ's witness to Himself overbears all criticism, except that of the record. Rationalism, whether orthodox or heterodox, consists in measuring revelation by something outside itself. But it must be borne in mind that revelation is a religious idea, that its counterpart and response is not knowledge, nor even poetry, but faith. It is for faith, it is not for science, that revelation is final. It is *the soul's* certainty and power that it assures. It is a religious finality that Christ claims. What He gives is peace with God. His revelation is final, not in compass, but in kind. All is revealed but not everything. It is a qualitative and not a quantitative finality. He declares the whole counsel of God, but not every counsel. He does not give us a program of history or a compendium of doctrine, as the Catholic and old-Protestant theory of a book-revelation is. He gives us a power of God, a certainty of faith, a quality of life, a finality of destiny, in contact with Him. Many things were unsaid, yet He said all — all that faith needs, but not all that knowledge craves; all that makes men, but not all that makes civilization — and yet all that makes civilization possible. He declares the depths of God's will, but not the details of His counsel. The revelation of Christ is final, and was by Him meant to be final, for all that concerns God's decisive will, purpose, and act for our salvation. Christ is Himself the final expression of that. He is not final in the sense of exhausting knowledge. To be exhaustive is just not to be final. It closes one region only to set our interest free for another. He is final because He is inexhaustible, and His silence has the same mastery, depth and suggestiveness as His speech. He is final in the sense of placing us sinful men in living, loving and trustful union with the final reality of life and the world. Our ragged rocks and roaring shoals are flooded into peace by His incoming tide. No higher revelation in kind is possible or thinkable. Later ages might extend the spiritual horizon, but nothing was left for later ages to do in the way of reconciling man and his destiny, man and God. Christ is final in respect of His undying personality and work. Whatever is to be done for human redemption He and no successor does it. Whatever comes to us in the way of revelation is the appropriation of Him. He is the ultimate impulse in the spiritual, and so in the whole progress of man. He cannot be forgotten while His work grows mighty and prevails. He cannot be parted from His work like any mere discoverer. His work is just to make Himself indispensable, to renew Himself in every age and every experience, to become in every life the one power which, amid the withering of all things, neither custom nor age can stale, but which from its throne evermore makes all things new. And He is final, furthermore, in virtue not simply of His harmony, but of His solidarity with the Father. He is thus the organ to us of a certainty which is the final certainty of life, and which would be impossible were He merely harmonious, as we all may hope to be one day, with the Father's will. The finality of His revelation and the absoluteness of our certainty are bound up with the uniqueness in kind of His person; which is to other persons what His revelation, considered as truth, is to all truth else — not so much compendiary as central, pervasive and dynamic.

Christian faith has never found the ground of its certainty in itself, but always in Christ. It does not even believe in Christ because of the Bible, for that would be believing because of the effect of Christ, or the Spirit's work, upon others. Rather does faith believe in the Bible because it believes in Christ, and it descends upon historic facts with a trust in the personal fact, Christ, which is more certain to our experience than any mere historical evidence can be. Whatever account an individual here or there may give of his religious moments, in the great classical instances of Christian experience, and in the large witness of the Church itself, it is Christ, the historic Jesus, that is experienced. It is an experience that cannot be explained away as a vision might. It becomes the new life itself. Paul and Luther did not simply see the Lord. That might have been a projection of their exalted selves. But it was a creative, not a created experience. It created a new life, it was not created by the old. Their experience for ever after was a self-consciousness of Christ, as Christ's was of God. He became not an episode to them but their world.

> This vision, far from perish, rather grows,
> Becomes their universe which sees and knows.

Moreover it was an experience without which they would have no saving knowledge of God.

But no human being ever did for Christ what He does for us all. There is nothing in His experience of any man analogous to our experience of Him. Revelation did not come to Him as He comes to us. He depended on none as we do on Him. There was a directness and a solidarity in the relations between Him and the Father which do not exist between the Father and us without Him. The self-consciousness of Christ in respect of God was not parallel to the God-consciousness in man. The source of religious knowledge was not the same for Him as for us. To judge from history He found His certainty in His consciousness; we find it in Him. For Him self-consciousness was the source of such knowledge; for us it is only its site. Revelation was not made to Christ, but to us in Christ. The matter of revelation was not a principle which He and we alike apprehend by the same method only with different degrees of completeness. It is not a truth which would thrive in our perception, even if the memory of Him grew dim. To take Him away from present religious reality is to cut off our spiritual supplies, and close in ice our waterway to God. No man is indispensable to truth; but Christ is. He is the divine truth of man. What He revealed was not a conviction, but Himself. His experience of God was His experience of Himself. He was God's self-expression in Humanity. He was that even more than the expression of Humanity in its ideal. He creates a new Humanity more than He embodies the old. His first purpose was not Shaksperian — to reveal man to man. The relief that He gives the race is not the artist's relief of self-expression, but the Saviour's relief of redemption. He did not release the pent-up soul, but rebuilt its ruins. It was another power than man remaking man; it was not tongue-tied man made happy at last in a rapt hour of complete self-realization.

He is absolutely essential to our personal realization of the principle of His revelation; and that not as its historic medium, but as its ever living mediator. He is not the founder of Christianity, but the living object of its faith and worship. He taught, He constrained, men to pray in such a way that their prayers turned in spite of themselves to Him. "I besought the Lord thrice." Was Paul there a saint-worshipper, an idolater? If Jesus never expressly invited worship, His Spirit led His nearest disciples to it by an irresistible necessity of faith. He hardly claimed Messiahship in so many words: but He so spoke of the kingdom, and so embodied it, that the conviction of His Messiahship became to His closest companions irresistible before He died. And so after He rose He came home to them as an object of prayer — by His own injunction indeed, but by His injunction in the shape of a necessity of faith. He is not an instance but a

portion of our highest religious consciousness. He is not our
ideal; for an ideal is imitable, and we cannot imitate our
Redeemer. He is not our ideal, for we transcend and leave
our ideal, when we have absorbed Him into ourselves. The
more like Him we grow, the more we can dispense with Him.
He does for us what it was in Him to do, what at a stage we
needed done; and we pass on, to remember Him with gratitude but not with worship, to find our freedom in escaping
from Him, and not in owning His sway. But the more we grow
like Christ the more indispensable He is to us. The closer we
come to Him in character, the more He rules us. Those
nearest Him have called themselves His slaves, and been
their own freemen and the world's in the act. The more
abundant our revelations the more of the revelation we
find Him to be; and the more we are redeemed the more
we know His sole power to redeem. The higher He lifts us
the loftier we find Him; and the more power He gives us
the more we spend it in submitting to Him. Ideal is no
name for what we find Him to be, and to be capable of
being, to us. It seems as if our likeness to Him were only
given us to enable us to realize our difference. It is in His
difference from us, rather than in His resemblance, that the
core and nerve of His revelation lie. Our resemblance only
provides the condition for appropriating it, and making it
intelligible. The flesh is there for the sake of the Word.
Why should we strive to reduce this difference? It brings
Him nearer than any resemblance can. It is just His difference from all men that He identifies Himself with every
man. The dearest and the most like us cannot come to us
as He can. He is our Saviour, not because He is our brother,
but because He is our Lord and our God. We are not His
peers. We are not even His analogue, when it is a question
of our knowledge of God. His experience is not simply a
glorified version of ours. Throughout the New Testament,
Father has a different meaning in relation to Christ, and in
relation to us, with an equal reality for both. The New
Testament Father is the God and Father of our Lord Jesus
Christ. He is our Father in Christ. "When *ye* pray say Our
Father." Did Christ ever say *Our* Father along with His

disciples, or in their name? Rather He spoke of "my Father and your Father." Part of the offense He gave was by claiming God as *"His own* Father, and so making Himself equal with God." There is a gulf between the Fatherhood of the New Testament and the sentimental fatherhood of literary theology and its popular Christianity. It really concedes the whole Unitarian position to say that God is the Father of every man in the same sense in which He is the Father of Christ except that He was His Father preeminently. "No man knoweth the Father but the Son, and he to whom the Son shall reveal Him." He *knew* the Father whom He *revealed* to men. It was not by revelation that He received what in Him is revelation to us. These words are not among the disputable portions of the Gospels; and they are decisive as to Christ's unique solidarity with the Father, and the dependence of all men on Him, as He depended on none, for the knowledge of God. As Paul puts it, Christ is the Son of God with power, while we are sons by adoption, in all that pertains to the moral relationship as distinct from the natural in creation. Exception may be taken to the metaphor of adoption, but to except to the fact and the difference it seeks to cover is to except to the consistent teaching of the New Testament. There God is revealed as Father, not in our feeling of childship, but in our certainty of sonship in Jesus Christ. He is essential to constitute the sonship, and not merely to aid us to discover it. The intrinsic quality of our religious act is our sense not of a divine principle, but of Christ revealing Himself in us. And revelation takes effect in us, not as an act of insight, but only as an experience of being redeemed. There are pure souls, reared in the lap of Christian culture, cloistered with thought, and unfamiliar with the deepest, darkest, and most passionate experiences either of sin, the soul, or the cross, to whom this may seem both unphilosophical and untrue. But in a long-established and hereditary Christian culture there is a new danger of a lofty and noble sort, lest the world by goodness know not God.

Revelation then may be defined as the free, final and effective act of God's self-communication in Jesus Christ for man's redemption. It is not simply an act of manifestation, or even of impressive representation, but it is a historic and eternal act of deliverance, prolonged in an infinite number of acts *ejusdem generis* in the experience by Christian people of their redemption in Christ. It is a free act as being wholly marvellous and unbought. It is a final act because it embodies, in an aforesaid sense, the whole purpose of God with man. And it is effective because it is only completed by its return on itself in man's experience and response. A sound returns void, but not a word, not a revelation. A Christ is not a Christ without a kingdom. It is, moreover, the self-communication of God, because it is not a witness to God by His closest intimate even in eternity, but God Himself at work as our Redeemer. God so loved that He gave Himself in His Son; not, God was so lovely that the Son could not help giving report of it to men. That would make Christ a religious artist more than the Saviour. Nor is it thus: God was so eager to redeem that the Son's heart filled with the design to give the helpless divine passion voice and course among men. That makes the Son the prophet of God, not to say that He came to God's rescue. But God in the Son conveyed Himself, not a report, nor an expression, nor an echo, nor an engine of His will to redeem, but His own present redeeming will. It is impossible to separate revelation from redemption. Revelation has no real and final meaning except as the act of redemption to the experience of being redeemed. Its response is by faith, not by scientific certitude, by faith as the certainty and experience of reconciliation. It is a religious and not a scientific act, and only by a religious act can it be met. Its express object in us is not to produce assent, nor to facilitate discovery, nor to vindicate a rational unity in things, but to establish soul-certainty. It has nothing directly to do with the identity of thought and being. It is free to discuss that and other questions because of a certainty which cannot wait for their solution before beginning to live and rule — the soul-certainty "if God be for us who can be against us?"

(From "Revelation and the Person of Christ," pp. 108-117.)

He becomes His own witness in us. What we then have is no more insight of ours into a revelation set down in the past. It is that revelation individualizing itself in our case. It is the eternal living act of the historic Christ still acting in a particular instance, as the body's life is repeated in the life of its cells. It is the same Christ carrying out in individuals the eternal act He did once at a historic point for the race, and completing revelation in response. No phenomenon in history is revelation except in so far as it comes home to individual souls, is understood and welcomed as revelation, and gives man the power amid all the pressure, illusion and blight of life to be his own freeman in Christ Jesus.

(Ibid., *p. 122*.)

IV: GOD

To bring sin home, and to bring grace home, we need that something else should come home which alone gives meaning to both — the holy. The grace of God cannot return to our preaching or to our faith till we recover what has almost clean gone from our general, familiar, and current religion, what liberalism has quite lost — I mean a due sense of the holiness of God. This sense has much gone from our public worship, with its frequent irreverence; from our sentimental piety, to which an ethical piety with its implicates is simply obscure; from our rational religion, which banishes the idea of God's wrath; from our public morals, to which the invasion of property is more dreadful than the damnation of men. If our gospel be obscure it is obscure to them in whom the slack God of the period has blinded their minds, or a genial God unbraced them, and hidden the Holy One who inhabits eternity. This holiness of God is the real foundation of religion — it is certainly the ruling interest of the Christian religion. In front of all our prayer or work stands "Hallowed be Thy Name." If we take the Lord's Prayer alone, God's holiness is the interest which all the rest

of it serves. Neither love, grace, faith, nor sin has any but
a passing meaning except as they rest on the holiness of
God, except as they arise from it, and return to it, except
as they satisfy it, show it forth, set it up, and secure it everywhere and for ever. Love is but its outgoing; sin is but its
defiance; grace is but its action on sin; the Cross is but its
victory; faith is but its worship. The preacher preaches to the
divinest purpose only when his lips are touched with the red
coal from the altar of the thrice holy in the innermost place.
We must rise beyond social righteousness and universal justice
to the holiness of an infinite God. What we on earth call
righteousness among men, the saints in heaven call holiness
in Him.

(*From* The Cruciality of the Cross, *pp. 22-23.*)

His is not the omnipotence that natural happiness requires,
far less that the natural imagination pictures; but it is the
omnipotence that His own *holiness* requires, His own purpose not of love simply but of holy love, the omnipotence
required by His own perfection, the omnipotence required to
establish in the world as we find it, in a sinful world, a
kingdom of complete communion with His Holy Self and
His Eternal blessedness. All power in heaven and earth is
delivered to the victorious *Holy* One, and to Him alone.

We thus begin with such notions of power as we imbibe
from our first contact with it in natural force, elemental
instincts, or imperious wills. And we carry that order into
our thinking. We construe omnipotence accordingly. We
form ideas of omnipotence which are suggested to us by
nature, and then we demand that a revelation from God
shall begin by accrediting itself to those natural notions —
especially by some miracle. But we demand an impossible
thing when we look for such a revelation in Christ — human being omnipotent in that sense. A human being with
natural omnipotence would be a monster. Christ did not
come with natural omnipotence either for His weapon or for
His credentials. He did not come with a power of unlimited
miracle, with a blank check on the universal energy. His
omnipotence was not of the kingdom of nature but of grace.

His power was both held and used under moral conditions, as we see in the cases where it was arrested by unbelief. He came much rather to convert that natural method, nay, to invert it. He revealed that holiness *was* the divine power, and did not wait on power; that the forces of creation had their end, charter, and scope in a moral redemption, and they could not exceed their terms of reference; that holiness, that moral Godhead, could only establish itself in the world by its own nature, and not by natural force; that *His* Church could only be established by its gospel, and not by anything at the disposal of states, or at the command of Empire. His kingdom was not of the world. This principle gave rise to a struggle within Himself, in the temptation He mastered; as it has done also within His Church, in the temptation to which she succumbed. The power He incarnated was the intrinsic, supreme, and final power of divine conscience, that is, of holy love, for the destiny of the world. This is the true power of God which was incarnated in Christ — this morally irresistible power of holy love.

In the natural, arbitrary, and unregenerate sense in which we understand the word, God is not omnipotent. All things do not work together for an omnipotent God, but for love's good on God's scale, for an absolutely holy purpose, to them that love God for His holy purpose (Rom. 8:28). At least the God of Christ is not omnipotent in any other sense than that. The God incarnate in Christ is not. He can do only the things that are congruous with His moral, His holy nature and purpose. But in this moral sense is He omnipotent over the world? Is He in final command of history? Is He secure of the reversion of time? Well, what omnipotence is required for that? Is it not the power of holiness, not to do anything and everything suggested by human egoism or fantasy, but to do everything required for its own effectual establishment on the world? The purpose of a world created by a holy God must be holiness, the reflection and communion of His own holiness. Can God secure it? What the world actually is we know, if we let our conscience speak its verdict on history. Is it in the power of the holy God, through the very holiness smitten by our sin, to secure such a world's holy destiny still? That is the ultimate question in life. That is what, in one form or another, occupies the first-class minds. And to that question Christ and His Cross are the answer, or they have no meaning at all. They reveal in their foregone victory the omnipotence of holiness to subdue all natural powers and forces, all natural omnipotence, to the moral sanctity of the kingdom of God. And if they do not reveal that, we are left without any ground of certainty about a holy ending for the world at all. And our guesses will be hopeful according to our sanguine temperament, our happy circumstances, our small insight, or our low demand. It is a tremendous revelation and achievement in the Cross of Christ. "How awful goodness is." The more we know about cosmic forces, antres vast, deserts horrible, Alps of thick-ribbed ice, seas, continents, vastitudes of every kind; of geological ages, stellar spaces, solar storms; of creature agonies, of social miseries, devilish wickedness, civilized triumphs, historic heroisms, the grandeur of genius and unquenchable love; of all the passion, for evil on the one hand, or, on the other, for the Eternal, Immortal, and Invisible good — so much the more we must feel how awful is the holy love of God, that has secured the grand issue for ever, that surmounts all principalities and powers, things past, present, and to come, every other omnipotence; surmounts, nay, exploits, them all, in the Holy One of God, who by His Cross is the same world-conqueror yesterday, today, and for ever. It is a tremendous claim. And the improbability of it is either a pious absurdity; or it is the quiet irony of a God who has it already done in the hollow of His hand. Like every ultimate interpretation of life it is a matter of insight — insight into the world, the Christ, and the Cross. What is lacking to the seers and geniuses of our time, like Swinburne, Meredith, or Hardy, is still lack of insight. They see into "Love in the valley" — and how lovely — what they do not see into is love *in excelsis.*

(From The Person and Place of Jesus Christ, pp. 227-229.)

What do we mean when we speak of the holy so often and so centrally as we here shall?

It is of course a religious idea — *the* religious idea; in what religion of our nature shall we seek the nature of religion?

For long it was sought in the region of theory — of the rational consciousness. What was asked about a religion was "Is it true?" That is to say, "How far does it fall in with those rational principles which make our *a priori* axioms and standards of scientific or philosophic truth?" And there are many who treat the question in this way still.

But the modern movement broke away from this quest for theoretic truth as the prime thing in religion. The day of orthodoxy went by, and with it the night of rationalism. With Kant came a new order of things. The ethical took the place that had been held by the intellectual. The notion of reality replaced that of truth. Religion placed us not in line with the rationality in the world but in rapport with the reality of it. And the ethical was the real.

As Kant handled the principle it was much hampered by the circumstances of his day, but his route was right. It is true that religion belongs neither to the rational, the aesthetic, nor the ethical side of the soul exclusively. It draws on the whole soul's being and energy. But the Christian religion at least involves if not the solitude at least the primacy of the ethical. If reality is to reach us it must be thus. And what Christianity means by the holy is best expressed in ethical terms as the absolute moral reality. We too are holy according to our relation to that power, or rather according to His relation to us.

Now it is distinctive of the moral consciousness that it is not, like the philosophic, single, simple, and harmonious, but double, divided, and even rent. It is not monistic but dualistic. A solution of the world which is determined to be theoretic above all must end in Monism, which is the death of religion; but if it be moral, if it be religious, it must begin with the experienced and certain fact of the divided conscience, a standing state of collision, war, and sin. It begins with a state of the consciousness anterior to its branches as theoretic, aesthetic, or ethical, a state underlying all these. It must begin with that fundamental antinomy of the conscience which emerges in the conflict of "must" and "ought," of instinct and obligation, of natural law and moral norm. To realize the deep distinction between law and norm, between our psychology and our conscience, between the make-up of our natural constitution and the state of our moral will, between our substance and our sanctions, to realize this is essential to a right start in the matter. And it leads us on to the further recognition not only that the distinction rises to collision but that the war between the law of instinct and the norm of duty is a civil war; it is waged within the unity of the person. The defiance of the moral norm seems to be as much bound up with our nature as obedience is. And this creates a problem quite insoluble for any philosophy as yet.

But apart from the success of philosophy in the matter of such a theodicy, our practical experience convinces us of the "ought" of the moral norm. The ideal is that that should rule. In God such an ideal is reached always, and in Him alone. Unless life is to be detached from reality and thrown into hopeless schism both with itself and the universe, Absolute Being must be identical with the absolute moral norm. God wills good because He is good, He is good because He wills good. That is the holiness of God, the identification of the moral norm and the ultimate reality of the world. The holy is the ideal good, fair, and true, translated in our religious consciousness to a transcendent personal reality, not proved but known, experienced immediately and honored at sight as the one thing in the world valuable in itself and making a world. It is a conception justifiable to no philosophy, as I say. For it seems to involve (what is a moral impossibility condemning any theory) that all reality, even that of evil,[1] should be a part of the absolute moral normality. It seems to require that the norm of all reality should cover what is contrary to a moral norm, that absolute reality, ruled by the moral norm, should yet have the morally abnormal among its appearances or products.

When we are dealing with the holy, therefore, we are in a region which thought cannot handle nor even reach. We

---

[1] Which can never be treated as a mere unreality and negation without ruining both the place of conscience and the agelong passion for redemption.

cannot go there, it must come here. We are beyond both experience and thought, and we are dependent on revelation for any conviction of the reality of that ideal which moral experience demands but cannot ensure. Life is ruined if our greatest moral ideals are not fixed in the greatest reality; yet we have no means in our own power of any conviction of such fixity. The holy is both urgent and inaccessible. It is imperative, yet unapproachable. The situation is only soluble by a miracle.

That is the miracle of revelation, of grace. The unapproachable approaches, enters, tarries, lives, dies, conquers among us and in us, knows us into our only knowledge of itself, subdues all things to its sanctity, and establishes its good and blessed self in us and on us all. The norms, the "oughts," become for us the motives that instinctive laws and "musts" used to be. We are ruled by the imperative and not the clamant, and we are united by love where we used but to meet in passion, and in passion slay.

But the effect on us of the moral ideal is not simply admiration; it is confusion; it is accusation; it is judgment. We do not only desire it, we dread it. Its very grandeur fills us with a sense of weakness, nay, of blame, shame, and despair. We are not only weak but helpless. And it is chiefly by our fault, crime, and sin. So we do not simply worship afar, we repent in the dust.

But what does that mean? It means that the revelation of the holy can only come through redemption by the holy; that to us, ruined by sinful act, the only truth that represents Him is an act; that the absolute reality of the active and mighty world in its actual case is expressible only in an Eternal Deed; that the holy nature of God comes home by no prophetic exposition, even through apostle or Saviour, but only by the priestly act in which the saving person consummates; that it cannot be taught us, it must be created in us by that act; that the Cross is the creative revelation of the holy, and the holy is what is above all else revealed in the Cross, going out as love and going down as grace; that the Holy Spirit's point of departure in history is the Cross; and that while our justification has its source in God's self-justification of His holiness there, our sanctification has the same source as both.

I shall often have to return to these points to expound and expand.

(From The Principle of Authority, pp. 4-7.)

LOVE AND HOLINESS

"God is Love" has in the New Testament no meaning apart from the equally prominent idea of righteousness, of God as the author and guardian of the moral holy law. The Christian principle of pardon is not forgiveness to repentance ... but to due repentance. And a due repentance means a repentance not only sincere (and certainly not equivalent), but containing some adequate sense of the evil done, ... recognition of majesty and inviolability of the law of holiness.... It is this practical and experienced recognition that is the atonement or expiation. It is ratifying by act and experience, by assent which was response and by a response which was lived and died, God's death sentence on sin.

(From The Atonement in Modern Religious Thought, pp. 74-75.)

The Cross was not simply a fate awaiting Christ in the future; it pervaded subliminally His holy Person. He was born for the Cross. It was His genius, His destiny. It was quite inevitable that, in a world like this, One holy as Jesus was holy should come to the Cross. The parable was spoken by One in whom the Cross and all it stands for were latent in His idea of God; and it became patent, came to the surface, became actual, and practical, and powerful in the stress of man's crisis and the fullness of God's time. That is an important phrase. Christ Himself came in a fullness of time. The Cross which consummated and crowned Christ came in its fullness of time. The time was not full during Christ's life for preaching an atonement that life could never make. Hence as to the *method* of God's free and flowing grace the parable has nothing to say. It does not even say that the father went seeking the prodigal. The seeking grace of God we find there as little as the redeeming grace. And so also you have not the mode of grace's action *on a world*. But, speaking of what you do have in the parable, the father knows no change of feeling towards the prodigal; yet could he go on making no difference? Could he go on treating the prodigal as though he never had become a prodigal? He did not certainly when he returned; and as little as he could before. His heart followed the prodigal, but his relations, his confidence, his intercourse were with his brother. So long as the son is prodigal he cannot be treated as though he were otherwise. Even repentance needs some guarantee of permanence. The father's heart is the same, but his treatment must be different. Cases have been known where the father had to expel the black sheep from the family for the sake of the others. Loving the poor creature all the same, he yet found it quite impossible, in the interests of the whole family, to treat him as though he were like the rest. So God needed no placation, but He could not exercise His kindness to the prodigal world, He certainly could not restore communion with its individuals without doing some act which permanently altered the relation. And this is what set up that world's reconciliation with Him. It was set up by an act of crisis, of judgment.

Remember always we are dealing with the world in the first instance and not with individuals. I constantly come back upon that, for the orthodox and their critics forget it alike. I suppose the prodigal was a slave, I suppose he had sold himself to that vile work of swine-feeding. When he returned I suppose he ran away from his master. But the prodigal world, of course, could not run away from its master, it could not run away from the power that it was enslaved to. "Myself am hell." Supposing now the prodigal had not been able to run away. Supposing he had been guarded as a convict is guarded, then he could only come back by being bought off. As soon as you go beyond the one theme of the parable, the absolute heartiness of grace, and begin to think of grace's methods with a world, this point must be faced by all who are more than pooh-pooh sentimentalists in their religion. We have to deal with a world in a bondage it could not break. If the prodigal could not have arisen to go to his father; if the elder brother had sold up the whole farm, reduced himself to poverty, taken the sum in his hand, followed the prodigal into the far country, and there spent the whole amount in buying his brother's manumission from his master before a judge; and if it was all done by mutual purpose and consent of himself and his father; would not that act be a great and effective thing, not so much in producing repentance but in a harder matter — in destroying a lien and making absolute certainty of the father's forgiveness? He is sure because the father not only says but pays. His mere repentance could not make him sure, could not place him at home again, could not put him where he set out. His mere repentance could turn his heart to his father, but it could not break the bar and fill him with certainty of his father's love and forgiveness. And that is what the sinner wants, and what the great and classic penitents find it so hard to believe. Now, the parable tells us of the freeness of God's grace, and its fullness, but the Cross enacts it and inserts it in real history. It shows to what a length that grace could go in dealing with a difficulty otherwise insuperable when we turn from a single prodigal to a world. The act which I have described by a New Testament extension of the parable — the act of Christ's Cross — is not simply to produce individual repentance, but it has its great effect upon the relations of the whole world to God. And the judgment, the payment, was on that scale. I will show you later that it was not pain that was paid but holy obedience.

What the elder brother does in the supposition I have made is twofold. First, he secures the liberation, he deals with the equitable conditions of the release. Secondly, he also acts upon the prodigal's heart and confidence. In the first case he meets certain judicial conditions, certain social conditions, ethical conditions, bound up with the existing order, the law of society in which the prodigal was living. But it is said sometimes that there the analogy fails, because the elder son, acting for the father, in my extension of the story, has to deal with a law which is outside his control and outside the father's control; he has to deal with the law of society, with the law of the land where the prodigal was. Whereas, if you come to think about God, there can be no social and moral conditions which are outside His control. There, it is said, your illustration breaks down. God could ignore any such impediments at His loving will. Now, that is just the crucial mistake that you make, that even Kant does not allow us to make. God could do nothing of the kind. So far the omnipotence of God is a limited omnipotence. He could not trifle with His own holiness. He could will nothing against His holy nature, and He could not abolish the judgment bound up with it. Nothing in the compass of the divine nature could enable Him to abolish a moral law, the law of holiness. That would be tampering with His own soul. It had to be dealt with. Is the law of God more loose than the law of society? Can it be taken liberties with, played with, and put aside at the impulse even of love? How little we should come to think of God's love if that were possible! How essential the holiness of that love is to our respect for it and our faith in its unchangeableness! If God's love were not essentially holy love, in course of time mankind would cease to respect it, and consequently to trust it. We need not a fond love, but a love we can trust, and for ever. What love wants is not simply love in response, but respect and confidence. In the bringing up of children today one often wishes they had more training in respect, even if less in affection. God's holy law is His own holy nature. His love is under the condition of eternal respect. It is quite unchangeable. It is just as much outside His operation, so far as abrogation goes, as was the law of the far country to the father of the prodigal.

(*From* The Work of Christ, *pp. 108-113.*)

FATHERHOOD, HOLINESS, AND THE CROSS

Fatherhood in the Old Testament neither demands sacrifice nor makes it, but in the New Testament the Holy Father does both. The holiness is the root of love, fatherhood, sacrifice, and redemption.

(*From* The Holy Father and the Living Christ, *p. 7.*)

We have been over-engrossed with a mere distributive equity, which has made God the Lord Chief Justice of the world. Or we have recoiled from that to a love slack and oversweet. But this lifts us up to a more spiritual and personal standard, to the Fatherly holiness whose satisfaction in a Holy Son is the great work and true soul of Godhead. The divine Father is the holy. And the Holy Father's first care is holiness. The first charge on a Redeemer is satisfaction to that holiness. The Holy Father is one who does and must atone. . . . He offers a sacrifice rent from His own heart. It is made to Him by no third party ("for who hath first given unto Him?"), but by Himself in His Son, and it is made to no foreign power, but to His own holy nature and law. Fatherhood is not bought from holiness by any cross; it is holiness itself that pays. It is love that expiates. Do not say, "God is love. Why atone?" The New Testament says, "God has atoned. What love!" The ruling passion of the Saviour's holy God is this passion to atone and to redeem.

(Ibid., *pp. 8-10.*)

The soul of divine fatherhood is forgiveness by holiness. It is evangelical. It is a matter of grace meeting sin by sacrifice to holiness, more even than of love meeting need by service to man. To correct and revive that truth, to restore it to its place in the proportion of faith, would be to restore passion to our preaching, solemnity to our tenderness, real power to our energy, and moral virility to our piety. . . . The chief lack of religion today is authority; and it must find that in the Cross or nowhere, in the real nature of the Cross, in its relation to the holy demand of God.

(Ibid., *pp. 13-14.*)

[Between us and God] there comes . . . sin. Sin, hell, curse, and wrath! The wrath and curse of God not on sin only, but on the soul.

(Ibid., *p. 22.*)

A soul can neither be saved nor sanctified without a world. To redeem the sin must be destroyed, a universe reorganized.

(Ibid., *p. 25.*)

There are debts that cannot simply be written off and left unrecovered. There is a spiritual order whose judgments are the one guarantee for mankind and its future. That law of holiness can by no means whatever be either warned off or bought off in its claim. God cannot simply *waive* it as to the past, nor is it enough if he simply *declare* it for all time. In His own eternal nature it has an undying claim to which He must *give effect* in due judgment somewhere, if He is to redeem a world. The enforcement of God's holiness by judgment is as essential to a *universal and eternal* Fatherhood as is the outflow of His love. . . . God in Christ judged sin as a holy Father seeking penalty only for holiness' sake. . . . The misery and death which the sinner bears blindly, sullenly, resentfully, was there understood with the understanding of Holy God; the guilt was seen as God sees it; the judgment was accepted as God's judgment, borne, owned and glorified before the world as holy, fatherly, just, and good. The final witness of holiness to holiness amid sin's last wreck, penalty and agony — that is expiation as the Father made it in the Son, not changing His *feeling*, but by crisis, by judgment, eternally changing His relations with the world.

(Ibid., *pp. 29-31.*)

If we could satisfy the moral order we disturbed, our insufferable self-satisfaction would derange it straightway.

(Ibid., *p. 32.*)

Penalty only expiates crime, not sin. There was owed that debt to holiness, that atonement to holiness, which is so misconstrued when we make it due to justice, or demanded by justice alone. Justice wants penalty, holiness wants holiness in the midst of penalty. It wants a soul's own perfect holiness in the midst of penalty due to other souls; it wants loving obedience amid the penalty of loveless defiance. God alone could fulfil for us the holy law He never broke, and pay the cost He never incurred.

And He has paid it, so freely and completely that His grace in forgiving is as full and free to us as if it had cost Him nothing, as if it had been just kindness. The cost is so perfectly and freely borne that it never appears in a way to mar the graciousness of grace, or deflower the Father's love. The quality of mercy is not strained.

(Ibid., *pp. 35-36.*)

The first condition of forgiveness is not an adequate com-

prehension of the atonement, and a due sense of the cost. . . .
The Cross becomes a theology only by beginning as a religion.
The condition of forgiveness is answering the grace and freedom of it with a like free, humble, and joyful heart. It is
taking the freedom of it home, and not the cost. It is commit-
ting ourselves to God's self-committal to us. It is taking God
at His word — at His living word, Christ — His urgent, ret-
icent, gracious, masterful word Christ.

(Ibid., *pp. 58-59.*)

Christ came not to *say* something but to *do* something. His
revelation was action more than instruction. He revealed by
redeeming. . . . It was to *effect* forgiveness, to set up the relation of forgiveness both in God and man. You cannot set up
relation between souls without affecting and changing both
sides even if on one side the disposition existed before, and
led to the act that reconciled. The great mass of Christ's work
was like a stable iceberg. It was hidden. It was His dealing
with God, not man. The great thing was done with God. It
was independent of our knowledge of it. . . . Doing this *for*
us was the first condition of doing anything *with* us.

(Ibid., *pp. 64-65.*)

Any conception of God which exalts His Fatherhood at the
cost of His holiness, or to its neglect, unsettles the moral
throne of the universe. Any reaction of ours from a too exact-
ing God which leaves us with but a kindly God, a patient
and a pitiful, is a reaction which sends us over the edge of
the moral world. And it robs us of moral energy. The fatherly
God of recent religious liberalism is indeed a conception for
which we have to bless Him when we look back on much
that went before. But the gain brings loss. It is a conception
which by itself tends to do less than justice even to God's
love. It tends to take the authority out of the gospel, the
sinew out of preaching, the insight out of faith, the stamina
out of character, and discipline out of the home. Such a view
of God is not in sufficient moral earnest — though nothing
could exceed the moral eagerness of many who hold it. It
does not descend into hell nor ascend into heaven. It does
not pierce and destroy our self-satisfaction. It has no spirit-

ual depth, real and sincere as the piety is of many of its
advocates. It has not what I have already called adequate
moral mordancy. The question at last is not of its particular
advocates but of the result that would follow if this became
the view of the whole church. "As is Thy majesty so is Thy
mercy," says the sage. But what I describe is a view of mercy
which does justice neither to the majesty of God, nor to the
greatness of man. It has certainly no due sense of the human
tragedy, the moral tragedy of the race. And, accordingly, it
takes from preaching the element so conspicuous by its absence today, the element of imaginative greatness and moral
poignancy. It lacks the note of doom and the searching
realism of the greatest moral seers. It is no more true to
Shakespeare than to the Bible, to Dante than to Paul. It robs
faith of its energy, its virility, its command, its compass, and
its solemnity. The temperature of religion falls. The horizon
of the soul contracts. Piety becomes prosaic, action conventional, goodness domestic, and mercy but kind. We have
churches of the nicest, kindest people, who have nothing
apostolic or missionary, who never knew the soul's despair or
its breathless gratitude. God becomes either a spectacular and
inert God, or a God who acts amiably; with the strictness of
affection at best, and not the judgment of sanctity; without
the consuming fire, and the great white throne. He is not
dramatic in the great sense of the word. He is not adequate
to history. He is not on the scale of the race. He is the center
of a religious scene instead of the protagonist in the moral
drama of Man and Time. The whole relation between God
and man is reduced to attitude and not action — to a pose, at
last. It is more sympathetic than searching. The Cross becomes
a *parergon*. We tend then to a Christianity without force,
passion, or effect; a surburban piety, homely and kindly but
unfit to cope with the actual moral case of the world, its giant
souls and hearty sinners. We cannot deal to any purpose with
the great sins or the great fearless transgressors, the exceed-
ing sinfulness and deep damnation of the race. Our word is
as a very lovely song of one that has a pleasant voice and can
play well on an instrument. And the people hear, but do not.
They hear, but do not fear. They are enchanted, but un-

changed. Moral taste takes the place of moral insight. Religious sensibility stands where evangelical faith should be. Education takes the place of conversion, a happy nature of the new nature. Love takes the place of faith, uneasiness of concern, regret of repentance, and criticism of judgment. Sin becomes a thing of short weight. It was largely our ignorance; and when we thought of God's anger we were misreading Him by reading into Him our choleric selves. Our salvation becomes a somewhat common thing, and glorious heavens or fiery hells die into the light of drab and drowsy day. Much is done by enlightened views in the way of correcting our conception of God, to fit it into its place in the rest of knowledge, and to lift it to a higher stage in the long religious evolution. But it is all apologetic, all theosophic. It aims at adjusting the grace of God to the natural realm rather than interpreting it by our moral soul and our moral coil. It is not theology; it is not religion, it is not vital godliness. It does not do much in the way of effectively restoring the actual living relation between God and the soul. I am compelled to recognize often that the most deeply and practically pious people in the Church are among those whose orthodox theology I do not share. I even distrust it for the Church's future. But they have the pearl of price.

(*From* Positive Preaching and the Modern Mind, *pp. 243-245.*)

V: CHRIST

PREEXISTENCE AND MEDIATION

Such a relation as we believe our Saviour now bears to the Father could not have arisen at a point of time. It could not have been created by His earthly life. The power to exercise God's prerogative of forgiveness, judgment, and redemption could never have been acquired by the moral excellence or religious achievement of any created being, however endowed by the Spirit of God. I confess (if I may descend so far) I had long this difficulty, which lowered the roof of my faith, and arrested the flight of devotion. And I am afraid, from the state of our public worship, I was not alone in that difficulty. I could not get the plenitude of New Testament worship or Catholic faith out of the mere self-sacrifice of the human Christ even unto death. Nor could I rise to it from that level. I was too little moved by His earthly renunciations to rise to the dimensions of the Church's faith, for I am not speaking of its creed, which was my own. The Cross of such a Christ, who was the mere martyr of His revelation, or the paragon of self-sacrifice, was not adequate to produce the absolute devotion which made a proud Pharisee, yea, a proud apostle, glory in being Christ's entire slave, and which drove the whole Church to call Christ Lord and God, in a devotion the most magnificent the soul has ever known. Such worship seemed too large a response to anything which Jesus, with all His unique greatness, did or determined in the course of His earthly life alone. The Synoptic record alone would not account for the Christian religion, nor produce the plerophory of Christian faith. Christ's earthly humiliation had to have its foundation laid in heaven, and to be viewed but as the working out of a renunciation before the world was. The awful volume and power of the will-warfare in which He here redeemed the world, and turned for eternity the history of the race, was but the exercise in historic conditions of an eternal resolve taken in heavenly places. He could never be king of the eternal future if He was not also king from the eternal past. No human being was capable of such will. It was Godhead that willed and won that victory in Him. If it was God loving when He loved, it was God willing as He overcame. The Cross was the reflection (or say, rather, the historic pole) of an act within Godhead. The historic victory was the index and the correlate of a choice and a conquest in Godhead itself. Nothing less will carry the fullness of faith, the swelling soul, and the Church's organ voice of liturgy in every land and age. If our thought does not allow that belief we must reduce the pitch of faith to something plain, laic, and songless, and, in making it more homely, make it less holy, less absolute, less adoring. The adoration of Christ can only go with this view of Him in the long run. Nothing lower takes with due seriousness the superhuman value of the soul, the unearthliness of our salvation, and its last conquest of the whole world. It would reduce the unworldly value of the soul if it could be saved by anything less than a Christ before the worlds. It came upon me, as upon many at the first it must have mightily done, that His whole life was not simply occupied with a series of decisions crucial for our race, or filled with a great deed then first done; but that that life of His was itself the obverse of a heavenly eternal deed, and the result of a timeless decision before it here began. His emergence on earth was as it were the swelling in of heaven. His sacrifice began before He came into the world, and His Cross

was that of a lamb slain before the world's foundation. There
was a Calvary above which was the mother of it all. His
obedience, however impressive, does not take divine magni-
tude if it first rose upon earth, nor has it the due compelling
power upon ours. His obedience as man was but the detail of
the supreme obedience which made Him man. His love
transcends all human measure only if, out of love, He re-
nounced the glory of heavenly being for all He here became.
Only then could one grasp the full stay and comfort of
words like these, "Who shall separate us from the love of
Christ?" Unlike us, He *chose* the oblivion of birth and the
humiliation of life. He consented not only to die but to be
born. His life here, like His death which pointed it, was
the result of His free will. It was all one death for Him. It
was all one obedience. And it was free. He was rich and for
our sakes became poor. What He gave up was the fullness,
power, and immunity of a heavenly life. He became "a man
from heaven." When Paul spoke so he was not thrusting
upon his Churches the rabbinical notion of an Adam Kad-
mon, or ideal man in heaven, in the same sense as Judaism
spoke of an ideal existence of the Temple itself, or the law,
or the Mother Jerusalem from above, or the heavenly city
which came down out of heaven from God. Probably enough
he knew the notion, but only to transcend it, to use it freely
as a suggestion and not succumb to it merely as a dogma.
God sent His Son, He did not emit Him, He did not think
Him. The heavenly side of salvation was not ideal simply
but historic, though it was premundane history. It was an
eternal and immutable transaction. Things were done there.
God sent; the Son came. And He came consenting to earn
a glory He was entitled to claim. In all most precious things
must we not *erwerben* what we *ererben*, and appropriate our
greatest rights? Godhead came in Him, only not in force
but in virtue, not gross and palpable but in moral power.
He could have had His legions of angels. He could have
come and taken possession of the world as a ἁρπαγμόν,
as an Alexander seized a country. He could have come as an
Apollo King, and taken the world as a prize of war, by moral
storm, manly beauty, and heroic action. But, though He

came as God, He came to win the world as His Father's gift, and by the Father's way of the Cross as part of the gift. The self-determination to be man went the whole divine length to the self-humiliation of the Cross. The Son expressed His true nature as a servant; but it was glorious as the service of the eternal Son. He was Son before He became man; even as in His earthly life it was His sense of Sonship that gave Him His sense of Messiahship. It is what He did in becoming man, more even than what He did as man, that makes the glory of His achievement so divine that nothing short of absolute worship from a whole redeemed Humanity can meet it. Nothing short of that heavenly deed can stir the absolute worship which is the genius and the glory of His kingdom. Nothing else can enable us to measure the love of God, the thoroughness, the finality, the eternity of it. When God spared not His own Son, and yielded not even to the prayer of Gethsemane, it was a piece of Himself that He forswore; and in the grief of Christ He cut off His own right hand for the sake of the kingdom of His holiness. What God felt and did then was not through some relation to us that came into being with Christ's earthly life, but it was through something that underlay it. For had it come into being then, to see and judge the world in Christ would have been a step so new as to affect the unchangeableness of God. Grace would have begun, and so been finite. But it was a step which lay in the nature of Godhead for ever, in the eternal, personal, holy, and obedient relation of the Son to the Father, and in the act of renunciation outside the walls of the world.

Of course, when we come to discuss the precise mode of the Son's preexistence with the Father, or the psychological process of the kenosis, we are entirely beyond knowledge. The act is a postulate of saving faith, but the mode of action is insoluble. Logical difficulties may be raised against any view. But a kenotic theory so far has less than some, as I hope we shall see.

(*From* The Person and Place of Jesus Christ, *pp. 269-273.*)

It is important at a time like the present that we should keep clearly in view the interest which is served by our belief in the preexistence of Christ. Why should we press it? Why was it pressed in the New Testament? Was it in the interest of some scheme, either of philosophy or theology, which aimed at making more definite God's relation to the created world? Was it to provide some explanation for Christ's miraculous power, and especially for His resurrection? Was it to provide a large system of dogma with a celestial warrant? Was it to equip a religion with a central figure calculated to impress and command the imagination? Was it because the impression made by the historic Christ was so weak that it succumbed to the current notions of preexistence which floated in from the surrounding air and settled down to germinate in the warm soil of faith? It was for none of these reasons that the idea took the place it did, and has kept it. It was not in the dogmatic interest that it arose or survived, but in the religious. It was to give full and infinite effect to the condescending love of God, and to give range to the soul's greatness by displaying the vast postulates of its redemption. *Tantae molis erat divinam condere gentem.* If we feed on Christ it is on bread which came down from heaven. The soul's saviour could be no less a power than the soul's creator. It all arose from a sense of soul-greatness, from a direct, intimate, and intense relation between the soul and the Saviour, to which we grow daily more strange. It arose out of that experience; and not from the necessities of a system, or the infection from systems around. These would have been easily ignored had they given no means of expressing the experience that worked so mightily. It points in the same way when we note that Paul, in Philippians 2, uses the idea, as it was forced on living faith, for the purposes of that faith's moral culture. To promote a self-renouncing love he dwells on the act of self-renunciation which gave them for a Saviour God Himself in a life of humiliation, and no middle being who was a mere emanation from God in a world process.

(Ibid., *pp. 276-278.*)

Redemption was effected by Christ for the whole race, and it changed not only its religion but its whole moral condi-

tion and idea. And it does this for the various races within
the race. It is well to convert a man, it is more to convert an
age.

(From Missions in State and Church, p. 177.)

The whole course of history is a vast missionary movement
to release Christ from the past, to spread Him, to establish
Him in the life of a world foreign to Him and far from
Him, tending to be earthly, dark, cruel, and miserable. It
is to set up the kingdom of God among the kingdoms of
this world and above them. What is the inference for
national life? Surely that nation has the future which has
most of this large translating spirit in its policy.

(Ibid., p. 185.)

There is a Christ of nations as well as of souls. The nation
with a real future is the nation with a real Christ, to which
Christ is a real Lord. The race that best serves Him best
serves the future, and best serves its own destiny.

(Ibid., p. 187.)

And it is by no idea or even sentiment of fatherhood, but
by something so narrow as Christ's filial *will*, that we enter
to the Father. That individual will, straitened to the Cross,
is the one channel to a habitual life with the Father. That
will, not imitated nor reflected, but trusted. The way to the
infinite God, the infinite heart, the way to absolute *certainty*
about it, and to continual *life* in it, is the narrow way of
the historic man Jesus Christ crucified.

(Ibid., p. 203.)

The prerogative of Christ is that He is alone universal
among men. He is exclusively universal. . . . Indeed, you cannot have universality without exclusiveness.

(Ibid., pp. 206-07.)

THE SELF-EMPTYING OF CHRIST

The Church has always taught an earthly renunciation
on the part of Christ, which takes its eternal value from the
premundane renunciation that made Him Christ. We have
to make our renunciations in life alone; but He made His

before life. We have no choice as to our birth; He had. His will to die was also His will to be born. It is only by such a moral *act,* and not in the course of some ideal *process,* that we can think of His entry from a world of power and glory upon the conditions of earthly life. Only by a moral act could He incarnate Himself in human life, which is in its nature a grand act, choice, and venture, which is moral at its core, moral in its issues, and moral in its crown. If it was a real and universal human life He lived, that could only be by virtue of a moral act which is at least on the scale of the race; and if He was to master the race His act must be on an even greater scale, greater than the whole race's best, and as great as Holy God. The act that consented to become man was a superhuman act, an act of God. He did become creaturely. He did not simply enter a creature prepared for Him. When He was born human nature was not trans- formed by a special creation into some superhuman thing for the Spirit of God to enter — as a foreign palace might, by great furnishing effort and outlay, be transformed into an English home to honor a visit from our king. Nor were the two streams parallel while unmingled. There could not be two wills, or two consciousnesses, in the same personality, by any psychological possibility now credible. We could not have in the same person both knowledge and ignorance of the same thing. It He did not know it He was altogether ignorant of it. But the everlasting Sun in heaven was focussed in Christ — condensed to burn the evil out of man. The divine energy was concentrated for the special work to be done. The fullness of the Son's Godhead was still the essence of Christ. That Godhead lost nothing in the saving act. It took the whole power of Godhead to save; it was not the Son's work alone; far less then was it the work of any im- paired Son. It was not the work of a God *minorum gentium,* as the Arian Christ is. It could not be the work of any created being, however great. The value of the soul would slowly and surely sink if we believed it salvable by any creature. It would lower the soul that the Most High made for Himself were it saved by a second-class God. Such is the ethical effect on society of a false theology. The divine nature must belong to the universal and final Redeemer, however its mode and action might be conditioned by the work it had to do. The divine qualities were there; though their action was at once reduced, concentrated, intensified with the conditions of the saving work. The divine qualities were kept, but only in the mode that salvation made necessary. Jesus did not know everything actually, empirically, but only what was needful for that work. But, as that is the central final work in human nature, the knowledge required for it contains the promise and potency of all knowledge. And, as to the exercise of power, He did what God alone could do in forgiving human sin, a salvation which is the nucleus and germ of all worthy power beside. His knowledge, His power, His presence were all adjusted to His vocation. His vocation was not to apply or exhibit omnipotence, but to effect the will of infinite love, and master all that set itself against that. And that divine vocation was only possible to one who had a divine *position*. The world's Redeemer must be the Son of God.

If we ask *how* eternal Godhead could make the actual condition of human nature His own, we must answer, as I have already said, that we do not know. We cannot follow the steps of the process, or make a psychological sketch. There is something presumptuous in certain kenotic efforts to body forth just what the Son must have gone through in such an experience. God has done things for His own which it has not entered into the heart of man to conceive. It is the miracle behind all miracle. All detailed miracle was but its expression. It is the miracle of grace. And it can be realized (little as it can be conceived) only by the faith that grace creates, that answers grace, and works by love. Let us not be impatient of the secret. Love would not remain love if it had no impenetrable reserves. Love alone has any key to those renunciations which do not mean the suicide but the finding of the Soul.

(*From* The Person and Place of Jesus Christ, *pp. 318-320.*)

The question is this — when we begin with the gospel, when we begin with God's holy and loving will for the world in Christ — how are we to secure its realization in man?

How are we to establish in man as a race Christ's mutual, personal, and loving communion with such a God? That is something which no prophet was ever able to do. Prophetism was a failure for such a kingdom; it could not establish a national, to say nothing of a racial, communion with God; how could a Christ merely prophetic succeed? Did Christ succeed by that part of His life which was chiefly prophetic — the part prior to His death? The result of His life and teaching was that they all forsook Him and fled; but the result of His Cross, resurrection, and glory was to rally them and create the Church in which He dwells. Is not the creation of God's kingdom a task beyond the power of any instrument, any creature? Is it not God's own work? Whoever did it must be God Himself. Godhead must directly perform and sustain the great act that set up such communion. God must do it in person. Only one who incarnated God's holiest will as His Son alone did could produce and establish in men for ever the due response to that will — the response of their whole and holy selves. Holiness alone answers holiness; and only the Holy God could make men holy; it could be done by no emissary of His. We cannot be sanctified by commission or deputy. No intimation of Himself by God (through the holiest of creatures) could effect such an end. His *news* of Himself must rise to His *sacrifice* of Himself; His self-sacrifice must further be His self-vindication as holy; and from that it must go on rising to His *self-communication*. The Father who *spoke* by His prophets must *come* to save in the Son and must *occupy* in the Spirit. He offers, gives, Himself in the Son and conveys Himself in the Spirit. He who is the end of all, humbles Himself to be the means, that He may win all. God in Christ asserts Himself in His absolute freedom ("I, even I, am He"); He limits Himself for His creature's freedom ("that blotteth out thy transgressions"); and bestows Himself to make that freedom communion ("For I am with thee, saith the Lord, to save thee"). It is all one holy love and grace, in this eternal threefold action, both within God and upon man. Only on this trinitarian conception of God can we think of such a salvation as ours. Only so can we think of Christ as God with us. But then also we must follow on to ask how such a Christ is relative to this eternal and invisible God.

We have no call today to prove the real manhood of Jesus. For that is universally owned; and it is all that many can own. Things were otherwise in New Testament times, when it was freely held that the manhood was phantasmal and unreal. It is against such a notion that the writings of John are directed, and especially his Epistles — a fact which makes them somewhat irrelevant when used against the Socinian position in our own time. They were directed on people who were more ready to admit the divinity of Christ than His humanity. And with such people we have at the moment little to do.

Nor are we always called to convince people of the uniqueness of the man Jesus. That is, in some sense, freely owned by most who consider the matter seriously at all. Everything turns on what is meant by unique, whether He is unique in degree or in kind, whether it is the difference between the created and the increate. I have more than once pointed out that what is denied today is not a superior revelation in Christ but the absolute finality of that revelation. What we have to stand by is that finality — not of course in the sense that evolution has come to an end, but in the sense that all evolution is now *within* God's final word and not *up to* it. It is unfolding the Christ and not producing Him. Christ is God's seventh and last day in which we now for ever live and labor in rest. That is to say, the divine revelation is final but the human religion which answers it is not final. The word is final, but the response is progressive. The finality is as to the kind of God revealed and not as to the compass, which always enlarges upon us as culture enlarges our grasp. It is a question of the explication of God's last gift of Himself. And what we have chiefly to keep in view is the sort of uniqueness in the man Jesus which is required for the final and personal gift of Godhead in Him.

Now for such a purpose a Christ merely kenotic is inadequate. We have already seen that all revelation is God's self-determination. For any real revelation we must have a loving self-determination of God with à view to His self-assertion and self-communication; and this self-determination must take effect in some manner of self-divestment. We have examined the kenotic, or self-emptying theories of such an act, and we have found them either more helpful or less. But whether we take a kenotic theory or not, we must have some doctrine of God's self-divestment, or His reduction to our human case. Yet, if we go no farther than that, it only carries us half-way, it only leads us to the spectacle of a humbled God, and not to the experience of a redeeming and royal God. For redemption we need something more positive. It is a defect in kenotic theories, however sound, that they turn only on one side of the experience of Christ, viz., His descent and humiliation. It is a defect because that renunciatory element is negative after all; and to dwell on it, as modern views of Christ do, is to end in a Christian ethic somewhat weak, and tending to ascetic and self-occupied piety. For we can be very self-occupied with self-denial; it is the feminine fallacy in ethics. We must keep in view, and keep uppermost, the more positive process, the effective, ascending, and mastering process which went alongside of the renunciation in Christ, nay, was interwoven with it, as its ruling coefficient. I mean that, besides the subjective renunciation, we must note the growth, the exaltation, of His objective achievement, culminating in the perfecting at once of His soul and our salvation in the Cross, resurrection, and glory. I should not decline to speak carefully of a progressive incarnation. We must have some view, which may be kenotic indeed, but must also be more positive than kenoticism alone.

(Ibid., *pp. 326-330.*)

THE PERSON OF CHRIST

It may be an aid to clearness if it is explained here that by Christ is meant the historic Jesus as the eternal and only begotten Son of God, and by the Christian principle the idea of sonship taken religiously as the sonship of Humanity, nature and inalienable however man may behave, and not received by a moral redemption in Christ alone and for ever. The principle of personality is not essential to it, and not necessarily eternal for individuals. In the one case man is God's son in his freeborn right, in the other for Christ's sake alone.

(From "Christ and the Christian Principle," p. 134.)

Can a historical person be the object of an absolute faith?

(Ibid., p. 135.)

The chief practical objection to putting a principle in front of a person is that the religious life thereby becomes a one-sided process rather than a mutual act, an evolution rather than a communion; and thus it loses its ethical value, and is relegated to the pensive and passive side of our nature.

(Ibid., p. 149.)

The historic revelation in Christ is that the real is what we know as transcendently moral, the holy. That is the meaning of the incarnation.

(Ibid., p. 152.)

With us personality is never a finished thing, but a thing in constant growth; and it is an error to treat it as a complete, limited, and standard thing, and then to proceed to declare an infinite personality impossible. It is really the only form in which we can conceive intelligence or spiritual life — infinite self-knowledge, self-sufficiency, and self-determination. But a principle has none of these.

(Ibid., p. 154.)

And it can never effect what is the Christian relation to God, personal communion. Than this there can be nothing higher; and nothing less than this is the fullness of Christianity; which is not contact with God, impression from Him, or influence either from a God or a principle; but life-communion with the eternal. This is only possible with a living person. And the faith that effects it is absolute and final.

(Ibid., p. 155.)

The principle of Christ's relation to man is not a natural identity by constitution. . . . His connection with Humanity is not one of continuous self-realization, as if He crowned the great human process, and used sacrifice as a means on due occasion; it is one of self-identification, by an initial and a compendious act of sacrifice possible only to a Person who has the absolute disposal of Himself. Christ was God giving Himself far more than man finding himself.

(Ibid., pp. 156-57.)

If the supreme principle is to be guaranteed by a supreme person it must be identical with it.... An ultimate can only be guaranteed by itself. That is the basis of the certainty, supremacy, and autonomy of religion in the soul.... Our final authority must be God Himself in direct contact with Humanity, i.e. with History.... The key to the person of Christ is to be found not in an intellectual conviction, philosophic or theologic, nor in a romantic piety, part mystical, part wise, but in a positive religious experience of Him and a crucial moral decision behind which we cannot go in the quest for life's reality.... If for our faith Christ have the value of God we cannot help assigning to Him in our thought the nature of God.... The phenomenon of Christ is ultimate, and the faith that grasps it is the same.

(Ibid., pp. 159-162.)

What faith has to do with is the personal unity in an equal Godhead of Son and Father, a unity which is moral, because holy, in its nature, though it is much more than moral harmony; a unity also on the great moral principle that subordination does not imply inferiority. There must be a metaphysic of it, indeed, but that is deductive from the experience of faith, and not primary in producing faith, and not fixed in its form. Dogma, and especially metaphysical dogma, does not produce faith. It is only a temporary register of it. The function of dogma is to express the mind of the believing Church, not to prescribe to the inquiring world. The person of Jesus, however it may be metaphysically explained, has its first value as an actual and complete manifestation of the absolute personality as holy love. The necessities and implicates of such a revelation made to experience form the only sure foundation of a doctrine of the Trinity. ... And Christ makes real for those who enter communion with Him what without Him were a mere possibility, a mere bias to God. He is that which in them is only destiny. He *is* the gracious destiny of all. . . . God truly was in Humanity before Christ was born, but as a presence and a power in contact, and not in communion; by His Spirit, but not, as He is in His Church, by His Holy Spirit.

(Ibid., *pp. 164-65.*)

But, however it may fare with our imagery, in Christ we have two things, the two grand actions of spiritual being, in final peace and eternal power. We have the whole perfect action of Godhead concentrated through one factor or hypostasis within it[1] and directed manward both to create and redeem; and we have also the growing moral appropriation by man's soul moving Godward of that action as its own, as its initial divine nature and content. In Christ's life and work we have that divine mobility[2] in which the living Son eternally was — we have that coming historically, and psychologically, and ethically to be. He came to be what He always vitally was, by what I have called a process of moral redintegration. He moved by His history *to* a supernal world that He moved *in* by His nature. We have that divine Son, by whose agency the world of souls was made, but now creating another soul for His purpose, but Himself becoming such a soul. Surely, as I have said, if He had it in Him to make souls in the divine image it was in Him to become one. On the one side we have a personality, originally existing under those spiritual and discarnate conditions (for which our individualist ideas of person are so inadequate and misleading) — we have that personality taking the form and conditions of a corporeal life, in order to be the arena and the organ of God's revelation and man's redemption. (You may observe that what we are dealing with is not a contrast of finite and infinite natures, but of corporeal and discarnate spirituality or personality.) And, on the other side, we have Him growing in this corporeal personality, this increate but creaturely life. We have His eternal person living under the conditions

---

[1] By what theologians used to call an *apotelesma* in the Son.

[2] I ask leave to use the word mobility to express that uncaused self-contained vitality, that changeless change, in God which is the ground of the manward movement of which I speak.

of corporeal personality; we have His divine mobility, therefore, translated into human growth. We have together within one historic life the gradual descent and the growing ascent, by a moral process in each case. We have them on a world scale, an eternal scale, the scale and manner of spiritual being insofar as experience tells us of spiritual being. And we have them in the unity of one historic person, to show that, however inadequate earthly personality is to heavenly, they are not incompatible, and they are capable of the supreme mutual act of love and grace. In the person of Christ we have the crisis and sacrament of divine and human love. Do not let us speak here of impossible contradictions in logic. Let us rather remember here again that the reconciliation of such rational antinomies as God's sovereignty and man's freedom only takes place in the unity of one active person which has equal need of both for full personal effect.

Christ thus embodies the two movements of spiritual reality in which man and God meet. Such movements are at bottom acts. For the world is not so much the abode of God as the act of God; and man's function in the world is not so much to settle immanently into it, even into its growth, as to overcome it, subdue it, and find himself for a transcendently active God in it. In either case the movement is a vast act, and the goal is a personal communion of acts. On either side the personality is put into a dual act and consummated there.

So much must be allowed to the idea of immanence; which is a very fertile idea if it is construed ethically as action, and not ontologically as mere presence or mere movement; if it is viewed as the personal action within the world of a Person who needs other persons and their free acts for the communion which in Christ He found absolute and eternal.

Creation is only maintained by the standing act of the one God in His grace; who is, therefore, duly answered only by a whole devoted life as the standing act of man in his faith. God is active in His work as its incessant Creator, just as in His kingdom He is incessant Redeemer; and man, too, subsists in action, and becomes what his action makes him; and he attains the kingdom by the constant act of faith which

integrates him into the act of grace. Life, history, at its
highest may be figured as a wire traversed in opposite direc-
tions by these two great spiritual currents, movements or
acts.

Let us mark still more carefully their coexistence in Christ.

First, we have man's movement to God, or man's action
on God, either in the way of aspiration and prayer, or in
the way of acquiring from God moral personality.

It should here be remembered that human personality is
not a ready-made thing, but it has to grow by moral exercise,
and chiefly, in the kingdom of God, by prayer. The living
soul has to grow into moral personality. And this should not
be ignored in connection with the moral psychology of Christ.
He no more than we came into the world with a completed
personality — which would be not so much a miracle but a
magic and a prodigy.

What He brought with Him was such a soul as was
bound morally (and not by a fated necessity) to grow, under
His life's vocation, to the personality that was the complete
and final revelation of God, the agent of man's redemption,
and the *locus* of man's communion with God. A soul of
Godhead is the necessary postulate of the redeeming personality; it is the necessary foundation for the growth of that
personality; and it is the necessary condition of the finality
of His work. It was a personality that differed from all
others by finding its growth to lie in the unaided and sinless
appropriation of that which it already was. The *potuit non
peccare* rests (but in no fated or mechanical way) on the *non
potuit peccare*. The ground of His inability to sin did not
lie in the immunity, and almost necessity, of a nature or
rank, but in the moral entail, the moral reverberation, of
His great, initial, and inclusive act eternal in the heavens.
His renunciations on earth had behind them all the power
of that compendious renunciation by which He came to
earth; even as His earthly acts of individual forgiveness,
before He came to the universal forgiveness of Calvary, had
behind them that cross which He took up when the Lamb was
slain before the foundation of the world. His relation to God
was immediate from the first, and perfect; but that did not

give Him any immunity from the moral law that we must earn our great legacies, and appropriate by toil and conflict our best gifts. We have to *serve* ourselves, heirs to the greatness of our fathers. *Non potuit peccare,* nevertheless. The intimacy of His connection with Humanity was in that respect but qualified. Yet to His own experience the moral conflict was entirely real, because His self-emptying included an oblivion of that impossibility of sin. As consciousness arose He was unwittingly protected from those deflections incident to inexperience which would have damaged His moral judgment and development when maturity came. And this was only possible if He had, to begin with, a unique, central, and powerful relation to the being of God apart from His own earthly decisions. So that His growth was growth *in* what He was, and not simply *to* what He might be. It was not acquiring what He had not, but appropriating and realizing what He had. It was coming to His own unique self. I have already said that I am alive to the criticism to which such a position has been exposed, in that it seems to take Him out of a real moral conflict like our own. And the answer, you have noted, is threefold. First, that our Redeemer must save us by His difference from us, however the salvation get home by His parity with us. He saves because He is God and not man. Second, the reality of His conflict is secured by His kenotic ignorance of His inability to sin. And third, His unique relation to God was a relation to a free God and not to a mechanical or physical fate, or to an invincible bias to good.

The second movement is God's movement to man.

In this connection we note, *first,* that God by His nature does so move.

He is no Deistic God. His changeless nature is not stock-stiff and apart. It has an absolute mobility. It has in it the power and secret of all change, all out-going, without going out of Himself. It is part of His *self-assertion* as the absolute God that He should *determine Himself* into *communicating Himself.* He moves, He was not moved, to give Himself in revelation to man. But was man, then, eternal in God, if in His gift to man He do not go out of Himself in this act?

That cannot be; for man is His creature and the creature is not eternal. But He went out always to His increate Son, in whom and through whom all creation is and all Humanity; in and through whom alone we have the revelation and actual gift of Himself; who was coming, and not merely prophesied, in the Old Testament, and in a less degree in other faiths.

Second, He moves to save.

The coming of Christ in the long course of history is the coming of God the Redeemer. Man's hunger for deliverance is the greatest movement in all the soul's life except one — God's passion to save, and His ceaseless action in saving. It is here alone that we grasp God's real presence and rest on it for ever. Valuable as speculative versions of the incarnation may be, we only really have it and believe in it when we sit inside it, by the saving action which sets us in Christ, and assures us of the incredible fact that we are included by God's strange grace in the same love wherewith He loves His only begotten Son. We are sure of the incarnation only as those who taste the benefit of Christ's death in union with Him.

What we have in Christ, therefore, is more than the co-existence of two natures, or even their interpenetration. We have within this single increate person the mutual involution of the two personal acts or movements supreme in spiritual being, the one distinctive of man, the other distinctive of God; the one actively productive from the side of eternal God, the other actively receptive from the side of growing man; the one being the pointing, in a corporeal person, of God's long action in entering history, the other the pointing of man's moral growth in the growing appropriation by Jesus of His divine content as He becomes a fuller organ for God's full action on man. The two supreme movements of spiritual being, redemption and religion, are revealed as being so personal that they can take harmonious, complete, and final effect within one historic person, increate but corporeal.

(*From* The Person and Place of Jesus Christ, *pp. 338-344.*)

THE FAITH OF JESUS

Yet for all His trust in God, we hear nothing of the *faith* of Jesus. The New Testament writers seem almost deliberately to avoid applying to His relation with God the distinctive word which expresses ours both to God and Him. He required from men a faith He never exercised. He sees God, knows God, hears Him, and so forth, but He never *believes* in God as He taught and enabled men to do. He never says, "Believe in me as I believe in the Father." The religion of Jesus was a very different thing, for the New Testament writers, from the best of ours. Faith is the creation of God in us, but the trust of Jesus is never spoken or thought of in that way.

And Schlatter's suggestion seems sound. In our faith we have to make our way over a kind of moral difficulty which for Jesus did not exist. We have a gulf to cross that He had not. His darkness had a different source from ours. The experience of God in His case rested on a spiritual continuity with Him which for us does not exist — whether by our nature or by our fault. For Him neither did thought create the difficulty nor will the distance that we find between us and God. He felt otherwise than we before the Holiness which He yet saw as we never can. He never quailed before that which humbles us to the dust. Not such was His humility. For us there is now no condemnation, because for Him there never was. From Him the confession of sin and of faith are alike absent. Where we believe, He knew. Ours is the confidence of faith, His of vision. Where we believe with effort and godly fear, He knew and rejoiced in spirit (Matt. 11:25-27). For us faith is much more dependent on fear than with Him. With us it dies as it casts out fear; for Him the Lordship of the Father had another effect, and He was at home with His holy majesty. There was no repentance in His faith; but ours is not faith without it. Revelation was one process for Him, it is another for us. He needed none of the grace which is its one form for us. Our love of God grows out of faith, His trust grew out of love. We find God *in* our experience, but God *was* His. For us God emerges in our self-consciousness, for Him God was His self-consciousness. There was nothing mediatorial in His religion, ours is essentially so. He was His own Christ — as some now hold Humanity to be.

So that, as Schlatter says, faith is associated with such visitations of God as reach men from without — even if they come with that inward outwardness which they have in coming through Christ the Spirit. Christ used the word for the attitude of those who sought God's help through Him; but it was an attitude which He occupied towards none, towards no phase of nature and no soul of man.

It is little we are given to know of the religion of Jesus as His personal experience. But we know enough to know how essentially different it is from ours. And when one hears, for instance, that a particular community has been congratulated as being so Christian because of the ardency of its imitation of Christ, without any reference to its faith in a Redeemer whom to imitate is to deny — one wonders if all the Churches of the Reformation are due to end thus, and, having received the Spirit by the hearing of faith, are to sink to the perfection of the works of a subtle law. The faith *of* Christ is beyond us, and anything in its nature can only come by faith *in* Christ.

(From "The Faith of Jesus," p. 9.)

VI: CREATION

GOD, PURPOSE, AND EVOLUTION

The evolutionary idea is certainly compatible with Christianity; but not so long as it claims to be the supreme idea, to which Christianity must be shaped. Evolution is within Christianity, but Christianity is not within evolution. For evolution means the rule of a levelling relativism, which takes from Christ His absolute value and final place, reduces Him to be but a stage of God's revelation, or a phase of it that can be outgrown, and makes Him the less of a Creator as it ranges Him vividly in the scale of the creature. There is no such foe to Christianity in thought today as this idea is; and we can make no terms with it so long as it claims the throne. The danger is the greater as the theory grows more religious, as it becomes sympathetic with a Christ it does not worship, and praises a Christ to whom it does not pray. A book so devout as Bousset's Jesus does for the Saviour what the one-eyed Wotan did so tenderly for Brunnhilde within the touching *Feuerzauber*, "Ich küsse die Gottheit dir ab," "I kiss thy Godhead away." To say that evolution is God's supreme method with the world is to rule out Christ as His final revelation. It is to place Christ but at a point in the series, and to find Him most valuable when He casts our thoughts forward from Himself to a greater revelation which is bound to come if evolution go on. But when Christ's finality is gone, Christianity is gone. Yea, and progress itself is gone. For there is no faith in progress permanently possible without that standard of progress which we have in Christ, the earnest of the inheritance, the proleptic goal of history, the foregone sum of the whole matter of man. Progress without any certainty of the goal is as impossible in practice as it is senseless in thought. It is mere motion, mere change. We need a standard to determine whether movement be progress. And the only standard is some prevenient form or action of the final goal itself. Our claim is that for religion the standard is God's destiny for man, presented in advance in Christ — presented there, and not merely pictured — presented to man, not achieved by him — given us as a pure present and gift of grace — and presented finally there.

(From The Person and Place of Jesus Christ, pp. 10-11.)

It is not strange that the doctrine of evolution should have taken a hold upon the present age, which has in many quarters become a tyranny. It is a grand and comprehensive idea, which has now been taught to speak the language of the palpable sciences to every ear. It also clears up several of the more obvious difficulties that have posed the ordinary intelligence in the natural world by indicating that creation is not yet done. And "every new idea," says Goethe, "acts like a tyrant when it comes to light: hence the gain it brings only too soon turns to loss."

It is a youthful mistake, of course, to suppose that the idea of evolution in nature entered through Darwin or even Lamarck. It was a philosophic idea long before it was scientific, and it was far more comprehensive. It did not even dawn with Hegel (who has room for Darwin's greatness in a side pocket). It plays an unformed and mystic part in the Neoplatonic systems of Alexandrian times, and, through Augustine, had much place in medieval thought. It was an intuition of speculative genius (like so much in Lucretius, for instance) before it was a biological theme.

There is no doubt, also, it still exerts a great imaginative fascination. No small source of its influence is outside of its scientific utility as a hypothesis. Its popular spell is largely aesthetic; and it is due to the imposing features read into it by the imagination, which quietly elevates it from a physical hypothesis to be a scheme of the world. It seems to bring life from the dead. It represents a kind of evangelical revival, if not indeed a reformation, in the scientific mind. It offers to the mind, in a world which had seemed to antiquity so finished and fixed, the spectacle of a universe in vital movement, a ζῶον, in movement, too, on a vast scale, and in an overwhelming crescendo. Creation seems at last to be on the march — nay, on the path of victory. It is as if we were lifted to a place where we could safely look down on the whole battlefield of existence and see in rapture the vast deployment of the fight. It replaces the old mechanical conception of the world by the more engaging idea of organic growth. At the same time, it spreads the realm of cause and law to cover the vast region of new knowledge laid open by the explorers in all kinds; so that our growing experience reveals still a universe ordered in all things and sure; controlled, not to say centralized, yet instinct with vitality and promise. Again, it calls upon every individual to show cause for its existence in its contribution to the whole; and this, even if it swamp the individual's ultimate right to be which is drawn from his relation to the absolute God, is in tune with other instincts of the age, and seems a useful curb upon unchartered egoism. It seems to show that the moral and social forces, which repress undue claims for self, are the great agents and guarantees of human progress, that godliness is not only good but useful, and profitable for both worlds if we look widely enough. And it appears to take some of the gloom from the struggle and pain of existence by showing that it is not all fruitless, not gratuitous and suicidal, but a condition of progress so far. It writes one aspect of the Cross, its sacrifice, on the whole area of life, and traces the roots of it among the minute crevices of all sentient being. It may at once be said that in principle the evolutionary idea has a place and value in science that can never be lost, however

questionable we may find it in philosophy. And it has fore-
gleams and points of contact for the nobler morality, fatal
as it may be to it on the whole (for its altruism has a strange
trick of suddenly doubling back into a hard egoism). But
to fight it or begrudge is no duty of religion, and no service
to it, so long as the theory is not elevated to be a new religion,
and a complete guide of life.

. . . .

At most, and even supposing the missing link or links
were found, the doctrine simply registers a method of past
procedure. It has no world goal. It has no teleology on one
great cosmic scale. There is nothing that gives us to know
the problem set us as living souls in the world, far less to find
ourselves in that problem. It does not explain the world, it
only marshals it. It is an organizer and not an interpreter.
It sets up the type in lines and pages, but it cannot read the
book or open its seal. It follows its grammar, but not its
logic; and it does not discern its spirit. It is not revelation,
but illumination. Knowledge of the world is one thing, and
that can be expressed in science; but the explanation of the
world is another thing, and it has to do with destiny. Even
the knowledge is as yet very incomplete. At the source of
each step is a variation whose cause is unknown, and whose
method of appearance is unexplained. Far less have we a
causal explanation of the origin of one particular variation
—consciousness; less still of the origin of self-consciousness
and spiritual, responsible life. There is no scientific bond con-
necting the finest movement with even a primitive consciousness. And the gulf is not bridged between the ideas
and duties in human thought and the pictorial conceptions of
the animals below. But supposing many of these gaps were
connected up, we should still have but a splendid sequence,
waiting for its true explanation in some great interpretive
Word. This word can only express an end, goal, or destiny;
and for such a word science not only has not, but cannot
have, the secret. Explanation has far more to do with purpose than with cause or method. *How* man was made does
not tell us *why* he was made, and cannot. History alone does
not give destiny. It is only in a modified sense that the

history of a truth is its criticism. We may ask what caused all this and marshals it, or we may ask what means all this and crowns it; and while science has a place in dealing with the first question, with the second it has nothing to do, nor anything to say upon it. The answer to the first does not necessarily answer the second, and the second must not arrest the first. Science seeks causes or methods, but not ends. She can but know and formulate the world so far as it has gone, she cannot interpret it by the end to which it is going. She must claim the region of etiology, but let teleology alone. The explanation of the world is in its nature revelation, and only faith can apprehend it. For it is an unfinished world, and a destiny corresponding to its vast scale cannot be forecast by us. But it may be foretold to us, and in principle it is — in the absolute revelation which breaks through the midst of history in Christ. The goal of the world is a spiritual power already in the midst of the world. The final whole is given us in Christ's spiritual whole. It is the perfecting, the universalizing of our present miraculous communion with the eternal God. It is the kingdom of God — which is given us and not achieved, which is matter of revelation and not of discovery. Redemption is man's destiny. The purpose of the world is the correction of a degenerate moral variation on its way to becoming universal. Only our responsive faith gives us that knowledge of the infinite whole in which evolution works as a partial procedure. Yet for explanation it is the whole that we need. I am not myself a true and whole self till I find my place in the whole. We need something on which man as evolved can stand while he construes the process of his evolution. For our security we ask, What is the vast power going to do with us at last? We need a moral, universal, and final teleology; and that is the gift in Christ. Let us only take care that we treat that gift as a teleology and a power. Let us not waste it upon questions of causes, to which it brings no direct answer. In this region its best service is the promotion of a true science, equipped for causal research, and counting among its first equipments those spiritual and ethical conditions in which alone a true science can rise and thrive.

And when we ask what progress means, what it is measured by, how it is distinct from mere movement, what shall we reply? What entitles us to say whether any increase of movement or complexity is progress?[1] Must the newest be the truest? We have from science no answer. Evolution is quite silent, because quite ignorant, as to its own goal and standard. It looks to yesterday with a smile, which fades whenever its glance turns to tomorrow. To what do we move? Over Niagara? To what do we climb? To the top of a slumbering volcano, on whose slopes the vines grow lush only because of its one-day fatal fires? What has the individual to reconcile him to all that is exacted from him in toil, suffering, and death to feed the progress of the race? What profit is there in his blood? What is the recompense of whole races and ages thus crushed and erased? What private, personal, inward, and spiritual gain have they won? Why should they toil and suffer for the sake of a posterity equally blank and barren? The struggle naught availeth. What is there to translate their cross into glory, their sorrow into hope? What is to transfigure their body of grief and death? What is to change them from victims into martyrs, and from martyrs into the seed of some triumphant Church? If there be any such integrating agent it must surely be something which is at once the final victory and the present power; some purpose which runs through all things as the truth in all and the crown upon all; some will which turns mere matter into purpose, which elects to proceed in the way of selection, and to sustain in the way of communion. We must find the end of living in the living God, the goal of all in the stay of all. And this is a power which we have only in the revelation of the Cross and its foregone (may I say its proleptic?) conquest. The empirical world is far too vast, complex, and tragical now for any philosophy of history to prophesy its goal from the necessities of speculative surmise and the categories of an irresistible ideal embedded in thought. We must turn for our certainty elsewhere where philosophy

---

[1] The very Church has come to confound size with power, and bustle with growth. It gets excited about a Church census, and it stupefies its ministers by incessant demands for what is slangily called "work."

fails as a foundation. We turn to historic faith and its experience. We are cast onward and upward to faith as our divine destiny. We were born to believe; and we are harried, as it were, into our heaven. We are carried reluctantly to our true glory, which is to know because we trust, rather than trust because we know. Our chief knowledge is of that whereby we are known. We are cast upon faith, neither as a *pis aller,* nor as a leap in the dark, upon a faith which finds in the historic work of the superhistoric Christ an absolute warrant of the kingdom of God as the close and crown of all. This realm will not be on earth; but it grows from earth, though planted from heaven. It is only evolved because it has been infused. It is one of the great gains of our time to have realized the organic continuity of the spiritual future with the growing present. The modern world but prolongs the soul of the seen through the crisis of death. And our heaven is more a fulfilment of our earth than its reward. Glory is but the consummation of grace, and grace arises in the very heart of nature and history, though it springs out of neither. The kingdom of God is to faith the immanent truth of things, their soul and *nisus,* subtly, slowly supreme on earth, and eternal in the heavens.

. . . . . .

There is, for life at its last and largest, an end of all things which is only given in the moral world. There are so many cases of maladaptation both in nature and society that it is impossible to base a fixed faith on a teleology which takes account only of the happy adjustment we can trace in either. It is not in nature at all that we can find nature's end. Nor is it in living society that we find the sure word of prophecy as to the social goal. And if it be in history, it is not in history as a series. It is not an induction from the whole area of history (which we see not yet), or the abstraction of an apparent tendency. It is at a point of history, where for once and all the soul becomes a personality as absolute and final as it is in God. In Jesus Christ we have the final cause of history, and the incarnation of that kingdom of God which is the only teleology large enough for the whole world. It is to faith, to the loving soul believing in Christ, that all things work together for good. Let the text be finished. All things cooperate for blessing to them that love a God in Christ reconciling the world, and are the called in His purpose. It is this frame of mind and heart that all nature and history are adjusted to produce at the long last. It is this order of heart that is the destined and called, according to life's original and final purpose in God. And it is this faithful union with Christ that affords to the individual soul power to rise up against the pressure of an environing world and an evolutionary past, and to assert itself with an originality which the vast process tends to stamp out. This is especially so in the case of repentance against a degenerate past. It is only faith, and faith in Christ, that enables the soul, lamed by its own schism and treason, to resist the tendency to go with the huge natural stream, and to submit to be classed as a thing among things. Each man, indeed, is a child of his age, but only so far as the form of his problems go. Their essence is perennial. And the answer must come from that in him which is both within and above his age, which links him to the Unseen and Eternal and gives him intelligence of its ways. Redemption is the one goal. Christ is the purpose of God for the world. The Redeemer Himself is already our redemption, the Saviour is our sanctification, who Himself is made unto us righteousness and perfection. Our salvation is to be in Christ, and we are complete in Him, in whom and for whom are all things.

Till science appreciate and explain the historic fact of Christ, it has not subdued the world. When He is explained we possess the world's explanation. Only, it is an explanation which to science as science is always impossible. For science cannot concern itself with ends or destinies. And these are the categories that explain Christ. It was in these He chiefly wrought. And the Christian explanation proceeds by the knowledge of faith, not of sight; by the faculty which interprets the value of facts, and not simply their cause or coordination. It appreciates the why of the world, and not simply its how. Science here is like the balance which says this is heavy and that is light, but cannot say if either be silver or gold.

So, besides the limitations of the evolution doctrine in its own area, there are great areas of existence and life to which it does not apply at all. What solves the biological problem does not solve the philosophic. The formula for the evolution of a section is not the norm for the evolution of the whole. The great conflict of the age is the battle for a spiritual interior, a spiritual totality, and a spiritual interpretation of life and the world. This is the test of every new doctrine which comes before us. Does it make for the spiritual value of life? Or does it discourage it? Or does it preclude it at the outset? And judged by this test the higher we rise towards man's spiritual life, the more inadequate does the evolutionary principle seem. It would be foolish to say that our spiritual life is unaffected by it; but it would be more foolish to say that it is expressed by it, far less explained. Evolution is not the complete formula for human progress. Righteousness and peace are worth more than mere progress and prosperity, and what does not bring them is neither a revelation nor a gospel.

. . . .

I have spoken of the inadequacy of evolution as a formula for the region of spiritual originality, and for that of the morally backward and forward. But there is another area besides where its writ does not run. I mean the whole world of the changeless which is so indispensable as a background, an interior, nay, a constant source for the world of change. The development of spiritual faculty it is that brings us into touch with this permanent world. As we rise in human affection we realize how fixed the primal passions are. The human heart beats to the same measure today as in the Eddas. "Homer's sun lights us, and we see it with the same eyes." The old and aching riddle of life is substantially the same for us as it was for Job. The refinement and flexibility of human relations demand more and more urgently a fixed moral world, an eternal and immutable morality, an authority that cannot be shaken, a standard that is not relative but absolute for the soul. Even change lends itself to a philosophy of development only in so far as it is methodic, calculable change, normal variation, going on by fixed laws, and partaking of the uniformity of nature. Parallel to all the change is a presence and permanency of law which gives it its scientific value. The laws of the persistence of matter and the conservation of energy are inseparable from every extension of the area of evolutionary change. Without this permanent element evolution is impossible. But it is an element which accompanies the evolutionary process rather than is subject to it. It holds change in a hand that knows no change. The very regularity of change lifts it out of the realm of change. And we are warned here of our approach to a region which is not subject to mutation, but is the source of those very fixtures and orders that convert variation into real progress and life. For the fixity that regulates such change is but an index of a spiritual fixity at once final and fluid, whose true name is the eternal God, leading all time and marshalling all space.

. . . .

For it is another drawback to evolution that it measures everything by present utility and treats nothing as an end in itself. It tends to exclude purpose and dwell in utility. Everything is viewed as it may contribute to some fashion of life conceived and not revealed. We cultivate an earthly other-worldliness. We aspire to a mere millennium at best. Some Utopia is our goal, not a present God. Nothing is of final and absolute value within life. This inevitably means a hardening and flattening of life, and it breeds that vehement restlessness of the hard, the tense, and the lean. We are not living, but always wanting to live. We live in gasps, dashes, and breathless moments. Our object is motion and not action; life is something we snatch at, and the iridescent bubble bursts as we seize. We live in a passion for the thrilling, the new, the next article. We crave for effects, sensation, all the monotonous kaleidoscope of the average man, and the dreary excitements of suburban mediocrity. Attention is monopolized not by life but by its lenitives, or by the means or living, or of aggrandizing life. The absolute value of the individual disappears. The mere fact of the individual, it is true, is exaggerated. He is insulated as atom from all the rest of the world by the absence of any but a causal nexus. He is knit into no fabric of purpose or destiny, of sympathy or glory. His existence, his demands are extravagantly emphasized. But meantime his *worth* is diminished. He grows as a unit, but he fades as a world. He has place and force, but no interior, no meaning. He is a quantity without quality. He issues, in the most favored cases, as the unmoral *Uebermensch*. The right of the weak vanishes, as does the pity for the weak. The infinite preciousness of the soul sinks. The value of life decays. With the soul's worth sinks the soul's freedom. Liberty is of small account. "Empire" and "firm government" engross men's thought and care, as ends and not means. Religious zeal and even unction are found to coexist with moral stupidity and vulgarity. These are fruits which we see only too palpably around us. And they are much due to the extent to which evolution has unconsciously become a theology, and has ceased to be a scientific hypothesis. It has spread, by an act of imaginative and nonmoral faith, from being a theory of nature to being a solution of the world, from a fact of observation to being a philosophy, even a guide of life, nay, a form of religion. From a sectional formula it becomes the principle of the whole. From a method it has become a doctrine, and then with the stalwarts a dogma. Have the extravagant claims of a narrow theology ever been more grasping and withering than this in certain well-known cases? It is a case of hasty idealization in which imagination plays as much part as knowledge, and dogmatism ousts philosophy. A leap is made for an aesthetic and imposing completeness of system which is a work of art more than science. We are supplied at best with an object of reverence rather than faith, and a source of enthusiasm rather than love, wherewith to replace the spiritual trusts and divine affections that have been thrown away on the plea of being outgrown.

(From "Christian Aspects of Evolution.")

CHRIST, THE INDIVIDUAL, AND THE RACE

But no society can permanently rest on the mere freedom of its individuals or preferences.

(From Marriage: Its Ethic and Religion, p. 14.)

Monogamy is the true index of civilization. That is the true nature of society, the nature which, through all its history, has been working to the top, where civilization, through Christianity, has now fixed it.

(Ibid., *p. 31.*)

A complete Humanity rests on men and women who do not simply fuse in passion, but who grow into each other in sacrifice as only souls can.... Man and wife are one flesh as one spiritual personality ... by each being the other's inner complement. They interpenetrate. They make up a joint personality by the harmony of an indelible psychic difference. And this dual, or complex personality (family ties) is the base of the corporate unity of society. And it is the point of attachment for those great spiritual analogies which connect Christ so intimately with a human society in the Church.

(Ibid., *p. 34.*)

Each soul is more than a product, more than a convergence. But it has an active, a *law-giving* power, a valuing, selective, nay, creative power, a power of growth and of mastery. A living soul is also a life-giving spirit. It has a self and only so is it spiritual — as it is personal. It has therefore a life peculiar to itself and autonomous. It has a creative function, which makes it a fresh contribution to the series at each point, a quite new departure, and which, therefore, places it outside the methods of physics, when we go to the heart of the matter. This is indeed one modern aspect of the same contention as appears in the old issue of the freedom of the will.

The analogy may be applied to the social soul, to the solidary mind, to society.... Each age is more than a redistribution of the forces of its past.... For society itself is composed of such souls, which find in it their higher unity. They find themselves in it, personality being super-individual. But it is a unity which, if it limit the individual, yet is the condition of his social life and freedom.... If souls were but atomic products, and not contributory sources, they could never form a society. They would form a mosaic but not a

tissue.... No true society can be formed by simple addition.
. . . .

They produce in a society a living creature which has something in the nature of personality. It has something with a
cognate yet superior kind of personality, such as theology
speaks of in the personal Godhead's relation to its inner
Trinity of Persons. The credibility of that doctrine is likely
to be favorably affected by the modern passage from the
metaphysic of static substance to the metaphysic of social
ethic, of personality, of spirits and their interpenetration;
and especially the metaphysic of growing personality enhanced by its congenial social medium, of the social spirit,
the corporate personality.

(*From* Theology in Church and State, *pp. 154-157.*)

But such a large conception of personality should become
easier as we leave that empirical, substantial, or atomic notion
of unity or reality, and find it in action — as we find the
fundamental unity to be that unitary and eternal Act of
God which is the universe itself — *die Welt als Tat.*

(Ibid., *p. 159.*)

It seems at first sight as though it were meaningless to
speak as if God could be wroth with the world and yet
gracious and loving to individuals. But I may be very angry
with a political party, yet I cherish respect and love for individuals belonging to that party. We must be on our guard
against narrow, individual views, against treating individuals
according to their public and collective condemnation. We
are created, redeemed, judged as members of a race or of a
Church. Salvation is personal, but it is not individual. (There
is another distinction for you, if you have come in off the
street.) It is personal in its appropriation but collective in its
nature. What did the Reformation stand for? Not for religious individualism. But I hear someone asking in the back
of his mind, Was not the Reformation the charter of private
judgment and individual independence? It was nothing of
the kind. It was the charter of personal direct faith and its
freedom. What the Reformation did was to turn religion
from being a thing mainly institutional into a thing mainly

personal. The Reformers were as strong as their opponents about the necessity of the Church for the soul — though as its home, not its master. They were not individualists. Individualism is fatal to faith. It was the backbone of the rationalism and atheism of the French Revolution. The Reformation stands for personal religion and social religion and not for religious individualism.

There is no such thing as an absolute individual. What is the change that takes place when we are converted? Our change is really from one membership to another, from membership of the world to membership of the Church. When we become a member of the Church we are not really changed from individualism, but from membership of the world. It is membership either way. The greatest egoist and self-seeker is a member of the world. He could not indulge his egotism if it were not for the society in the midst of which he lives and into which he is articulated. He is a member of the world who exploits his membership instead of serving with it. When we are converted we are not converted from a sheer and absolute individual. There never was such a person. Certainly Robinson Crusoe was not. We are converted from membership of the world to membership of Christ. Before our conversion and after we *belong*. We are not absolute, solitary individuals. We are in a society, an organism. We are made by the past. And our selfish, godless actions and influence go out, radiate, affect the organism as they could not do were we absolute units. They spread far beyond our memory or control. In the same way we are acted upon by the other people. We are members one of another both for evil and for good. When you are told that evil is only selfishness it is worth while bearing this in mind. Even as selfish men, as egoists, we belong — only to a pagan order instead of to Christ. The selfish man is a member of a kingdom of evil. There is no such thing as an absolute individual. Hence, to save us, to reconcile us, involves the whole race we belong to. Before God that race is an organic unity. It is not a mere mass of atoms joined together by various arbitrary relations, sympathies, and affinities. Hence, as the race before God is one, a personal God is able to do for the race some one thing which at the same time is good for every person in it.

But now, if the race is a unity, where does its unity lie? Does it lie in our elementary affections for each other, in the palpable relationships of natural life with our parents, brothers, lovers, and friends? Or is the unity of the race simply its capacity for being organized by skillful engineers? Is the unity of the race like the unity of machines? No. The unity of the race is a moral unity. Therefore it is a unity of conscience. If you want to find the trunk out of which all the loves and practices of Humanity proceed, you must go to conscience at the center. That is where the unity of Humanity lies. It is in the conscience, where man is member of a vast moral world. It is the one changeless order of the moral world, emerging in conscience, that makes man universal. What have you to preach if you have no gospel that goes to the foundations of human conscience? What ground have you for a social religion? The most universal God is one that goes there, not to the heart in the sense of affections, but to the conscience. The great motive for mission of every high kind is not sentiment, but salvation. It is dangerous to take your theology from poets and literary people. You quote, "One touch of nature makes the whole world kin." Well, if you are going to build a religion on that, it will have a very short life. In the long run nature means anarchy when taken by and for itself. But it was never meant to be taken by itself. It was meant to go in an eternal context with supernature. It is not the touch of nature that makes us kin enough for religion, for eternity, but the touch, and more than a touch, of the supernatural — not nature, but grace. What makes the world God's world is the action and unity of God's moral order of which our conscience speaks.

Now, if that order be broken, how can it be healed? If I slit the canvas of this tent it can be patched. I make a fissure, but it is not irremediable. I simply get someone to stitch it up. At the worst I can have a new width put in. But if the moral order, and its universal solidarity, its holiness, is broken, how can that be healed? That cannot be patched up. It is not merely a rent in a tissue, a gap in a process, which the same process goes on to heal into a scar. The moral law differs from all natural law in having in it a demand, a claim, an "ought" of a universal kind. It is all of one piece. We use the word law in a loose kind of way. We apply the same word to gravitation and to the moral law of retribution. It is that ambiguity of terms which leads us astray. The moral law differs from every other law in having a demand, and a universal demand, a claim upon us for ever. And that has to be made good as well as the rents and bruises in us from our own collision with it. It is not a gap that has to be made good and sound. It is a claim, because we are here in a moral and not a natural world. It is one thing to make good a gap and another thing to make good a claim. The claim must be met. It will not do simply to draw the edges together by mere amendment, to have God here and man there, and gradually bring them together till they unite. It is two moral persons with moral passions we have to do with. It is moral relationship that is in question; communion, trustful mutuality, is the object of the divine requirement. It is a case of moral, holy reconcilement. It is the expression of God's holy personality whenever God makes His claim.

(*From* The Work of Christ, *pp. 119-124.*)

THE JUSTIFICATION OF GOD

The radical questions of a belief are forced upon us anew by each crisis of the world. And the first task of the Church, before it go to work on the situation that a crisis leaves behind, is to secure the truth and certainty for its own soul of its faith in the overcoming of evil by good; an operation which may mean the recasting of much current and favorite belief. Is there a divine government of such a world, a world whose history streams with so much blood, ruin, and misery as to make civilization seem to many doubtfully worth while? That question means for its answer another, Is there a divine goal of the world? Because, if there is, God who secures it has the right to appoint both its times and its means; and a good government of the world is what helps best in our circumstances to bring us there. But is there such a goal, and where do we find it? How shall we be sure of it? Are we to believe in it only if we can sketch its economy, and trace the convergence of all lines, whatever their crook or curve, to that point? Do I believe that all *is* well with my soul only in so far as I see that all *goes* well? Can we be sure that all is well with the world only if the stream of its history run through no dreadful caves, nor shoot wild cataracts, nor ever sink to a trickle in the sand of deserts horrible? Is there, in spite of all appearance, a divine teleology for the soul and for the race? The evolutionists seem driven more and more to a teleology of the world. Is it a divine one, found in the moral soul and in its eternal destiny for the image of God?

These, I have said, are questions which it is the business of a practical religion to answer — or, more exactly, of the revelation which is the heart and source of such religion. A revelation will be great, universal, and final just as it does answer such questions, and pacifies even the soul it does not yet satisfy. "What I do, thou knowest not now, but thou shalt know hereafter."

(*From* The Justification of God, *pp. 42-43*.)

Is there any divine visitation that puts us in possession, *in petto,* of the goal of all surmise? Is there any divine gift and deed that fixes the colors seen by genius in the eternal purpose and kingdom of God, where all earth's hues are not mere tints but jewels — not mere purpureal gleams, but enduring, precious foundation-stones?

To all such questions Christianity answers with an everlasting yea, however Christendom may blue or belie it. The eternal finality has become an historic event. There is a point of time at which time is no longer, and it passes into pure but concrete eternity. That point is Christ. In Christ there is a spot where we are known far more than we know. There is a place where God not only speaks but comes, and not only vouches but gives, and gives not only Himself to the soul, but, by a vast crisis, the soul to itself and the world to His Son. Our error and uncertainty go

back at last for their power to our guilt, and they pass away
in the gift of the grace that destroys it. The grace that
magnifies the guilt in the act of mastering it takes away the
doubt. Trust gives us the security denied to sight. We
escape from evidences to realities. Our dreams of good
become the certainty of God. In Christ God is not preached
but present, and not only kind but mighty, not only willing
but initiative, creative. He does more than justify faith, He
creates it. It is His more than ours. We believe because
He makes us believe — with a moral compulsion, an invasion
and capture of us. He becomes our eternal life. To live is
Christ. He is our destiny. He is our career. And He is the
same yesterday and for ever. The soul's goal is always the
soul's God. The world's perpetual destiny is the world's
Eternal Redeemer. We inherit "a finished work." We
receive, in advance, the end of our faith, which is the
salvation of our souls in the salvation of a world. We
receive, in the *Holy* Spirit (the Spirit of a perfection which
is always completely its own end), the pledge and installment
of our common heritage. This talk is scriptural in phrase,
but it is not antiquated in sense — except as we may have
come so to regard the whole miracle of the Spirit, who is
always changing time into eternity, and turning the Christ
of the past into the soul's real present. We possess, in a
living and present Christ, God's goal and destiny of the
soul and of the world. We are put (miraculously, it is true,
by the Spirit) in possession of a God whose holy self-
sufficiency secures the certainty of His purpose, and whose
purpose is the world's salvation to Himself in a kingdom.
It is not a salvation to prosperity, nor to civilization, nor to
idealism, but to Himself, to His obedience, His communion,
His realm. In this revelation, the economy of salvation
becomes the principle of the movement of the universe.
Nature is but a draft scheme of salvation with the key on
another sheet, where the eternal act of redemption is found
to carry and crown the long process of creation. It is God's
salvation of the world that dominates the long history of
the world — infallibly, if not at every point palpably. Such
is the position of Christian faith, and it is the ground of all

our good hope and sure outlook for the future. Such is the nature of Christian teleology. It rises from our experience of the Christian revelation.

The more recent trend of the philosophy of history points this way. The temptation is strong for many today to construe life on a scheme of evolution borrowed from the natural world, and passing through the normal points of birth, bloom, and death. But we are arrested in this scheme by several facts when we are dealing with personal life. For instance, the beginning of that life is not with birth, but with the first exercise of the soul in an act of free choice. Then its development does not lie in natural process, but in a series of such acts of choice, in which the personality asserts itself against the processes that would but hurry it, as a thing, down a stream. Its culmination, again, is not mere blossom, it is not in the easy, unconscious play of forces, but in the deliberate harmony of the self-asserting will with an ideal conceived, pursued, and more or less attained. And finally, death is not simply failure as blameless decay, but it is bound up with a failure with which we charge ourselves; and our best life is a gift in the midst of such failure, a gift of mercy, forgiveness, redemption, eternity.

(Ibid., *pp. 47-49.*)

If our problem is Job's, the historic answer has now gone much further than what he received. The Cross of Christ has come and gone; and we do not simply bow with Job under a sublime majesty more sure and impressive than the mercy. But in the Cross of Christ, as is His majesty so is His mercy. That is to say, He is gracious with all His might, and not in an arbitrary interval of His power. The solution there to the question of a teleology is not simply a *tour de force* of revelation; it is a moral victory and redemption; it is *the* moral victory which recovered the universe. The Vindicator has stood on the earth. It is the eternal victory in history of righteousness, of holiness, of the moral nature and character of God as Love. It is therefore the solution also to the teleological question in its more pointed form, as to a theodicy. It justified not man merely but God. The divine destiny of the world was not simply revealed in Christ but secured; and in a way which not only respected the holiness of God, but put it into action and leading action. The solution is equally religious and moral, as the Christian idea of the holy must be. It is evangelical, with the note of guilt, tragedy and glory. It is soteriological. It is a matter of judging grace, and of grace *taking* judgment. It is in the faith of God as a holy Saviour, and our deliverance from guilt in His Cross, judgment, and resurrection. God's justification of man opens our eyes to His justification of Himself. Both are one and the same act. The power of God unto salvation is the revelation and the energy of the righteousness of God (Rom. 1:16-17). It is holy love at work in final judgment, i.e. in the rectification of all things. The Cross of Christ creates in faith the assurance that the whole course of the world which entailed it is, before everything else, the explication of His work — a vast means for man's separation from his sin and union with his God. And thus by the Will and Act of God history fundamentally and finally serves His purpose of holy love. If it all seems very slow, and justice seems for periods even turned backwards, that only means that, since we do not see sin as God sees it, we have misconceived the problem. Those who are disappointed with the social success of Christianity must challenge the action of any beneficent power in history to the same extent. But, further, it is not *beneficence* but holiness that makes God God, and prescribes His action with the moral soul, with its intractability at worst, and at best its docility instead of its repentance. The most anomalous thing, the most poignant and potent crisis that ever happened or can happen in the world, is the death of Christ; the whole issue of warring history is condensed there. Good and evil met there for good and all. And to faith that death is the last word of the holy omnipotence of God. There is nothing hid from the light of His grace there, and nothing outside its service, its ethic, and its final mastery. The whole world is reconstituted in the Cross as its last moral principle, its key and its destiny. The

Cross is at once creation's fatal jar and final recovery. And there is no theodicy for the world except in a theology of the Cross. The only final theodicy is that self-justification of God which was fundamental to His justification of man. No reason of man can justify God in a world like this. He must justify Himself, and He did so in the Cross of His Son.

No reason of man can justify God for His treatment of His Son; but whatever does justify it justifies God's whole providence with the universe, and solves its problem. He so spared not His Son as with Him to give us all things. The true theology of the Cross and its atonement is the solution of the world. There is no other. It is that or none. And that theology is that the Cross is not simply the nadir of incarnation, but that it is God's self-offering (under the worst conditions that love could feel for evil man) to His own holy name. The just God is the chief Sufferer and sole Doer. The holy love there is in action everywhere. The most universal thing in the universal Christ is His Cross. Everywhere, according to God's ubiquity, immanence, or what you will, His holy love is invincibly at issue with death, sin, and sorrow. Everywhere is redemption. And that is the only theodicy. The purpose of salvation is the principle of creation; and the ruling power of the world is the purpose of God.

It is no light problem that faces the Creator in His world. There was never such a fateful experiment as when God trusted man with freedom. But our Christian faith is that He well knew what He was about. He did not do that as a mere adventure, not without knowing that He had the power to remedy any abuse of it that might occur, and to do this by a new creation more mighty, marvellous, and mysterious than the first. He had means to emancipate even freedom, to convert moral freedom, even in its ruin, into spiritual. If the first creation drew on His might, the second taxed His all-might. It revealed His power as moral majesty, as holy omnipotence, most chiefly shown in the mercy that redeems and reconciles. To redeem creation is a more creative act than it was to create it. It is the last thing omnipotence could do. What is omnipotence but the costly and inevitable action of holiness in establishing itself everywhere for ever. The supreme power in the world is not simply the power of a God but of a holy God, upon whose rule all things wait, and may wait long. It is no slack knot that the Saviour had to undo. All the energy of a perverse world in its created freedom pulled on the tangle to tighten it. And its undoing has given the supreme form to all God's dealing with the world. But at the same time the snarl is not beyond being untied. Man is born to be redeemed. The final key to the first creation is the second; and the first was done with the second in view. If moral freedom is the crown of the first creation, spiritual, holy freedom is the goal of moral; and it is the gift in the second creation. The first creation was the prophecy of the second; the second was the first tragically "arrived." There was moral resource in the Creator equal to anything that might happen to the creature or by him. And that resource is put forth in Christ — in His overcoming of the world on the Cross, and His new creation of it in the Spirit. All God's omnipotence is finally there. The great goal is not the mere fruitage of the first creation, but another creation more creative still. The first does not glide into the second; there is a crisis of entirely new departure.

This was a salvation in which God first justified Himself, hallowed His own name, and made His eternal purpose good in those heavenly places which rule earthly things. His holy love is not there just as the instrument of man's salvation, but man's salvation is there to the glory of God's holy love. Man is only saved by God's holiness, and not from it, not in spite of it. He is saved by the tragic action of a holy God, by the honor done by God in Christ to His own holy name and purpose. There is a brief phrase in Julian of Norwich which has a whole theodicy in it: "God will save His Word." He is true to false man because He is first true to His own nature and promise. His justification of man is only possible by a practical justification of Himself. We should be more sure of man's salvation if we sought first God's righteousness — as He Himself does — if we were more concerned to secure His kingdom than man's weal. There is nothing so good and wholesome for man as the kingdom of God and its holiness, which Christ sought first, and won. Nothing else assures man's destiny, or realizes all that it is in him to be. The great and final assurance we need is that God will save, must save, has saved His own holy purpose, gospel, and glory; and that history is the action of that salvation, surely however obscurely, irresistibly however slowly. With that faith we are sure of man's future. And only so. Man could never come to himself till God came to His own. If we first hallow God's name, as Christ did first, as God in Christ did, we are delivered from all evil, and all things are ours.

(Ibid., *pp. 121-125*.)

In this ultimate matter of a theodicy, philosophy well points out that we have two questions; and before each it is brought to a complete standstill. We have the question of evil as suffering and the question of evil as sin. They are distinct though closely connected. All sin is an ill, but all ill is not sin, nor is it caused by it. Suffering abounded in the animal world before man appeared with the moral freedom that makes sin possible. Pain came before sin, and, as it has no connection with freedom, it is nonmoral. And in any theodicy, or justification of God, His treatment of the two is different, to our Christian faith at least. The power in Him can convert suffering to a sacrament, but it must destroy sin. It can transcend and sanctify suffering while the suffering remains, but sin it must abolish. The Cross of Christ can submerge suffering, and make it a means of salvation, but with sin it can make neither use nor terms; it can only make an end of it. God in Christ is capable of suffering and of transmuting sorrow; but of sin He is incapable, and His work is to destroy it. And, by a mystery hard to search, His conversion of the one is the same act as His destruction of the other. His transfiguration of suffering in the Cross is also His conquest of sin. No doubt insoluble problems remain. Why in His creation must the way upward lie through suffering? Why, on this hard hill road, should we be met by sin descending upon us, seized, and flung into the abyss? But at least we can say that it is only one of these, it is the sin, not the suffering, that impugns the holiness which makes God God. A holy God might ordain the pain He took on Himself, but He could not ordain the sin. Suffering He could bear directly, but sin only sympathetically. Or though He might sweep away the good and the bad in some great catastrophe of nature, how can He allow the moral perdition even of those who were on the way to goodness, the fall even of the saint?

These questions are quite unanswerable. That is why a book on such a subject is at a disadvantage. We can but fall back on the last choice and committal which we call faith. And that seems to suggest a sermon rather than a discussion. Yet when God came to deal with the position practically and finally it was by the folly of preaching. He took the dogmatic note and not the dialectic. He did not put thought on a new line, but the thinker in a new life. The situation is insolubly irrational, so far as we are concerned. The solution is in action, as Carlyle said, — but in God's, as he did not say. We can but trust God, who by a saving Act masters the thinker and His world, as possessing an answer for thought that He does not yet see fit to give. And above all we must regard Him as having destroyed sin in principle by a way which carries with it also the end of pain. We must regard Him also as destroying evil in practice by methods which seem to us often very devoid and inadequate when we criticize His campaign, but which to Him are perfectly adequate and victorious. We can give God the glory even when He does not increase our joy; for our great object is not the delight of our soul but the glory of God. That sense of sin destroyed He does give us in the experience of our own faith and conscience; but He does not let us pierce with our theoretic reason the deep method and long strategy of His saving Will with the whole world. We may be more sure of our theodicy than clear about our theology. If a science of history be hardly possible, far less possible is a science of God's vindication in history drawn by induction from its course.

Some hard humility becomes our reason here. For its efforts

at a solution almost always run out into a slight on conscience. They move the previous question. They pass into a denial of the great crux, either by postulating a limitation on the power of God other than He imposes on Himself (which is to reduce His deity), or by denying the fundamental principle of the conscience, which is the radical and eternal antagonism of good and bad. The philosophic temperament, like the mystic, is too often accompanied by a certain lack of poignant moral sensibility, a certain acquiescence in the morally intolerable, and a lack of the sense of moral tragedy, as of concern for the soul. It is more interested in process than in action, in cohesion than in crisis, in order than in miracle, in growth than in grace. Its tendency is to substitute the aesthetic class of consideration for the moral. It seeks for connection rather than cultivates communion. It does not feel the sting of sin so much as the nuisance of it. It feels it to be an impertinence rather than a revolt. And it is tempted to regard the gulf between the holy and the sinful as more apparent than real, as adjustable in due course by some bridge of device rather than to be closed by a moral crisis and redemption, as something that will yield to evolutionary treatment, to nursing and not operation; as if sin would in due course be abolished like a dangerous blood clot in the general circulation. Sin becomes but a relative stage like everything else, and therefore a relative boon — were it only as something to push against in our ascent. Any notion of an absolute incompatibility and eternal conflict of good and bad is therefore an illusion in this point of view. Progress, culture, will dispel that illusion, and these extreme estimates will vanish, and their antagonisms converge, as they are drawn up into the ascending stream of things. That is to say, ethical values must yield to the mere dynamic movements of a *natura naturans,* quality being submerged in force. This to most will seem the relapse into barbarism. It is always barbarism where moral considerations must be submerged in the natural expansion of a power, a system, or a race, as Germany has shown.

This theory of a development essentially dynamic and not moral is a mere faith in progress now getting out of date. It *is* a faith — but of the inferior and ungrounded kind which easily becomes credulity. This destiny to endless progress cannot be a matter of knowledge; and it may be a superstition, if it has no guarantee beyond a presumption more or less high, and no certainty of a goal. It is at least an illusion, which many cherish, that history must mean advance and not mere movement, and that civilization carries in it progress as a sort of natural law. Civilization and progress are identical to so many, that it costs them a great effort to think the two apart. Hence the shock from the war as the outcome of civilization. We have an almost incurable belief, partly innate, partly inbred, in a Golden Age awaiting society; and it takes much historic thought to discern that the belief in progress was not in antiquity at all, and to realize what an importation it is from Christian faith, and how little there is to sustain it in historic sight. Before Christianity, and outside Israel, the Golden Age was only in the past. When we take a large enough survey, and especially a survey with the ethical eye, the tendency to relapse and degenerate is but little less apparent than the tendency to advance, as Ranke says. And at certain points it gets the upper hand, as it does today. The salt and sterile sea rushes up the stream with a huge "bore." At any rate, the value before God of each race or stage is not that which can be set forth in terms of civilization. It is not even to be expressed in terms of culture intellectual and aesthetic. It is something interior to most that is called progress, something which may cause God to think less than we do of our wondrous age, and more than we do of ages that we consider we have long outgrown. A time process like progress cannot be of first moment to the Eternal Spirit who has no after or before. What is of such moment to Him is timeless acts like grace, redemption, faith, and love. Christ can make good and godly men under any system. Eternity is a much more powerful factor in history than progress. At any rate, the value of an age or people for God (who is an Eternal Simultaneity) is not just what it contributes to other and later stages, but its own response and devotion to Him; and His connection with progress though real is indirect. Progress is much more rapid in the more external and less eternal things; which indicates how little stay it has in itself. Europe has arrived at a crisis in which the expansion of civilization has rent its crust. Its pace has ruptured its heart. Its collapse reveals the spiritual hollowness and the moral perdition within. And the painful process of restoring to progress eternal values is judgment.

It is practical and moral interests of life that raise these great questions. They did not condense out of the blue sky of abstract themes and speculative dreams. Therefore it is in the region of the soul's moral life that any solution must be found that enables us to go on. It is in the region of faith and in the terms of its theology. The secret of the Lord is not with the philosopher (though God whispers in his ear, it is not that He whispers), but with the prophet.

(Ibid., *pp. 135-139.*)

Isaiah is called on for a theodicy. He has to vindicate the ways of God to men. He has to take up the prophets' and apostles' task in every age, and force home the conviction that the absence of God is not the sleep of God, nor His hiding of Himself His absence, nor His silence His unrighteousness, nor His slowness His feebleness. The slowness of God is the patience of God. His silence is His omnipotence. His hiding is the subtlety of His omnipresence. His absence is a form of His vigilance. His forebearance is a stage of His judgment and a phase of His wise justice. If the thunder of judgment does not follow fast on the flash of sin, it is not because the Judge is not at the door. At least He is in the town, and is making His way to the inquest in your house. God's procedure is a great procedure. It is perfectly infallible in its working, and sure in its event. But it will not be hurried for outcry or for defiance. He is not a passionate God, like His accusers and sceptics. There is everything to be considered, and everybody, and the righteousness not of the moment but of the long last. With Him a thousand years are as one day, and one day as a thousand years. There is method in His procedure. There is plan, patience, completeness. He stays to gather up everything, to take everything with Him, to bring everything home. The home of everything is its place in the justice of God, its function in His judgment.

This is what Isaiah had to bring home to his public, as we have to ours. We have our resources; he had his. And ours are vaster, more complete, than his, though we do not use them as he did. We have God's own theodicy in Christ, in the justice and judgment of the Cross. But Isaiah and his prophet's vision, his insight into Providence, his sound judgment of God's judgment, his inspiration for judging of the Judge (which is God's Spirit reading Himself aloud). Isaiah had his sense of reality — of the reality of common life, and the reality of the spiritual principles beneath it. He had his gift of speech, of vivid observation, of fiery, fearless passion, of packed phrase. He had the skill of homely, deep parable that settles never to be dislodged, and teems from its place with God's truth pervading men's ways. And Isaiah put his theodicy in the shape of a parable from the commonest pursuits of rural life. It was there that he found the principles to God's dealings, not by excogitation, not innate in the soul, but saturating the healthy occupations of men, and ruling their practical relations with the good brown earth. He did not only illustrate his truth from their familiar toil, but he found *the same principles* in their work and in God's with the world. Just as in our fatherhood we have the rudiments of God's.

Listen, he says, you who think God sleeps because His chastisement is not incessant. Is the ploughman *always* ploughing? Is there no rest for the soil? Is there no sowing after the ploughing? Does he not let the earth alone after the sowing too? Does he fold his hands when he has torn up the ground and levelled its clods? No, he proceeds, only he changes his procedure. He puts in his seed. And he puts in different seeds different ways. He not only goes on; he discriminates as he goes on. He scatters the fitches, and the cummin; the wheat and the barley he sets with more care in rows; and the spelt he puts in for a border to these. How comes he to do this? God hath taught him, says the prophet. We should say now he has learned by long experience. Both are right. If we do learn from experience, it is God's laws that we learn, and we learn by God's schooling. If the experience of generations has taught us, it is none the less God's teaching. Creation by evolution is as compatible with a Creator as creation by a stroke. God taught him this, says the prophet. And God taught him so, because it is God's own way. God's theodicy is rooted in the very soil. His righteousness springs from the earth. God's way with the earth is His way with its dwellers. It is just so that God tills man and farms history. Providence is the Great Husbandman. We are God's planting and God's estate. As you do not for ever plough down the soil and break up the ground, so neither does God. There is in His procedure both method and discrimination. His judgment is not a monotony of chastisement. It is not His way to mow down Samaria and Jerusalem at one sweep. He does not treat the scoundrelism of Judah in just the same way as the drunkenness of Ephraim. Drunkenness does bring a swifter judgment on a people (as on a man) than rascality, though not a surer. But as after the ploughing comes sowing, and after sowing a time of rest ere the sprout appear, so God rests and lets men rest. This is His mercy, His wisdom. He will give the one judgment time to have its effect on men before the next comes. There is method and patience in His ways as in yours which He taught you. There is method, but no monotony. There is discrimination. He is not moved by passion, else He would sweep clean the whole wicked earth. He adjusts judgment to time, place, people, and the great end in view — the great harvest at the close of all. What indeed is judgment but adjustment? God does not move like a man in a hurry, by short cuts. He does not go to His end with blunt directness like your common plain-dealer, who sees but one small near thing to do, and straightway does it and is done. With God each judgment contributes to the next, and the next may be less severe or more, according as the interval is used. The Almighty is the Almighty strategist. He moves in great orbits and roundabout ways. But His forces are always on the spot at the right time. The hour comes and the God. And He sweeps the country clean as He advances. He leaves no foe to harass His rear. His judgments are slow, circuitous, lingering, it may be, but they are patient, merciful, final in their nature. They serve a purpose, they follow a plan, they discriminate; they strike here, they lift there, here they pull men up, there they let them go. Some they only shake, some they tread, some they crush and grind to powder.

(From "The Slowness of God," pp. 219-220.)

VII: THE WORK OF CHRIST

ON INTERPRETING THE CROSS

We do need to go back to our spring for our light and strength. Every age has its own spiritual problem. It interrogates the unseen with a new demand. It appeals to it with a new need. It taxes it for new power. Our age has a question and a need of its own. It is not the same as that of the Reformation. It is not exactly that of the first century. Jesus dealt with a Jewish civilization, the apostles with a Pagan, and Luther with a Catholic. Luther arose amidst a Europe long exercised about questions of sin, penance, and the means of grace. His gospel to that age was the gospel of a gracious God to a sinful experience. He spoke to people who were in a church and who knew sin. But we stand in a different Europe, a modern Europe, scientific, critical, ethical, and social. We have the same gospel, rich to all, but it faces a different need. The sense of sin has died down for the time; and the ruling idea of God, if not holier, is purer than it was, richer, broader, humaner, more intimate to men and things. We speak to people who are not in a church, or who care little for the church they are in. Many of them will change their church and minister for a better tennis green on the

121

other side of the town. The church and its message form no part of life's reality for them, but only of its decency at best. They do not deny, but ignore the Christian God. The time's demand, therefore, is not for a diviner idea of God; it is for power to realize, in experience, conduct, and thought, an idea already more divine than we can either take home or carry home in practical effect. It is not a more ideal God we need, but a more real God, actual in and over life. We know, or we dream, more things about God than we know how to use, trust, or obey. The question is not as to the ideality of Christ's character, for all own that; but it is as to the reality of His gospel, the authoritative reality, amid things, of a holy God whom our best ideas only desire, surmise, or depict. Especially it is a question as to the reality of a holy God, gracious in action, not to the church alone, but to society. With all the humane and philosophic enlargement of the idea of God during the last two or three centuries, we are still left without the certainty that it corresponds to the deep eternal reality of the stirring world. It should not be forgotten that agnosticism is the child of idealism, and not of empiricism or materialism alone. Spencer held neither. In such a world as this ideals are apt to become incredible and impracticable in proportion to their greatness; and we have to ask what is to translate the idea into experience and action; what will make an effectual power of it, make of it a religion more near and real to us than life itself is with its tremendous avidity today? It is little that a lofty idea of God will do to fortify or rule the youth who launches out into the torrent of energy and opportunity sweeping men along in a time like this, when man, nature, the world, and a career are mightier than ever before. No mere idea of God is strong enough to cope with the passionate experience of such a world — a world with such vitality in it, such capacity, such facilities, such fascination, and such fire. It needs that the divine idea become a hearty moral experience also, and a part of the man's moral reality, before it can be a guiding and saving authority in his immersion in such life. It must, however large, however imposing, become personal, searching, and real, before it can become effective, before it can cope with the personal reality of a man's imperious self. No Christian view of life, however ardent, no enthusiasm about Christ, will do the work of personal faith which unites a man in Christ with the central moral reality of a saving God.

And so we ask anew, from our own position — What was it that Christ came to bring? It is feeble now to say He came to bring a new thought of God. He brought little for the world of thought; for the moral world, *where reality lies,* He brought everything. He came with God Himself, and not with a picture or a guess about God; with God, not as a finer vision, nor as a necessity of thought, but as a mightier power, as the Holy One, as the ultimate moral energy, as the searching, judging, saving, and final reality, active in history and life. He was not a herald, but a plenipotentiary. God did not reveal His nature to Christ. Christ was neither a thinker before a problem nor a poet before a dream, but a doer before a task. God was in Christ, reconciling. Christ had not His knowledge of God by way of revelation. His consciousness was part of the self-consciousness of Godhead. His action was God's act. And through Christ, God was, and now is, in history — at its real spring, in its main stream. This Christ is the supreme contemporary of every age and its ruling power. The spinal cord of history is redemption. The course of total history is the evolution of grace. Christ came with God not only in evidence but in action, in decisive, final, continuous action on the active, historic, total soul of man. I say Christ came with God, but I mean that God came in Him, came for a world career, and came to abide at the throne of things.

And such a gospel meets the demand of today — not for an ideal God, but a real God. We have to secure not a new conception of God, but a new recognition of Him — a new position for Him in that sense. And that position must be in the conscience, amid the action in which we touch reality at last, amid the drama of things. The people that count are the serious people who play the game instead of watching it; and they are forced to feel that the reality of God comes home to us only in experience, in action, in the moral region. Judgment is there; and salvation is where judgment is. The nature of reality for living men is morality. And the real power that is demanded by our actual moral condition, our sinful condition, the only God relevant to it, is the holy historic God in His act of judgment-grace — the God in the Christ we inherit, given us and not discovered, given by Himself and not procured even by a Son, given to meet our moral perdition, and given in the flood of life and action's storm, in the Cross which entered a nation's politics, challenged its government, sealed its dream, broke at once its delusion and its history, and in so doing secured mankind's destiny. This indispensable power is given in the Cross as the spiritual fact and power in history, searching and judging to the last reality, gracious and saving to the uttermost eternity. If the world's history be the world's judgment, the Cross of Christ is the *nodus* of that judgment. The point may be clear. Reality is in morality; and morality lies in action, in history; and the need and the core of moral history, as we actually find things, is redemption — the gracious, pardoning, delivering God.

(From "The Reality of Grace," pp. 828-831.)

The Cross of Christ, with its judgment-grace, its tragic love, its grievous glory, its severe salvation, and its "finished work," is God's only self-justification in such a world. But is it not a salvation full and free? Surely. Full of the passion which sets the soul free for Himself. Free? It was of His own will. Hard? Yes, but hardest of all for Him. He took on Himself there more than He ever inflicts; and His infliction from us there He turns into His redemption. The Cross meant more change in God than in man. It was His own Act of changing judgment into mercy, His own miracle. And its first concern was His holy love, not ours. Real and thorough religion is theocentric more than anthropocentric. Thus, you see, the revision of our expectations involves the revision of our Creed. It is impossible even to discuss the theodicy all pine for without the theology so many deride. I shall venture to suggest that a call has come to the Church to set its own house in order, and show some deeper sense of the real moral problem — the problem within God, the

problem of judgment as atonement — ere it venture to adjust
to the conscience the damaged moral order of the world.
It is invited by events to discard light solutions, easy beliefs
and endings merely happy; now to rise above its cowardly
dread of depth on the ground that it is obscure; to win
from God's answer in Christ at least some profounder sense
of the world problem and some higher sense of the one
and eternal morality; to put down into their proper place
the small empirics and the mild mystics who have never
descended into hell and therefore do not know the price of
heaven, who never tasted damnation and therefore knew
not the authentic taste of grace. Unfortunately, the
Church's treatment of her truth has allowed it to come to
this, that when we use the only language that fits the moral
case of mankind, the language of the New Testament, we
are supposed by very many who should know better to be
discussing theses and holding a brief for some system of
theology, instead of handling the last moral powers of
heaven and earth, and setting out the final relations of God's
conscience and man's.

(*From* The Justification of God, *pp. 37-38.*)

This idea of judgment was very current when Christ
came; and it colored much of the first Christian preaching,
through the turn it took from the expectation of Christ's
speedy return, and through the way in which apocalyptism
took the lead of the old prophetism. The new feature in
Christianity was this — that the final judgment (whether as
a historic, even cosmic, catastrophe, or as the close of each
individual life) was effected in Jesus Christ, and consummated by Him (John 5:22). So much so that a great deal of
Christian thought was given to the question how a future
judgment of believers could comport with the facts of the
Christian salvation, final and secure. The ideas of responsibility and retribution must be adjusted to the assurance of
justification. The election of Israel and its pardon did not
give it immunity from judgment. The end of the law in
Christ did not destroy the final judgment, but it provided
the final standard. The idea of a judgment is bound up

with a moral order of a very real, immanent, and urgent, not to say eternal, kind. Yet how does it comport with grace? Is the gracious God judge at all in His grace? How can Christ be at once the living embodiment of the moral law (and so both standard and judge) and also the living grace of God and the agent of reconcilement? This is the issue in the Cross, and for many it has been its offense. And the line of answer is that the grace is the judgment; that grace, acting by way of atonement, has in its very nature a moral element, which does not leave the indifferent immune, but becomes their judgment. Judgment is the negative side of love's positive righteousness.

In the great and final inquest the judge is Christ the justifier. And the judgment falls on the Church and its faith, rather than on the world and its no faith. But it falls on the Church largely in respect of that which brings it into living and loving contact with the elemental human need (Matt. 25:31).[1] The same judgment is at once universal and individual. And for the individual there is no sound certainty of salvation, none beyond the risk of illusion, but that which will bear the test of a final judg-

---

[1] With reference to Matthew 25, it may be observed (though not without hesitation):

1. It concerns, perhaps, works of love to poor and afflicted Christians rather than to the poor of Humanity. The dividing line goes through the Church. Cf. Matthew 7:21, "Lord, Lord." The heathen make but a background of spectators.

2. The ultimate value of the service is not its Humanitarianism, but its Christianity, its being done to Christ — done not out of humane pity but out of Christian faith, however indirectly — done not to men but to Christians, because Christians are the people in Christ's presence. The real final saving thing is the doer's relation to Christ. Inhumanity is not surprising in the natural man, but in a Christian man or people it is damnable.

3. This is not the sole thing which determines judgment. For Christ praises other qualities and virtues — as in the Beatitudes — and promises them blessedness. Hence this must have been "occasional," and must refer to a situation which demanded prominence for these philanthropies. Christians were not such because of this, but this is what showed if their faith was the true righteousness, the true relation to Christ.

ment of moral finality (Matt. 7:21). So I Corinthians 4:4. We
may be judged at last (though not justified) by what may
be below our own conscious motive. "When saw we Thee
an hungered?" We are to God more than we know. It is
certainly not by individual acts we are judged, nor by their
balance tested by a mere law (I Cor. 3:15). The ultimate,
the fundamental, judgment is an adjustment between persons — God's and man's. It is not between a soul and a
law. It is a judgment of our faith and its personal relation
to the true Christian, rather than of our works, which are
the fruit of the relation. Lip confession of Christ is nothing;
but soul confession, life confession, there must be. The
great judgment is not upon works, but upon the standing
life-act which practically and eternally disposes of the person. It is Rome's error to say that justification is by law, and
that grace is merely to supply us with the power to keep the
law after a free pardon of original sin in baptism. Obedience
to Christ is the product of love and personal relation to Him
(John 14:15; I John 4:17; 5:3).

There is then a goal of history and a theodicy in the
grand style; and it is a last judgment (whatever form it
takes) according to God's grace. God vindicates Himself
by a righteous grace. His answer to human sin was — Christ
as crucified. The grace of God is the greatest judgment
ever passed on the world. That is the nature of the Cross —
God's grace (and not God's law), in moral, saving judgment
on man. When we have entered the kingdom through the
great judgment in the Cross, we do not escape all judgment;
we escape into a new kind of judgment, from that of law to
that of grace. We escape condemnation, for we are new
creatures, but chastisement we do not escape. Our work may
be burned, to our grief, that we may be saved (I Cor. 11:32).
We are judged or chastened with the Church to escape condemnation with the world. And at the last must there not be
some great crisis of self-judgment, when we all see Him as
He is, and see ourselves as His grace sees us?

(Ibid., *pp. 179-181.*)

CHRIST AND GOD'S HOLINESS
CHRIST JUDGED FOR SIN

We are to be redeemed by judgment from wrath. Not *over* but *through* judgment. Salvation must be salvation not *from* judgment but *by* judgment. The agent of judgment becomes the object of judgment, and so becomes the agent of salvation. As Judge of all the earth, as the Conscience of the conscience, Christ is absolute in His judgment, unsparing and final in His condemnation. But as the second Adam and Man of men He attracts, accepts and absorbs in Himself His own holy judgment; and bears, in man, and for man, the double crisis and agony of His own two-edged vision of purity and guilt.

(*From* The Atonement in Modern Religious Thought, *p. 81.*)

Atonement is substitutionary, else it is none. Let us not denounce or renounce such words, but interpret them. . . . We may replace the word substitution by representation or identification, but the thing remains. Christ not only represents God to man but man to God. . . . Representation apart from substitution implies a forgone consent and election by the represented, which is not Christ's relation to humanity at all.

. . . .

Sin is punished by suffering. And it was because of the world's sin that Christ suffered. . . . The suffering was penal in that it was due in the moral order to sin. It was penal to Christ's personality, to His consciousness, but not to His conscience; . . . it was the consequence attached *by God* to sin — sin's penalty; and He so recognized it. . . . But it was not substitutionary *punishment*. There is no such thing in the moral world. The worst punishment is to see the penalty we brought on Christ — whether we see it with faith in a saving way, or without faith to our deeper condemnation.

(Ibid., *pp. 83-85.*)

How should a man feel who was alive, alone, in a world of the dead? . . . His solitude was that of *the Life* amidst the dead world. The more He was the life the more power He had to feel death. . . . I do not say the death was *total* as yet; there was still greatness and goodness among men, even

among some who failed to see His. But it was universal; all
were infected by it....As it was *universal, He* was involved
in it — involved, though not diseased, not captured. His life
as Man was a real life, and He was bound to feel the last
reality of man's deadness. And He alone *could* feel it. *They*
were too dead in sin. Alone He fulfilled the condition of
feeling a moral death utterly universal, and therefore dreary,
cold, loathsome, to such a soul as His....Dying for every
man means that He shared in soul (though not in conscience) a universal moral death.

> (*From* The Taste of Death and the Life of Grace, *pp. 26-32.*)

The physical death only showed forth the spiritual. It was
there that the value lay. And a spiritual death, in absolute
obedience, amid an atmosphere of unfaith, when it is really
tasted and not merely sipped, means fog and gloom, sour and
chill, formless fears and failing force—no visions, no raptures,
no triumphs, no flush of energy, no heroic glow. That was
the blood of Christ. And you cannot dwell too much on the
blood of Christ so long as you are sure it was Christ's blood,
the Lamb of God carrying the sin of the world.

> (Ibid., *p. 42.*)

In conferring death on Christ the Father took the Son into
His own unapproachable grace and perfection of giving
Himself for the world to the uttermost. The death of Christ
was a function, and not merely a commission, of a supreme
power, grace and glory. It was an act of God, and not merely
of God's agent. God did not send the Son, He came as the
Son. What reconciled the world was God in Christ. God does
not suffer by deputy, or sacrifice by substitute. It is not His
prerogative to receive sacrifices greater than any He makes.
He does not delegate redemption; He redeems in the Son
with whom He is one.

> (Ibid., *pp. 46-47.*)

In our modern psychology we start from the primacy of
the will, and we bring everything to the test of man's practical and ethical life. And so, here also we start ethically from
the holiness of God as the supreme interest in the Christian
revelation. The standpoint taken by the Church is that

which I believe to be the position of the New Testament. That book represents a grand holiness movement; but it is one which is more concerned with God's holiness than ours, and lets ours grow of itself by dwelling on His. Christianity is concerned with God's holiness before all else; which issues to man as love, acts upon sin as grace, and exercises grace through judgment. The idea of God's holiness is inseparable from the idea of judgment as the mode by which grace goes into action. And by judgment is meant not merely the self-judgment which holy grace and love stir in man, but the acceptance by Christ of God's judgment on man's behalf and its conversion in Him to our blessing by faith.

By the atonement, therefore, is meant that action of Christ's death which has a prime regard to God's holiness, has it for its first charge, and finds man's reconciliation impossible except as that holiness is divinely satisfied once for all on the Cross. Such an atonement is the key to the incarnation. We must take that view of Christ which does most justice to the holiness of God. This starting-point of the supreme holiness of God's love, rather than its pity, sympathy, or affection, is the watershed between the gospel and the theological liberalism which makes religion no more than the crown of Humanity and the metropolitan province of the world. My point of departure is that Christ's first concern and revelation was not simply the forgiving love of God, but the holiness of such love.

(From The Cruciality of the Cross, *p. viii.)*

And, therefore, God's way of carrying home His love to the world was by a person who was realized in one act corresponding to the unity of the person and the scale of the world; a person whose consummation of Himself was in the great man's way of crucial action; an action giving effect to His whole universal personality and therefore having effect on the whole of man's relation to God. God in Christ's Cross not only manifests His love but gives effect to it in human history. He enters that stream, and rides on its rage, and rules its flood, and bends its course. He reseats His love in command upon the active center of human reality. He does

the thing which is crucial for human destiny. Christ effected
God's purpose with the race, He did not merely contribute
the chief condition to that end. The Cross *effects* the reconciliation of man and God; it does not simply announce it, or
simply *prepare* it. It does not simply provide either a pre-
liminary which God needs in a propitiation, or the stimulus
man needs in a spiritual hero, or a moving martyr. The
propitiation is the redemption. The only satisfaction to a
holy God is the absolute establishment of holiness, as Christ
did it in all but the empirical way. The Cross is the redemption in principle and effect. It does not avert the great last
judgment, it is the action of that judgment. Do not persist in
thinking of the last judgment as mainly dreadful and damnatory. In the Bible and especially in the Old Testament, I
have already said, the day of the Lord is an awful joy, as the
final vindication of goodness, the final establishment of righteousness. Judgment is the grand justification, not prepared
by the Cross, but effected and completed on the Cross and
the justification there. The justified have the last judgment
behind them. There the eschatological becomes ethical, the
remote near, the last first. The justification in the Cross does
not produce the salvation; it is the salvation. In Christ we
have no mere preface or auxiliary to the supreme crisis of
Humanity. We have that crisis. The day of the Lord is here.
We are in its midst. Only as the race is living out Christ's
death, for weal or woe, can we truly say *Die Weltgeschichte
ist das Weltgericht*. The work was finished there as well as
begun. But it was finished more than begun. It began its
career as a finished work. But to this point I must return
later.

(*From* Positive Preaching and the Modern Mind, *pp. 237-38.*)

In His death Christ not only acted and redeemed, He suffered and atoned. He acted as only a divine sufferer could.
His act of sacrifice became an endurance of judgment. Nothing else than atonement could do full justice to Love. Love
might do much, but if it did not suffer, and suffer not only
pain but judgment, it could not do its divine utmost. That is
to say, it might have contact with us, and blessed contact,

but it would be short of identification with us. It could not
enter into our self-condemnation. But surely love divine
could not stop short of such an identification with our suffering as made Christ's suffering judicial. Must a divine love
not go so far with us and for us as to enter the wrath of holiness? Even that was not beyond Christ's love. He was made
sin. God did not punish Christ, but Christ entered the dark
shadow of God's penalty on sin. We must press the results of
God's holy love in completely identifying Himself with us.
Holiness is not holiness till it go out in love, seek the sinner
in grace, and react on his sin by judging it. But love is not
divine identification with us till it become sacrifice. Nor is
the identification with us complete till the sacrifice become
judgment, till our Saviour share our self-condemnation, our
fatal judgment of ourselves in God's name. The priest, in His
grace, becomes the victim, and completes His confession of
God's holiness by meeting its action as judgment. To forgive
sin He must bear sin.

As He took the suffering He took and bore the sin that
caused it — the sin and not its consequences only. If He could
not confess sin, He could and did confess, in experience and
act, the holiness of God in its reaction on sin. He confessed
the holiness, but the guilt He could not confess in the same
sense. He could but realize it, bear it, as only the holy could,
and so expose it in all its sinfulness. The revelation of love is
a revelation no less of sin, because the love is holy love. That
holy confession in act of the injured holiness, amid the conditions of sin and judgment, was the satisfaction He made to
God. And the necessity for it lay in God's holy name. It was
thus that He offered to God, and acted on God. He not only
acted from God on man, but from man on God. I do not
mean that He changed God's *feeling* to the race. That was
grace always, the grace that sent Him. But He did change the
relation between God and man. The reconciliation of one
always means a great change for both parties. He made communion possible again on both sides. To do this He had to
bear the wrath, the judgment, the privation of God. He
could not otherwise enact and reveal love, and do the revelation justice. The more love there is in a holy God, the more

wrath. Sin, in the sinner He loves, against the law of His
own nature, which He loves better still, could not leave Him
either indifferent, or merely pitiful. For Love would then
desert its own holiness. And being holy, God's concern with
sin is more than pity, and more than pain. It is holiness in
earnest reaction. It is wrath unto judgment. That wrath
Christ felt, not indeed as personal resentment, but as the
dark valley, as the horror of thick darkness. And He felt,
moreover, that it was God's will for Him, not indeed inflicted,
so far as His conscience was concerned, but still laid on Him
by God through His sympathy with us. It was not merely a
darkening of His vision of the Father; it was desertion by the
Father in sympathy with the complete fulfilment of their
common task. As one might in certain circumstances say "I
love you, but I must leave you," "I love you, but for the sake
of all that is at issue I may not show it." And it was by recognizing, honoring, this very desertion as the wise, righteous,
loving will of God, that Christ converted it for us all into a
new and deeper communion. It was thus He approved His
Godhead, and achieved the redemption. The real incarnation
lay not in Christ's being made flesh for us, but in His being
made sin. And the dereliction was the real descent into hell,
the bottoming of salvation. Here beneath the depth of sin is
the deeper depth of God. "If I make my bed in hell, Thou
art there."

Love, then, must go to entire identification (short of
absorption). And Christ, in identifying Himself divinely
with sinful man, had to take the sin's consequence, and
especially its judgment, else the identification would not be
complete, and the love would come short. He must somehow
identify Himself in a sympathetic way, even *with man's
self-condemnation which is the reflection of his judgment by
God*. I need hardly allude to the familiar illustrations in the
shame which innocent people feel through the crime of a
kinsman. If the chief function of Christ's love was to represent man in a solidary way, a priestly way, He must make
offering to God; He must offer to God's holiness by a holy
obedience, and not merely to God's love by loving response.
He could not experience sin, for then He would be short of

holy identification with God; yet He must experience and endure God's wrath against sin, else His love would be short of sympathetic identification with us. And unless He felt God's holy wrath and reaction against sin, He could not show forgiving love in full. No one can forgive in full who does not feel the fullness of the offense. To feel the fullness of the offense as the Holiest must, is also to feel the wrath the Holiest feels. But for one in perfect sympathy with man to feel what the Holiest feels is to feel the divine wrath, not as its holy subject only, but as its human object. Christ could not show the power of forgiving love in full unless He felt the weight of God's wrath in full, i.e. not God's temper but God's judgment; which for Him was God's withdrawal, the experience of God's total negation of the sin He was made. Grace could only be perfectly revealed in an act of judgment — though inflicted on Himself by the Judge. Atonement to God must be made, and it was only possible from God.

No one can feel more than I do that if all this be not absolute truth it is sheer nonsense. So it sifts men.

This aspect of the matter is not indeed vital to personal Christianity, but it is to the Church's total message and to the final prospects of Christianity. It presents the last issue in the moral war of God and man. It is essential to a full interpretation of God's love. God so loved the world, not quantitatively but qualitatively, not only so intensely, but in such a unique manner, that He gave His Son to be a propitiation. It is the provision of a propitiation that is the distinctive mark of God's love as transcending humane pity or affection in holy grace. Surely it must be so. The greater the love the closer it must come to life, and to the interior of life. It can the less ignore the realities of life. It does not leave us to ourselves, in a careless affection; it enters our ways, and sounds our depths, and measures all our tragic case. It has a comprehending, and not merely a kindly pity. It does not merely feel for our case, it assumes it wholly. Therefore, it must regard the last reality of sin, and deal with it according to *all* circumstances — especially those visible to holiness alone, and to us in proportion as we are redeemed into holiness. So dealing with sin it forgives it; and forgives it effectually — not by way of amnesty, not by mere pardon, not by way of mere mercy upon our repentance, but by the radical way of redemption; not by indulgence, not by treating it as a matter of ignorance, weakness, misfortune, but as the crime of our freedom, grave in proportion to our freedom, most heinous in the face of the grace that gives our freedom. And as grace is far more than indulgence, so sin is far more than indifference. It is the nature of indifference to go on to become hate, if it be given time and occasion. The mercy, therefore, comes as no matter of paternal course, as no calm act of a parent too great and wise to be wounded by a child's ways. God is fundamentally affected by sin. He is stung and to the core. It does not simply try Him. It challenges His whole place in the moral world. It puts Him on His trial as God. It is, in its nature, an assault on His life. Its total object is to unseat Him. It has no part whatever in His purpose. It hates and kills Him. It is His total negation and death. It is not His other but An other. It is the one thing in the world that lies outside reconciliation, whether you mean by that the process or the act. It cannot be taken up into the supreme unity. It can only be destroyed. It drives Him not merely to action but to a passion of action, to action for His life, to action in suffering unto death. And what makes Him suffer most is not its results but its guilt. It has a guilt in proportion to the holy love it scorns. The greater the love the greater the guilt. And the closer the love the greater the reaction against the sin, the greater the wrath. Hence the problem of reconciliation — both of God and man — a problem so integral to Christianity, and so foreign to even the finest kinds of theism. It is not the reconciliation of man with his world, the establishment of his moral personality against nature. That were mere apologetic. But it is the reconciliation of man within himself and God. The channel of holy love must be the bearer, the victim of holy wrath. To bear holy love to us He must bear holy wrath for us. The forgiver of sin must realize inwardly the whole moral quality of the guilt — as Christ did in His dereliction in the Cross. Inwardly he must realize

it, experimentally, not intellectually. No otherwise could a
God, a love, be revealed, which would not let us go, yet was
in absolute moral earnest about the holy.

It may freely be granted also that the reconciliation of
God (by Himself in Christ) is not very explicit in the New
Testament — for the same reasons which forbid the missionary preaching to his heathen on such a theme. The New
Testament represents but the missionary stage of Christian
thought and action. But the idea is not therefore untrue.
If not explicit in the New Testament, it is integral to the
gospel. It is involved in the moral quality of holy forgiveness and in its divine psychology. In this respect it is like
the full doctrine of the Trinity, and many another. The
holiness of God, moreover, does not explicitly occupy the
same supreme position in the New Testament as it does in
the Old. Yet it is the very Godhead of God. It is the essence
of Christ's idea of God. And (I think I have said) it really
receives in the New Testament a position above any it had
in the Old Testament. For it forms much more than an
attribute of God. In the Holy Spirit it becomes a constituent
element in the Godhead, on its way to become at last a
coequal person in the Trinity.

(Ibid., pp. 248-253.)

The drift of our plea has been this. Christianity, especially on its ethical side, is regeneration. Regeneration is by a way
of justification. Justification is righteousness by grace. Grace
is the merciful act of the holy love facing defiant sin and
not responsive love. Being the great act of the *holy* love, it
and its justification is the action of the absolute righteousness, of the eternal and immutable morality. And it deals
with the actual man at his moral center. It is God's historic
treatment of the sinful conscience, of the race as it historically
is. It is the greatest moral Act of time and eternity, the
most real and creative. The second creation is much more
creative than the first because it meets not a material chaos
but a moral crisis. Being so ethical and so historic it has in
it, therefore, the last moral principle of history and human
affairs. And its revelation and principle in the historic Cross

is the focus of Christian ethic, especially on the public scale, the national scale, which the Sermon does not touch.

(*From* The Christian Ethic of War, *p. 182.*)

The teaching of Jesus is not the foundation of Christian ethic but is to be interpreted by that which is — namely the redemption of the Cross as the moral crisis of the world and the creator of the new conscience in historic conditions. Our present confusion is the debacle of the didactic or epideictic theory of Christ's work, the view that treats even the Cross as but the supreme object-lesson and most impressive display of the love of God. When the idea of holy love's saving, atoning judgment in Christ's blood has gone out of the center of Christian ethic it takes severe judgments to bring it back.

(Ibid., *p. 193.*)

CHRIST'S CONFESSION OF HOLINESS

Our will alone is our ownest own, the only dear thing we can and ought really to sacrifice. The blood as life means the central will, the self-will, the whole will, in loving oblation. This is the sacrifice even in God. The Cross does not in the New Testament exhibit God as accepting sacrifice so much as making it. And it is never in the New Testament represented as the extremity of suffering, but as the superlative of death; it is not the depth of agony but the height of surrender; and that again is represented as the triumph of eternal life. It is the absolute active death of self-will *into* the holy will of God; but also *by* that will; the complete, central, vital obedience of the holy to the holy in a necessary act on the eternal scale. A necessary act. It was in an act, and not in a mere mood of resignation. And in an act not gratuitously done (however voluntarily), not blindly done just to get some outlet for an irresistible instinct of self-sacrifice. It was an act made necessary by the organic pragmatism and moral unity of Christ's whole life; which was a whole life rooted in the organic context and moral necessity of a national history; which history again was integrated into the spiritual necessity of God's holy purpose for the whole race and its redemption. Christ must die not simply of the blindness and blunders of men, but because by God's will He was the incarnation of that holiness which, as it moves through history, necessarily makes sin so sinful and wickedness so furiously to rage. The *must* was not merely in the Jewish nature, but in the nature of holiness, as soon as it came to close quarters with human sin. The real nature of the incarnation lies in what might (with some violence perhaps) be called the moral polarity, the reciprocal identity, of Christ's holiness with the holiness of God. The holy God alone could answer Himself and meet the demand of His own holiness. So Paul felt in his own relation to Christ's holiness. "Not I, but Christ living in me."

(From The Cruciality of the Cross, *pp. 92-93.)*

So the act of Christ had this twofold aspect. On the one hand it was God offering, and on the other hand it was man confessing. Now, what was it that Christ chiefly confessed? I hope you have read McLeod Campbell on the atonement. Every minister ought to know that book, and know it well. But there is one criticism to be made upon the great, fine, holy book. And it is this. It speaks too much, perhaps, about Christ confessing human sin, about Christ becoming the Priest and Confessor before God of human sin and exposing it to God's judgment. The horror of the Cross expresses the repentance of the race before a holy God for its sin. But considerable difficulties arise in that connection, and critics were not slow to point them out. How could Christ in any real sense confess a sin, even a racial sin, with whose guilt He had nothing in common? Now that is rather a serious criticism if the confession of sin were the first charge upon either Christ or us, if the confession of human sin were the chief thing that God wanted or Christ did. I think it is certainly a defect in that great book that it fixes our attention too much upon Christ's vicarious confession *of human sin.* The same criticism applies to another very fine book, that by the late Canon Moberly, of Christ Church, *Atonement and Personality.* I once had the privilege of meeting Canon Moberly in discussion on this subject, and ventured to point out that defect in his theory, and I was relieved to find that on the occasion the same criticism was also made by Bishop Gore. But we get out of the difficulty, in part at least, if we recognize that the great work of Christ, while certainly it did confess human sin, was yet not to confess that, but to confess something greater, namely, God's holiness in His judgment upon sin. His confession, indeed, was not in so many words, but in a far more mighty way, by act and deed of life and death. The great confession is not by word of mouth — it is by the life, in the sense, not of mere conduct, but in the great personal sense in which life contains conduct and transcends death. Christ confessed not merely human sin — which in a certain sense, indeed, He could not do — but He confessed God's holiness in reacting mortally against human sin, in cursing human sin, in judging it to its very death. He stood in the midst of human sin full of love to man, such love as enabled Him to identify Himself in the most profound, sympathetic way with the evil race; fuller still of love to the God whose name He was hallowing; and, as with one mouth, as if the whole race confessed through Him, as with one soul, as though the whole race at last did justice to God through His soul, He lifted up His face unto God and said, "Thou art holy in all Thy judgments, even in this judgment which turns not aside even from me, but strikes the sinful spot if even I stand on it." The dereliction upon the Cross, the sense of love's desertion by love, was Christ's practical confession of the holy God's repulsion of sin. He accepted the divine situation — the situation of the race before God. By God's will He did so. By His own free consent He did so. Remember the distinction between God's changeless love and God's varying treatment of the soul. God made Him sin, treated Him as if He were sin; He did not view Him as sinful. That is quite another matter. God made Him to be sin — it does not say He made Him sinful. God lovingly treated Him as human sin, and with His consent judged human sin in Him and on Him. Personal guilt Christ could never confess. There is that in guilt which can only be confessed by the guilty. "I did it." That kind of confession

Christ could never make. That is the part of the confession that we make, and we cannot make it effectually until we are in union with Christ and His great lone work of perfectly and practically confessing the holiness of God. There is a racial confession that can only be made by the holy; and there is a personal confession that can only be made by the guilty. That latter, I say, is a confession Christ could never make. In that respect Christ did not die, and did not suffer, did not confess, in our stead. We alone, the guilty, can make that confession; but we cannot make it with Christian effect without the Cross and the confession there. We say then not only "I did this," but "I am guilty before the holiness confessed in the Cross." The grand sin is not to sin against the law but against the Cross. The sin of sins is not transgression, but unfaith.

(*From* The Work of Christ, *pp. 148-152.*)

So also of holiness, there is a confession of holiness which can only be made by God, the Holy. If God's holiness was to be fully confessed, in act and deed, in life, and death, and love transcending both, it can only be done by Godhead itself.

Now the object I have in view in this lecture is to press a former point as furnishing this unity — that the active and effective principle in the work of Christ was the perfect obedience of holy love which He offered amidst the conditions of sin, death, and judgment. The potent thing was not the suffering but the sanctity, and not the sympathetic confession of our sin so much as the practical confession of God's holiness. This principle (I hope to show) coordinates the various aspects which have been distorted by isolation. This one action of the holy Saviour's total person was, on its various sides, the destruction of evil, the satisfaction of God, and the sanctification of men. And it is in this moral medium of holiness (if I may so say) that these three effects pass and play into each other with a spiritual interpenetration.

Thus Christ's complete victory over the evil power or principle. His redemption is the obverse of His regenerating and sanctifying effect on us. To deliver us from evil is not simply to take us out of hell, it is to take us into heaven. Christ does not simply pluck us out of the hands of Satan. He does so by giving us to God. He does not simply release us from slavery, He commits us in the act to a positive liberty. He does not simply cancel the charge against us in court and bid us walk out of jail, He meets us at the prison-door and puts us in a new way of life. His forgiveness is not simply retrospective, it is, in the same act, the gift of eternal life. Our evil is overcome by good. We are won from sin by an act which at the same time makes us not simply innocent but holy.

So also we must see that the third — our regenerate sanctification — is the condition of the second — the complete satisfaction of God. The only complete satisfaction that can be made to a holy God from the sinful side is the sinner's restored obedience, his return to holiness. Now, the cheap and superficial way of putting that is to say that penitent amendment is the only satisfaction we can give to a grieved God. But future amendment does no more than the duty of the future hour. And rivers of water from our eyes will not wash out the guilt of the past; nor will they undo the evil we have set afloat in souls far gone beyond our reach or control. Yet it remains true that nothing can atone to holiness but holiness. And it must be the holiness of the sinner. It must also be an obedience of the kind required by the whole situation, moral and spiritual. It must be the obedience not of improvement but of reconciliation, not of laborious amendment but of regenerated faith. But faith in what? Faith in One who alone contains in Himself a holy obedience so perfect as to meet the holiness of God on the scale of our sin; but One also who, by the same obedience, has the power to reproduce in man the kind of holiness which alone can please God after all that has come and gone.

(Ibid., *pp. 201-203*.)

THE CROSS AS GOD'S ACT

So much of our orthodox religion has come to talk as though God were reconciled by a third party. We lose sight of this great central verse, "God was in Christ reconciling

the world unto Himself." As we are both living persons, that
means that there was reconciliation on God's side as well
as ours; but wherever it was, it was effected by God Himself
in Himself. In what sense was God reconciled within Himself? We come to that surely as we see that the first charge
upon reconciling grace is to put away guilt, reconciling by
not imputing trespasses. Return to our cardinal verse, II
Corinthians 5:19. In reconciliation the ground for God's
wrath or God's judgment was put away. Guilt rests on God's
charging up sin; reconciliation rests upon God's nonimputation of sin; God's nonimputation of sin rests upon Christ
being made sin for us. You have thus three stages in this
magnificent verse. God's reconciliation rested upon this, that
on His eternal Son, who knew no sin in His experience
(although He knew more about sin than any man who has
ever lived), sin's judgment fell. Him who knew no sin by
experience, God made sin. That is to say, God by Christ's
own consent identified Him with sin in treatment though
not in feeling. God did not judge Him, but judged sin upon
His head. He never once counted Him sinful; He was always
well pleased with Him; it was part, indeed, of His own holy
self-complacency. Christ was made sin for us, as He could
never have been if He had been made a sinner. It was sin
that had to be judged, more even than the sinner, in a world-
salvation; and God made Christ sin in this sense, that God
as it were took Him in the place of sin, rather than of the
sinner, and judged the sin upon Him; and in putting Him
there He really put Himself there in our place (Christ being what He was); so that the divine judgment of sin was
real and effectual. That is, it fell where it was perfectly
understood, owned, and praised, and had the sanctifying
effect of judgment, the effect of giving holiness at last its
own. God made Him to be sin in treatment though not in
feeling, so that holiness might be perfected in judgment,
and we might become the righteousness of God in Him; so
that we might have in God's sight righteousness by our living union with Christ, righteousness which did not belong to
us actually, naturally, and finally. Our righteousness is as
little ours individually as the sin on Christ was His. The

thief on the cross, for instance — I do not suppose he would
have turned what we call a saint if he had survived; though
saved, he would not have become sinless all at once. And the
great saint, Paul, had sin working in him long after his conversion. Yet by union with Christ they were made God's
righteousness, they were integrated into the New Goodness;
God made them partakers of His eternal love to the ever
holy Christ. That is a most wonderful thing. Men like Paul,
and far worse men than Paul, by the grace of God, and by a
living faith, become partakers of that same eternal love
which God from everlasting and to everlasting bestowed upon
His only-begotten Son. It is beyond words.

(Ibid., pp. 82-84.)

Therefore we press the words to their fullness of meaning;
"God was in Christ reconciling," not reconciling through
Christ, but actually present as Christ reconciling, doing in
Christ His own work of reconciliation. It was done by Godhead itself, and not by the Son alone. The old theologians
were right when they insisted that the work of redemption
was the work of the whole Trinity — Father, Son, and Holy
Spirit; as we express it when we baptize into the new life of
reconcilement in the threefold name. The holiness of God
was confessed in man by Christ, and this holy confession of
Christ's is the source of the truest confession of our sin that
we can make. Our saving confession is not merely "I did so
and so," but "I did it against a holy, saving God." "I have
sinned against heaven and in thy sight," sinned before infinite holiness and forgiving grace. God could not forgive
until man confessed and confessed not only his own sin but
confessed still more — God's holiness in the judgment of sin.
The confession also had to be made in life and action, as the
sin was done. That is to say, it had to be made religiously
and not theologically, by an experience and not an utterance.
A verbal confession, however sincere, could not fully own an
actual sin. If we sin by deed we must so confess. It is made
thus religiously, spiritually, experimentally, practically by
Jesus Christ's life, its crown of death, and His life eternal.
The more sinful man is, the less can he thus confess either

his own sin or God's holiness. Therefore God did it in man
by a love which was as great as it was holy, by an infinite
love. That is to say, by a love which was as closely and sympathetically identified with man as it was identified with the
power of the holy God.

(Ibid., *pp. 152-153*.)

The essence of holiness is God's perfect satisfaction, His
perfect repose in eternal fullness. And the Christian plea is
that this is Self-satisfaction, in the sublimest sense of the
phrase. For us, mostly, the word has an ignoble sense. But
that is only because what we meet most is an exclusive self-
satisfaction, an individual self-sufficiency. But when we have
an entirely inclusive self-satisfaction, an eternal and complete
adequacy to Himself in the most critical situation, we have
the whole native fullness of God blessed for ever, with men
beneath the shadow of His wing. The perpetual act of holy
God is a perpetual satisfaction or accord between His nature
and His will at every juncture, and a satisfaction from His
own infinite holy resource — a Self-satisfaction. God is always
the author of His own satisfaction: that is to say, His holiness is always equal to its own atonement. God in the Son is
the perfect satisfaction and joy of God in the Father; and
God the holy in the sinful Cross is the perfect satisfaction of
God the holy in the sinless heavens. Satisfaction there must be
in God's own nature, whether under the conditions of perfect
obedience in a harmonious world, or under those of obedience jarred and a world distraught. God has power to secure
that the perfect holy obedience of heaven shall not be
eternally destroyed by the disobedience of earth. He has
power to satisfy Himself, and maintain His holiness infrangi-
ble, even in face of a world in arms. But satisfied He must
be. For an unsatisfied God, a dissatisfied God, would be no
God. He would but reflect the distraction of the world, and
so succumb to it.

But a holy God could be satisfied by neither pain nor death,
but by holiness alone. The atoning thing is not obedient suffering but suffering obedience. He could be satisfied and
rejoiced only by the hallowing of His name, by perfect and

obedient answer to His holy heart from amid conditions of
pain, death, and judgment. Holy obedience alone, unto
death, can satisfy the holy Lord.

(Ibid., pp. 204-206.)

We are set to inquire of what principle we could secure, not
the continuity of evolution, but the supremacy of God's loving glory, and how we are to avoid a mere sanctified Eude-
monism and the passion for having a good time in a decent
way. We are bidden to recognize that God's demand on man
takes the lead of man's demand on God. And both are over-
ruled by God's demand on God, God's meeting His own
demand. And we learn unwillingly that only God's justification of man gives the secret of man's justification of God. The
justification at the root of all other is God's self-justification.
In a word, there is but one theodicy, and it is the evangelical.
For the Gospel has the only universal and eternal ethic in its
heart, the true, real, and final moral relation of God and man.

(From The Justification of God, p. 40.)

We still await a culture on Christianity, i.e. less on Christ's
teaching than on the moral regeneration flowing from God's
moral act and crisis of the Cross, creative and supreme for
the whole race, and rich with all the fullness of Christ. It
is through this act alone that we rise to the faith, fullness,
and power of the incarnation[1] that is within it. It is His
atonement in its experience value, it is the rich and regenerative oblation of the race's conscience there, it is the eternal
life created in us as moral beings there, that give us access to
the real meaning of His incarnation and found the true, the
evangelical, Catholicism. It is such faith that finds meaning
in the incarnation as a moral act, beyond mere prodigy,
meaning for the moral soul that makes us men — even if
guilty men. However we speculate, we know nothing of any
incarnation except what our conscience finds in the atoning
redemption and its implicates of reconciliation. A holy God
self-atoned in Christ is the moral center of the sinful world.
Our justification by God has its key in God's justification of
Himself. If we begin with culture we shall end with crises;

---

[1] Experience is the method but not the measure of faith.

but if we be begin with crises at the Cross all culture is added to it.

(Ibid., pp. 93-94.)

CHRIST'S MORAL VICTORY

And what I am suggesting from the viewpoint of a theodicy is that, if righteousness remain, there could remain for such a situation but judgment, that the wonderful thing is not the judgment but its delay, that the amazement would be if no judgment did come. The surprise would be if everything went on in a godless civilization as if men were waiting on the Lord instead of using Him to wait on them. But is there such a world righteousness in supreme and final command? My case is that there is no certainty of it till we are sure of more. We cannot trust a world righteousness till we are sure of God's holiness. And the certainty of that is a matter of religion, and of atoning and redeeming religion. It is *the* matter of religion, the matter of *the* religion, of religion equally moral and mystic, of evangelical religion, of faith in the final crisis and victory of the moral soul, God's and man's, in the Cross of Christ, who has overcome the world for good and all in an eternal act of love, judgment, grace and glory. He starts the new ethic in creative mercy, the new Humanity in regenerative forgiveness; and the forgiveness has its moral ground in atonement to the living law, to the holy God, the God of the whole moral universe, and of the Church in so far as the Church is the earnest of a whole and holy world. The Cross is not a theological theme, nor a forensic device, but the crisis of the moral universe on a scale far greater than earthly war. It is the theodicy of the whole God dealing with the whole soul of the whole world in holy love, righteous judgment, and redeeming grace. There is no universal ethic but what is based in that power and deed. There is no sound theology but what moves in universal righteousness to a universal kingdom of peace and joy to the glory of the holy name. This is a point, or rather a center, to which we must return before we are done.

(Ibid., pp. 132-33.)

The Holiness of Christ was the one thing damnatory to the Satanic power. . . .

It was not His dying that saved, but the holiness of it. In the Cross took place the holy judgment which made Christ sin's destroyer and the spiritual Master of the universe. His exorcism of Satan was in the same act His conquest of man. "Now is the judgment of this world," He said Himself. And what we call the last judgment is only the completion of the deadly judgment passed on collective evil in the Cross.

. . . .

The judgment at the end of history is only the corollary of the judgment at the center of history, and the close of that daily judgment in which we live. . . . The mainspring of missions is not the judgment that *will fall,* but the judgment that *has fallen* in the Cross. . . . Christ has judged the prince of the world and doomed its principle. He did so by taking on Himself the judgment of the world. What Christ did was to immortalize the good, and ban the evil, and paralyze Satanic power. And He did it by active holiness. What He won was God's moral victory in sinful man. It was a victory of conscience; and conscience is the most universal thing, the most missionary thing, of all.

(*From* Missions in State and Church, *pp. 13-17.*)

So far was the death of Christ from having its chief effect on man that it acted primarily in the spiritual world. And there it acted not solely on God, but on the power of evil gathered and personalized.

(Ibid., *p. 60.*)

To see sin, sorrow, and death continually under the Cross, to see the grace of God triumphing over them in it, is the very soul and victory of faith.

. . . .

There is much more in the Cross than such a darkling faith has fathomed. The infinite, ultimate love of God is there. The gift and grace of God for the whole world are there. It is not simply nor chiefly the love of Christ for His brethren that is in the Cross. That was indeed uppermost in Christ's life; but in His death that is not direct but indirect; and the primary thing is Christ's obedience to God, and His action, therefore, as the channel of God's redeeming love.

(From The Taste of Death and the Life of Grace, *pp. 68-70.)*

CHRIST AND THE RACE

CHRIST MADE SIN FOR US

In being "made sin," treated as sin (though not as a sinner), Christ experienced sin as God does, while He experienced its effects as man does. He felt sin with God, and sin's judgment with men. He realized, as God, how real sin was, how radical, how malignant, how deadly to the Holy One's very being. When Christ died at sin's hands it meant that sin was death to the holiness of God, and both could not live in the same world. When He rose it meant that what was to live and rule in the world was the holy God. Dying as man, Christ placed His whole self beside man under the judgment of God. He was beside man in court but on God's side in the issue, confessing God's holiness in the judgment, and justifying His treatment of sin. Justifying God! A missionary to the North American Indians records that having seen his wife and children killed before his eyes, and being himself harried in bonds across the prairie amid his tormentors, he "justified God in this thing." I do not know a sublimer order of experience than from the heart to bless and praise a good and holy God in despairs like these. It is to this order of experience that the work, the blood, of Christ belongs. And there is no justification of men except by this justification, this self-justification, of God. Never is man so just with God as when his broken, holy heart calls just the judgment of God which he feels but has not himself earned; and never could man be just with God but through God's justification of Himself in the blood of Christ.

We cannot in any theology which is duly ethicized dispense with the word satisfaction. It was of course not a quantitative replacement of anything God had lost, nor

was it the glutting of a God's anger by an equivalent suffering on who cares whom. It was no satisfaction of a *jus
talionis*. But it was the adequate confession, in act and
suffering, "Thou art holy as Thou judgest." That man
should confess this vicariously and victoriously in Christ
crucified and risen is the reestablishment of God's holiness
in the world. We can only understand any justification of
man as it is grounded in this justification — this self-justification — of God. The sinner could only be saved by something
that thus damned the sin. The Saviour was not punished,
but He took the penalty of sin, the chastisement of our
peace. It was in no sense as if *He felt* chastised or condemned
(as even Calvin said), but because He willingly bowed,
with a moral understanding possible only to the sinless,
under the divine ordinance of a suffering death and judgment which was holily ordained to wait on the sin of His
kin. The blood of Christ cleanseth from *all* sin. The metaphor denotes the radicality, totality, and finality of the
whole action in the realism of the moral world — which
even high sacrifice, not resisting unto blood, only slurs or
shelves — when it does not toy with it.

(*From* The Cruciality of the Cross, *pp. 101-103.*)

The wrath of God is not a mode of passion, but a
phase of Providence; not a temper, but a treatment on
God's part as the Holy Redeemer. What was to be extorted
was not punishment, but the true practical recognition of
God's holiness. Without that God cannot remain God; He
would be Father, but a partial not sovereign Father. But
it is the very thing that sinful man cannot and will not
give. It is an expiation which must be found by God, and
not by man; therefore in God. Jesus Christ is the human
revelation that it is so found. In Him God honored within
man the law of His own changeless holiness; He condemned
sin in the flesh. He made human response to His own holiness, and a response damnatory. It is too much ignored
that the revelation in Christ, being a revelation of holy love,
must be condemnation as earnestly as mercy. In Christ God
did not simply show pity on men, but God was **in man**

expiating sin to His own holiness. He revealed the fact that power to do even that was not sought with God in vain.

The extinction of our guilt is a pure, unbought, inexplicable act of miraculous grace. And the revelation of such extinction can only be the transfer of that act of grace into our personal experience. Its transfer, observe, not its declaration. This is a work that no mere declaration could do, no mere exhibition of pure or even devoted love. Only a person's act and experience can be a revelation to a person. Nor is it real till it be transferred within us. In this case it is God's active experience that must be brought home to us and repeated in us. Such is the work of Christ — to realize and transfer to us the experience of God's holy love in the conditions of sin. It was not to give an equivalent for sin, but to effect in man God's own sense of what sin meant for His holiness. Christ's sorrow and death were a sacrifice offered by God to His own holiness. Christ did feel His death as a divine necessity, a necessity in God, not as an earthly necessity divinely borne. And this feeling on His part, in willing, utter obedience, was God's practical recognition of His own eternal holy nature. Christ accepted sorrow and death at the hands of God's holiness, and bore sin's damnation in humble obedience. And He did so because He knew it was the divine purpose to carry home to us by the effect on Him the holiness of God's love. It was not the sorrow that saved, not even the negative sinlessness of it, but its positive and complete obedience. It was not even the death that saved, but the living act of obedience in it. It was Christ's recognition of it as a divine necessity, which was God Himself meeting the law of His nature and satisfying in man His own holiness.

In some such way may redemption be treated as revelation, without becoming a mere exhibition of God's pitiful desire for man, but remaining a work and act of God demanded by His own nature and calculated in its effect to bring us to true saving repentance. As the sole organ of this repentance Christ represents us before God, no less than He represents God to us; and so He is the sole condition of our repentance being saving repentance with

God. Nothing here said is meant to impugn the uniqueness
of Christ's work for us all. As His religion was essentially
different from that of other men, so was His sacrifice. It
was not simply the classic instance of the cross we have all
to bear. When we have done all, something has to be done
in our stead, something unique in its bearing on human sin
before God.

In what sense the person of Christ is revelation, is therefore only to be understood when we appreciate in experience
the value of His work for us as sinful men. It is no final
revelation for sinless intelligence. The philosophical discussion of this person is full of intense interest and all but
supreme value; but for our moral need, which is *the* need
of Humanity, it is comparatively sterile. Only the beneficiaries of the Cross can effectually discuss the Cross, and
through it the incarnation — of which the Cross, and not the
birth, is the key; the Cross, and not the miraculous birth,
because the one can be verified in our Christian experience,
while the other is a question of the record alone, and cannot.
It is the one and not the other that is *used* in Scripture. It
is in the one, not in the other, that our certainty lies, and
so our revelation; for nothing is revelation in the close use
of words, which is not verifiable in our Christian experience.

(From "Revelation and the Person of Christ," pp. 141-143.)

CHRIST OUR MEDIATOR

The reconciling and redeeming work of Christ is, indeed,
our grand avenue to His person in its fullness; but it does
not exhaust it, unless that work be interpreted as the new
creation *in nuce*. And certainly if (like so many good but
bornés souls today) we reduce the reconciling work of Christ
to His earthly life, character, and teaching, apart from their
consummation in a death which was more than worth them
all, if we cherish a "simple" sermon-on-the-mount Christianity, it is quite impossible to erect on that basis a personality
so great as its advocates really revere. The greater the personality the more impossible it is to give it full expression
in life. We have already seen how large a part of the activity
of His person Christ reserved in the secrecy of His private

and personal contact with the Father. And we may also observe that, as the crisis of His death drew on, it was this hidden life that overspread His soul. He became less and less engrossed with His prophetic effect on man, and more and more with such priestly gift to God as God alone could offer, and no man.

By all the deepest experience of the Church the benefit from Christ is not exhausted in the satisfying of the heart or in the pacifying of the conscience. Christ does more than fill or fortify us; he sanctifies. His work, consummated on the Cross, is yet larger than a deliverance at a historic point. It is the energy of the whole eternal person who culminated in that act. He does more than release us; He has to uplift and transform us. He does more than inspire the race, He completes it. He brings it to the glory for which it was destined by God. And for this no saintliest man could be enough. Nothing lower than the holy God could rehallow the guilty human soul. Only the creator of our destiny could achieve it. Of course, the *extent* at any one time of the Church's response to Christ, or the soul's, may be limited. The horizon of its experience may be partial and confined. But what is of more moment is the *nature* of that experience. It is not psychological, but theological. It is not an experience of the soul's old past, nor even so much of its new self, but of its new creator and king, its Lord and its God. That changes the nature of the experience from a subjective to an objective, from me to one who makes me. It is not simply the experience of an immense impulse, a vast promotion in goodness, a change of sentiment towards God, the clearing up of misunderstandings, and the wiping of the slate. What is cured is not merely distance, nor merely estrangement from a loving God, but the obsession by hostility to a holy God, and the guilt of it all. The forgiveness is an absolute gift, but it is not an amnesty; nor is it a revival; but in its nature it is a new creation. Christ does not bring us mere absolution, He is the giver of a new eternal life. His charge is the second creation, and the divine consummation of humanity.

Now for this creative work no mere man is sufficient. The

creators of the greatest works of genius are quite unable
to create the new heart within us, the new communion, and
to put us beyond all cavil as to our final destiny in God.
They cannot make themselves the guarantee and surety of
that destiny. But Christ does do this. And He has never
ceased to do it. Throughout the ages there is a ceaseless
succession of confessors of such a theological salvation and
not only a psychological only, of a new act of creation and
not a quickened process.

If, then, such be the benefit begun and assured, the
agent of that blessing no more began His work when He
appeared on the earth, than He ceased it when He left the
earth, as man's way is. A man might reconcile me to God;
but could any greatest man so keep me as to ensure that
we did not fall out again; or that if we did the due reconciler
would again appear? A man might reconcile us to God
but he could not unite us for ever with God in the way
that an eternal holiness requires. He could do no finished
work. The greatest thought and passion of the Church,
its experience, and not its philosophy or its theology alone,
has been driven to postulate behind all the acts of Christ's
will on the earth, behind all His pity and power, an act of
His (not merely of His God and ours), eternal in the heavens,
an act which held all these earthly acts within it. His person has been felt to be greater than these earthly acts
could express. They had all a volitional foundation in the
heavens, which, because it was action and not mere substance, did not impair their reality but enhanced it. They
had a moral substratum in the act of His premundane personality, whose power was not exhausted in our rescue
alone — unless that rescue be viewed as the first stage of a
New Creation which had all the consummation of Humanity
in its scope.

We are thus driven, by the real existence of an eternal
Father and our experience of His grace, to demand the
existence of an equally real eternal Son — both being equally
personal and divine. The question, then, is what is the
relation between the Godhead of the eternal Son and
the man Jesus Christ, and how did it come to pass. Such

questions at once arose among believers; and they engrossed
the Church's thought during the early centuries in the many
Christological systems that succeeded the Trinitarian strife.
There was a teeming variety of opinions on the subject in
the redeemed community — as indeed there must always
be; and room must be made for them. Christian faith insists
on the reality of the incarnation as a fact if we take in all its
seriousness the experience that we have in Christ a gracious
and holy God truly with us; but the mode of its process is
an open question, on which it cannot be hoped, and hardly
wished, that all the Church should think alike. And we
may have occasion to note that many who reject the incarnation do so not only because they wrongly require from
it the satisfaction of a philosophic rather than a religious
demand, but, even more, because they cannot see *how* such
a process could take place. Which is much as if we refused
to act on a cable from across the ocean because we do not
understand the modes of electric action and transformation.

It is impossible with due reverence to speak in any but
the most careful and tentative way of the relations within
the Godhead. It has not pleased God to make these matters
of revelation. As we know of Christ only what He chose
to reveal in His vocation and work, so we really know of
God only what He chose to reveal in His Christ. We
practice ourselves a reserve about our inmost experiences
and relations which may make intelligible, at least in some
measure, God's own reserve with the sons of time. On the
other hand He wills to be inquired of. It is not the questions
that are intrusive. We are not called on to sacrifice our
intellect, if only we do not idolize it. And we are not de-
barred in advance from all inquiry as to the conditions
of Christ's supramundane existence. St. Paul did not feel
so hampered. We are surely free at least to say some things
which it could not be — could not be consistently with such
an idea of God as Christ Himself revealed. There was that
in the earthly personality of Christ which in the heavenly
could not be. For instance, in the earthly personality there
was growth; in the heavenly there could be none — unless
perhaps He were an Arian Son, a being created prior to the

world's creation. What is of Godhead does not grow: it is from eternity to eternity. The indubitable movement and change in the living personality of God does not take the form of growth. Growth belongs only to corporeal personality; and in His incarnation the Son of God did not become for the first time personal but only corporeally personal, personal under the limited conditions which involve growth. He did not enter personal conditions but historic. If growth be essential to personality in every form there can be no personal God; and our question then becomes of a quite different kind. There may therefore be in eternity a personal Being that does not come to Himself and His perfection by growth. Whether two or more such can cohere in the one God is again another question, with its own methods of discussion. But the growth of a divine personality in eternity is a much more impossible thing than the coexistence of three.

In Jesus Christ we have one who was conscious of standing in an entirely unique relation to the living God. It is the prophet's prophecy that reveals God, but it is Christ's person; and as *the* Son it reveals Him as *the* Father. If His Father be *the* Father, His Sonship is *the* Sonship. He held a relation to God as Father that never existed in any man before. Nay more, it was one that no man can ever reach again. Geniuses are repeated, but Christ never, the Son never. *For this relation constituted His personality.* He was not a person who became a Son, or was destined to be a Son, but His whole personality was absolute Sonship. This is not true of us. We are not sons and nothing else. The relation made the personality in Christ's case. I do not mean that the relation *made* Jesus grow into a personality, but it made up *His* personality, made the essential thing in it. That is not so with us. His personality had another foundation in God than ours. His person is born of God, ours is created. We are indeed related to a personal God, as His offspring, in a way that necessitates our being persons too. But not such persons. We can reach and develop personality without reference to God; He could not. Destroy His Sonship and you destroy His personality. His personality shaped His work, our work shapes our personality. Indeed His work was identical with His personality. Not so with us, whose work is always less than our personality. Our work is a means for our personality, His personality was the means of His work, Of no man can it be said that his relation to God constitutes the whole personality. But in the case of Jesus the whole relation to the Father, namely, Sonship, did constitute that personality. Think it away and nothing is left. His whole relation to the Father would be an abstract phrase were it not embodied in an actual personal Sonship, correlate with the living Father, knowing the eternal Father as the Father knows Him, and at every point in eternity, therefore, so knowing because so known.

(*From* The Person and Place of Jesus Christ, *pp. 280-286.*)

CHRIST AND HUMAN RESPONSE

Christ is certainly no less concerned than Nietzsche that the personality should receive the fullest development of which it is capable, and be more and more of a power. The difference between them lies in the moral method by which the personality is put into possession of itself and its resources — in the one case by asserting self, in the other by losing it; in the one case by self-pleasing, in the other by self-renunciation. Christianity is interested in the first degree in the modern emphasis on personality, because it is its chief creator. But the influence I allude to is more than that. It lies, secondly, in the conviction that the *strength* of personality, after an early stage, is damaged by the mere *force* of individualism, and is a social product. Personality does not come into the world with us ready made, but it has a history and a growth. Education is not merely its training, it is its creation. In all of us the personality is incomplete; and it misleads us in the most grave way when we use it as an analogy for the ever complete and holy personality of God. We are but persons in the making. Personality is created by social influences, and finds itself only in these. We complete our personality only as we fall into place and service in the vital movement of the society in which we live. Isolation means arrested development. The aggressive egotist is working his own moral destruction by stunting and shrinking his true personality. Social life, duty, and sympathy are the only conditions under which a true personality can be shaped. And if it be asked how a society so crude, imperfect, unmoral, and even immoral as that in which we live is to mould a personality truly moral, it is here that Christ comes to the rescue with the gift to faith both of an active Spirit and of a society complete in Himself, which in Him is none of these evil things, the society of the kingdom of God, which plays a part so great in the modern construction of the gospel. We are saved only in a salvation which set up a kingdom, and did not merely set it on foot. We have the kingdom not with Christ but in Christ. Do not leave Christ out of the kingdom, as if He were detachable from it like any common king. The individual is saved only in this social salvation. And the more you insist that a soul can only be saved, and a personality secured, by Christ's finished work, the more you must contend that the kingdom of God is not merely coming but is come, and is active in the Spirit among us now. There is the closest connection, if not identity, when you go deep enough, between the theology of salvation and the moral principles of social regeneration. The principle of our salvation is the principle of human ethic, not only of private, as has long been seen, but of public ethic, as we now come to see.

(*From* Positive Preaching and the Modern Mind, *pp. 178-180.*)

I have been illustrating one of the finest things in human nature, and I am asking whether, if that were multiplied indefinitely, we should yet have the effect which is produced by the death of Christ, or which is still to be produced by it in God's purpose. No, there is a difference between Christ's death and every case of heroism. Christ's was a death on behalf of people within whom the power of responding had to be created. Everybody thrills to that story I told you, and to every similar story. The power of response is lying there in the human heart ready — it only needs to be touched. There is in human nature a battery charged with admiration for such things; you have only to put your knuckle to it and out comes the spark. But when we are dealing with the death of Christ we are in another position. Christ's was a death on behalf of people in whom the power of responding had to be created. We are all afraid of death, and rise to the man who delivers us from it. But we are not afraid of that worse thing than death from which Christ came to deliver us. Christ's death was not a case of heroism simply, it was a case of redemption. It acted upon dull and dead hearts. It was a death which had to evoke a feeling not only latent but paralyzed, not only asleep but dead. What does Paul say? "While we were yet without strength, Christ died for us" — without power, without feeling, as the full meaning is.

Let me illustrate. Take a poet like Wordsworth. When he began to publish his poetry he was received, just as Browning was received later, with ridicule and contempt. The greatest critic of the time began an article in the leading critical organ of the day by saying, "This will never do." But it has done; and it has done for Jeffrey's critical reputation. Lord Jeffrey wrote himself down as one who was incapable of gauging the future, however much he might be capable of understanding the literature of the past. Some of you may remember — I remember perfectly well — the same kind of thing in the penny papers about Browning when he was fighting for recognition. I remember, when I was a student, reading articles in luminaries like *The Standard* which sneered and jeered at Browning, just as smaller men today would sneer at men of like originality. But Wordsworth and Browning have conquered. I take another case. Turner was assailed with even more ridicule when he exposed his works to the British public. What would have happened to Turner if Ruskin had not arisen to be his prophet I do not know. His pictures might not even have been mouldering in the cellars of the National Gallery. They might have been selling at little second-hand shops in back streets for ten shillings to anyone who had eyes in his head. Wordsworth, Browning, and Turner were all people of such original and unprecedented genius that there was no taste and interest for them when they appeared; they had to create the very power of understanding themselves. A poet of less original genius, a great genius but less of a genius, like Tennyson, comes along and he writes about the "May Queen" and "The Northern Farmer," and all those simple, elementary things which immediately fetch the handkerchiefs out. Now no doubt to do that properly takes a certain amount of genius. But it taps the prompt and fluent emotions; and the misfortune is that kind of work is easily counterfeited and abused by those who wish to exploit our feelings rather than exalt them. It is a more easy kind of thing than was done by those great geniuses I first named. Original poets like Wordsworth and Browning had to create the taste for their work.

Now in like manner Christ had to make the soul which should respond to Him and understand Him. He had to create the very capacity for response. And that is where we are compelled to recognize the doctrine of the Holy Spirit as well as the doctrine of the Saviour. We are always told that faith is the gift of God and the work of the Holy Spirit. The reason why we are told that, and must be told it, lies in the direction I have indicated. The death of Christ had not simply to touch like heroism, but it had to redeem us into power of feeling its own worth. Christ had to save us from what we were too far gone to feel. Just as the man choked with damp in a mine, or a man going to sleep in arctic cold, does not realize his danger, and the sense of danger has to be created within him, so the violent action of the Spirit takes men by force. The death of Christ must call up more than a responsive feeling. It is not satisfied with affecting our heart. That is mere impressionism. It is very easy to impress an audience. Every preacher knows that there is nothing more simple than to produce tears. You have only to tell a certain number of stories about dying children, life-boats, fire escapes, and so on, and you can make people thrill. But the thrill is neither here nor there. What is the thrill going to end in? What is the meaning of the thrill for life? If it is not ending as it should, and not ending for life, it is doing harm, not good, because it is sealing the springs of feeling and searing the power of the spiritual life.

What the work of Christ requires is the tribute not of our admiration or even gratitude, not of our impressions or our thrills, but of ourselves and our shame. Now we are coming to the crux of the matter — the tribute of our shame. That death had to make new men of us. It had to turn us not from potential friends to actual, but from enemies into friends. It had not merely to touch a spring of slumbering friendship. There was a new creation. The love of God — I quote Paul, who did understand something of these things — the love of God is not merely evoked within us, it is "shed abroad in our hearts by the Holy Spirit which is given to us." That is a very different thing from simply having the reservoir of natural feeling tapped. The death of Christ had to do with our sin and not with our sluggishness. It had to deal with our active hostility, and not simply with the passive dullness of our hearts. *(From* The Work of Christ, *pp. 15-19.)*

We are saved, men and peoples, as we enter on that righteousness; and this we do by a faith which is really a union with Him, the Faithful to death. This union is not mystic and rapt chiefly, but moral, a union not with His static person but with His dynamic work and His soul outpoured. . . . He unsinned humanity in His own moral victory in a national issue; which victory was so constant, so universal, and so final that He became the Conscience of the race and its moral Providence.

(From The Christian Ethic of War, *p. 187.)*

Man is not a mass but a mosaic of nations destined to be members of each other. Men in nations must serve the kingdom, and not merely as individuals, groups, or Churches; for a nation has a personality of its own. Human history, the history of peoples, transpires within redemption. It is slowly bent into the history and evolution of God's forgiveness of man by judgment which makes it a new creature. The New Humanity comes by the loving and saving judgments of God in the world. History, thus read, thus made, is the passage of Christ writ large. *(Ibid., p. 189.)*

VIII: THE CHRISTIAN LIFE

THE GOSPEL OF GRACE

The conflict concerned the nature of grace and the corresponding nature of faith. The Catholic view of grace is sacramental, the Protestant is evangelical. In the Catholic idea grace is, as it were, a new substance infused into the soul, first by baptism, then by the mass (*gratia infusa*). It is a sort of antiseptic influence made to pervade the spiritual system like new blood. The blood of Christ is understood in a material way, though in the way of a very refined material. It does not give a new righteousness, but power to please God by the old. And the faith that answers it is an acceptance of the Church's power to convey this rarefied and spiritualized substance. The love or charity so produced is thought of in the like way as a sort of spiritual ether infused into the soul. But in the Protestant and evangelical idea grace is not an infusion, but an act and way of God's treatment of us. *It is not infused, but exercised.* It deals with man as a will, not as a substance. It is the same as mercy, the mercy of God, the forgiveness of sin, the cancelling of guilt, the change and not the mere pacifying of the conscience. In a word, for Catholicism grace is magic, for Evangelicalism it is mercy. The grace of Evangelicalism is Christ the gospel, the Word. The faith that answers that is living faith in a living person directly in converse with the soul ... a new type of religion. ... It is faith changed from assent to trust.

(From Rome, Reform and Reaction, *pp. 56-57.)*

We are evangelical; we find Christianity not in the Church but in the gospel. We are Churchmen; and we find in the gospel alone the true charter and freedom of the Church. We are evangelical Free Churchmen. If we follow the Reformers by going to the Bible before the Church, we have no room for the priest because the New Testament has none.

(Ibid., *p. 69.*)

Do not preach the duty of love, but the duty of faith. Do not begin by telling men in God's name that they should love one another. That is no more than an amiable gospel. And it is an impossible gospel till faith give the power to love. They cannot do it. Tell them how God has loved them. Bid them as sinners trust that. Preach faith as the direct answer to God's love. The first answer to the love of God is not love, but faith. Preach faith and the love will grow out of it of itself. Loving, *as a gospel,* is Catholic. The Protestant and evangelical gospel is believing. Believe in Christ crucified and the love will come. Love must come if we believe in love. But it has first to be believed in before it is imitated.

(Ibid., *p. 104.*)

In a religion everything turns on the nature of the revelation. ... What was the Christian revelation? A system or an act? a theology or a redemption? a visible Church or a spiritual reformation? a truth or a person? grace as the capital with which God set up the Church in business, or grace as His act on the individual soul? The whole question between Protestant and Catholic turns on the nature of revelation.

. . . .

What made him [Luther] groan in his monk's cell was

not the bondage, tyranny, narrowness, immorality of the Church, but the burden of his own soul, his own self, his own guilt. It was the load of guilt that was killing him, not the load of the Church. He turned on the Church only when he found that it could do nothing real and final for misery and sin.

(Ibid., pp. 125-128.)

I am going on the assumption that the gift to men in Christianity is the gospel deed of God's grace in the shape of forgiveness, redemption, regeneration. *Im Anfang war die That.* But I should perhaps define terms.

By grace is not here meant either God's general benignity, or His particular kindness to our failure or pity for our pain. I mean His undeserved and unbought pardon and redemption of us in the face of our sin, in the face of the world-sin, under such moral conditions as are prescribed by His revelation of His holy love in Jesus Christ and Him crucified.

And by the gospel of this grace I would especially urge that there is meant not a statement, nor a doctrine, nor a scheme, on man's side; nor an offer, a promise, or a book, on God's side. It is an act and a power: it is God's *act* of redemption before it is man's message of it. It is an eternal, perennial act of God in Christ, repeating itself within each declaration of it. Only as a gospel done by God is it a gospel spoken by man. It is a revelation only because it was first of all a reconciliation. It was a work that redeemed us into the power of understanding its own word. It is an objective power, a historic act and perennial energy of the holy love of God in Christ; decisive for Humanity in time and eternity; and altering for ever the whole relation of the soul to God, as it may be rejected or believed. The gift of God's grace was, and is, His work of gospel. And it is this act that is prolonged in the word of the preacher, and not merely proclaimed. The great, the fundamental, sacrament is the sacrament of the Word.

What I say will not hold good if the chief gift to the world is the Church and its sacraments, instead of the work and its word. Wherever you have the ritual sacraments to the front the preacher is to the rear, if he is there at all. In Catholicism worship is complete without a sermon; and the education of the minister suffers accordingly. So, conversely, if the preacher is belittled the priest is enhanced. If you put back the pulpit, by the same act you put forward the altar. The whole of Christian history is a struggle between the apostle, i.e. the preacher, and the priest. The first apostles were neither priests nor bishops. They were preachers, missionaries, heralds of the Cross, and agents of the gospel. The apostolic succession is the evangelical. It is with the preachers of the Word, and not with the priestly operators of the work, or with its episcopal organizers. Our churches are stone pulpits rather than shrines. The sacrament which gives value to all other sacraments is the sacrament of the living Word.

(From Positive Preaching and the Modern Mind, pp. 3-4.)

There is another counterpart of authority than certainty, and one more spiritual than obedience. It is humility, which is freedom's elder twin and guide. That we should have all but lost this sovereign feature from so much of our religion of the kingdom is not surprising in the decay of authority or its debasement, and especially in the abeyance of that superlative form of authority which the mystic of the conscience calls holiness, and which enjoins us, if we would be perfect as our Father, to be holy as He is holy, and humbled to the very Cross. The holiness of God is beyond our definition, for it is God the holy; and we cannot define a person, far less the absolute Person. It is not simply His perfection either in thought or act. Its appeal is to something beyond both mind and will. It carries us deeper into God and man. We cannot define it, we can but realize it. And, as it is the last reality, we can but realize it in the last and highest energy of the soul. It is that in God which emerges upon us and comes home to us only in our worship. It changes that worship from dull abasement before God's power, or dumb amazement at the wealth of His nature, to the deepest adoration of what He personally is, and is for us.

Its counterpart in us and our religion is the humility that worship at once rears and perfects. And it is as much beyond righteousness in Him as humility is beyond mere obedience or justice in us. Humility is not a chain of submissive acts, but the habitual and total and active obedience of the whole soul to the Holy in His act, to that which alone both abashes and exalts the whole soul, and severs it from the world by every step of its assumption into God. Religion never confers such distinction upon the soul as in its humility, since nothing so exalts the common to the choice as the dignity placed upon us by the communion of the Holy; whose very anger turned on the world is a patent of nobility for it,[1] whose judgment is its glory, and His saints its peers. The true authority cannot return to order, secure, and distinguish society without a religious revolution. It cannot till humility pull down self-satisfaction on the one hand or lift up self-prostration on the other, and take the place of self-worship or self's dishonor. Yet it is never the mere breaking of self that makes humility, as it does not make true repentance or confession; it is the sight, sense, and confession of that ineffable sanctity which comes home to us but in adoration, and makes such hours the ruling and creative hours of life. For in that holiness we are neither passive, soft, nor weak; we are touched by the one authority and reality of life; and in the amazement, the miracle, that He should come to us who is sublimely separate from all the sinful world, we have the exalted humility which teaches us to love the world in godly sort, and is the secret of the obedience that at once controls life and inspires it. To know such a God is to be crushed, to be known of Him is to sit in heavenly places. This holiness is that in love which humiliates us, not in gratitude merely, but in adoration; and in the act it takes us into the fellowship of what is the one power and reality of life and eternity. The last authority of the soul for ever is the grace of a holy God, the holiness of His gracious love

---

[1] "Was Thine anger against the rivers or Thy wrath against the sea?" (Hab. 3:8).

in Jesus Christ. And this is the last reality of things, the last rest of all hearts, and the last royalty of all wills.

(From The Principle of Authority, *pp. 417-419.)*

FAITH

This man acts on the heart. He wakes admiration, fear, love, and, above all, faith, trust. He is found to haunt life as no other does. He becomes an unseen spectator and standard of all we do and devise. His beauty, terror, dignity, and invincibility pervade us. His love, mercy, faithfulness master us. His indomitable grace survives death and rises again in us. He becomes an imaginative ideal, and then a moral imperative. His principle of divine Sonship becomes the base of a new religion.

(From The Holy Father and the Living Christ, *p. 114.)*

A living faith is not mere sympathy with a historic Christ. It is not admiration, reverence, love of that great ideal. It is not the acceptance of His principle, or the assent to His truth. Nay, response to a merely historic Christ is not adequate even to that Christ. It does not meet His claims. It is not the whole response His teaching awakes, or His work evokes, or His character compels, or His soul sought. Faith in the Christian principle is not the living faith in Christ. We may hold truth as it is in Jesus, and miss it as Jesus, miss Jesus as Himself the Truth alive for evermore.

(Ibid., *p. 116.*)

Living faith is faith in a living Christ. . . . Faith in Christ is faith neither in Christendom (or a Church) nor in Christianity (or a system of creed or conduct). But it is in the practical reality of His unseen Person, now living, reigning, guilding from His unseen throne the history and the hearts of men to the kingdom of God.

(Ibid., *pp. 118-19.*)

That is our need of a Redeemer, of a living human Redeemer, a moral owner and King, a living Christ, a Lord and Master more immortal than ourselves, and the root of all that makes our immortality other than a burden. We need a living Redeemer. We need Him for a living faith. And we need Him, as I have already said, *for a living God* — for the reality of a living God.

Yes, to lose the living Christ is to lose the living God, and so on to lose our human soul and future.

(Ibid., *pp. 136-37.*)

The priestly atonement of Christ was final, but it was final in the sense of working incessantly, insuperably on, not in its echoes and results with us, but in the self-sustained energies of His own almighty and immortal Spirit. This is the priesthood which is the end of priesthood, and its consummation the satisfaction of the priestly idea.

(Ibid., *pp. 143-44.*)

He must be personal to us. He must be *our* Saviour, in *our* situation, *our* needs, loves, shames, sins. He must charge Himself with *our* souls. We believe in the Holy Ghost. We have in Christ as the Spirit the Sanctifier of our single lives, the Revealer of our hearts, the Helper of our most private straits, the Inspirer of our most deep and sacred confessions. ... We need, O how we need a Lord and Master, a Lover and King of our single, inmost, shameful, precious souls, the Giver and the Goal of our most personal salvation, a Conscience within our conscience, and a Heart amidst our heart and its ruins and its resurrection. That is the Christ we need and have.

(Ibid., *pp. 146-47.*)

You cannot treat Christ adequately by the historic sense, psychic research, cosmic emotion, the canons of natural ethic, or tender affection. The only adequate treatment of a fact so unique as Christ is the treatment proper to the moral nature of such a fact, the treatment it elicits and inspires, the treatment to which in the first disciples we owe anything that we know about Him, the treatment by faith. You must trust Him ere He seem worthy of your trust. He is really God only to the faith which has confessed Him as Saviour. His incarnation is an evangelical and not a logical demand. The Church's views about His person were forced upon those whom He not only impressed but regenerated, forced on them by the logic of living faith poring on the new creation that had passed them from death into life. It was only the scientific forms of these views that were affected by the philosophy of the hour, which did not, and cannot, give the certainty of their substance. It was a real redemption, making the Church's experienced life of faith, that Athanasius sought to express by the metaphysical Trinity. And the experienced verdict (and not merely the orthodox deposit) of His living Church in history is, that He is the incarnate holiness of the world and of eternity; that Christ is no mere part of past history, but the soul of the race's total life; and no mere starting-point for the ideal, but the living object of each age's absolute faith. To trust Him is not a leap in the dark, but it is a venture none the less. It is a venture of courage and not of despair, of insight and not of bewilderment. In an age like this the greatest moral courage lies, not in challenging faith, as the crude public believes, which believes in little more than pluck. That is cheap heroism now. But true courage lies in pursuing, amid the dullness of the public, the desolations of criticism, the assaults of foes, and the treason of friends, such faith as still places the precious soul, the wondrous age, and the cosmic world for ever and ever in those hands which twenty centuries ago were nailed for our advantage to the bitter cross. To do that with open eyes today is a very great achievement of the soul, a very great venture of faith, and a very great exercise of moral courage of the silent and neglected sort. The world knows nothing of its debt to those who for the soul's sake are incessantly facing and laying the specters of the mind.

(From The Cruciality of the Cross, *pp. 79-80.)*

What Christ offers to God is, therefore, not simply an objective satisfaction outside His revolutionary effect on the soul of man in the way of faith, repentance, and our whole sanctification. As the very judgment He bore for us is relevant to our sin by His moral solidarity with us, so the value of His work to God includes also that value which it has in acting on us through that same solidarity, and in presenting us to God as the men it makes us to be. He represents before God not a natural Humanity that produces Him as its spiritual classic, but the new penitent Humanity that His influence creates. He calls things that are not yet as though they were. In Him a goodness of ours that is not yet, rising from its antenatal spring, brings to naught the sin that is. There was presented to God, in Christ's holiness, also that repentance in us which it alone has power to create. He stretches a hand through time and seizes the far-off interest of our tears. The faith which He alone has power to wake is already offered to God in the offering of all His powers and of His finished work. That obedience of ours which Christ alone is able to create, is already set out in Him before God, implicit in that mighty and subduing holiness of His in which God is always well pleased. All His obedience and holiness is not only fair and beloved of God, but it is also great with the penitent holiness of the race He sanctifies. Our faith is already present in His oblation. Our sanctification is already presented in our justification. Our repentance is already acting in His confession. The effect of His Cross is to draw us into a repentance which is a dying with Him, and therefore a part of the offering in His death; and then it raises us in newness of life to a fellowship of His resurrection.

He is thus not only the pledge to us of God's love but the pledge to God of our sure response to it in a total change of will and life. We see now how organic, how central to Christ's gospel of atonement, is Paul's idea of dying and rising with Him, how vital to His work is this effect of it, this function of it. For such a process, such an experience, is not a mere moral sequel or echo of ours to the story of the Cross, it is no mere imitation or repetition of its moral greatness; nor is it a sensitive impression of its touching splendor. To die and rise with Christ does not belong to Christian ethic, to the method of Jesus, but it has a far deeper and more religious meaning. It is to be taken into His secret life. It is a mystic incorporation into Christ's death and resurrection as the standing act of spiritual existence. We are baptized into His death, and not merely into dying like Him. We do not echo His resurrection, we share it. As His trophies we become part of Christ's offer-ing to God; just as the captives in his procession were part of the victor's self-presentation to the divinity of Rome. God leadeth us in triumph in Christ (II Cor. 2:14). It is, indeed, for Christ's sake we are forgiven, but for the sake of a Christ who is the Creator of our repentance and not only the Proxy of our curse. And it is to our faith the grace is given, yet not *because* of our faith, which is no more perfect than our repentance. It is to nothing so poor as our faith or our re-pentance that new life is given, but only to Christ on His Cross, and to us for His sake who is the Creator and Fashioner of both. Our justification rests on this atoning creative Christ alone. And when the matter is so viewed, the objection some have to the phrase "for Christ's sake" should disappear.

No martyrdom could do what the death of Christ does for faith. No martyrdom could offer God in advance the souls of a changed race. For no martyr as such is sure of the future. It is easier to forget all the martyrs than the Saviour; and their power fades with time, while His grows with the ages. With the martyr's death we can link many admirable reflec-tions, exhortations, and even inspirations. What it does not give us is the new and eternal life. It is not the consummation of God's saving purpose for the world.

(From The Work of Christ, *pp. 192-196.)*

FORGIVENESS

Every remission imperils the sanctity of law unless he who remits suffers something in the penalty foregone; and such atoning suffering is essential to the revelation of love which is to remain great, high and holy.

(From The Atonement in Modern Religious Thought, *p. 88.)*

"Forgive us, as we forgive. . . ."

We ask, believing that God has broken sin in principle once for all. In grace He has forgiven the world. We ask that this may be carried home to us. . . . It is a great thing to realize that the forgiving grace of God is the deepest, mightiest, most permanent and persistent power in the moral world. . . . There is a universe of moral forces and soul powers about us, shaping us more really than our own physical world does, and all its forces. . . .

The rite lasts because it signifies the thing which lasts. . . . In the Lord's Supper God's forgiveness is not simply remembered by us, but offered us, carried home to us anew. The rite is the property of the whole Christian Church, and is its witness, its acted proclamation, of the gospel of forgiveness. God in the course of history offers Christ, the fount of history, anew. There is a long continuity in this historic act. Man repeats it, but it is a continuous act with God. . . . [Forgiveness] is the condition of our fellowship with the eternal life. We lay hold of that fellowship according as we lay hold of forgiveness, and show it forth. We enter the family of the eternal grace by becoming *blood relations of Jesus Christ.*

(*From "The Problem of Forgiveness in the Lord's Prayer," pp. 190-91.*)

We need for the kingdom of God in Humanity a love capable of doing the like — a love which forgives men before they wrong us, a heart so altered and disposed towards men that wrong falling on it awakes forgiveness before resentment has time to grow. . . . There is the hunger of the conscience for forgiveness, sin crying for mercy, for peace with God, for moral harmony within, and reconcilement with the eternal conscience with which we have for ever to do. That is the passion which outlives all, and is greater than all passions beside — except one. . . . For the greatest passion in heaven or earth, time or eternity, is the passion of God to forgive, the passion in the passion and death of Christ to redeem. . . . That is the ruling passion in the moral and spirtual universe. Thus God's great passion meets ours.

(Ibid., *pp. 204-05.*)

Let us only flee the amateur notion that in the Cross there is no ultimate ethical issue involved, that it is a simple religious appeal to the heart. The pulpit is doomed to futility if it appeal to the heart in any sense that discredits the final appeal to the conscience. I mean it is doomed if it keep declaring that, with such a Father as Christ's, forgiveness is a matter of course; the only difficulty being to insert it into men's hearty belief. There is no doubt that is a very popular notion. "How natural for God to forgive. It is just like Him." Whereas the real truth is that it is only like the God familiar to us from the Cross, and not from our natural expectation. Real forgiveness is not natural. Nor is it natural and easy to consent to be forgiven. The more quick our moral sensibility is the more slow we are to accept our forgiveness. And that not through pride always, but often through the exact opposite — through shame, and the inability to forgive one's self. Is it Newman who says that the good man never forgives himself? I wish a great many more said it. We should then have a better hold of the forgiveness of God. We should realize how far from a matter of course forgiveness was for a holy, and justly angry, God, for all His love. A free forgiveness flows from moral strength, but an easy forgiveness only means moral weakness. How natural for God to forgive! Nay, if there be one thing in the world for ever supernatural it is real forgiveness — especially on the scale of redemption. It is natural only to the Supernatural. The natural man does not forgive. He resents and revenges. His wrath smoulders till it flash. And the man who forgives easily, jauntily, and thoughtlessly, when it is a real offense, is neither natural nor supernatural but subnatural. He is not only less than God, he is less than man.

Is not God's forgiveness the great moral paradox, the great incredibility of the moral life, needing all the miracle of Christ's person and action to make us realize it when we grasp the terms? A recent authority on preaching warns us that the effective preacher must not be afraid of paradox. For the politician, or the journalist, on the other hand, nothing is more fatal. But that is the region of the ordinary able man, for whom all things must be plain — with a tendency to be dull. In that world an epigram is a frivolity, an antithesis mere ingenuity, and a paradox is mere perversity.

(*From* Positive Preaching and the Modern Mind, *pp. 200-01.*)

Now holy forgiveness is the greatest moral paradox, the most exalting, pacifying paradox, the greatest practical paradox, in the world. Do not think that the word of your gospel is not a moral paradox — law and love, the just and the justifier of the unjust, the holy and the sanctifier of the unholy, holy severity and loving mercy, yea, the Holy made sin. Of their union the Cross is not only the evidential fact but the effecting fact. It not only reveals it, it brings it about. That God might be just and also the justifier of the sinner meant all the moral mystery of the Cross, and all its offense to the natural moral man. The natural moral man either does not forgive — and there are none more unforgiving than some sticklers for morality; or else he forgives as he shaves — "I suppose I ought to"; or as he dines — "because I like to." He believes in a God who either does not forgive, or who forgives of course — *c'est son métier*. But the true supernatural forgiveness is a revolution and not an evolution — yea, it means a solemn and ordered crisis within God Himself. But crisis is Greek for judgment. The forgiveness of the world can only be accomplished by the judgment of the world. That is the indispensable paradox whereby Christianity makes morality spiritual. And not to realize that means a step back and not forward in the great modernizing drift which moralizes spiritual things.

(Ibid., *p. 204*.)

The history of the world morally viewed is a tragedy. All the great tragedy of the world turns upon its guilt. Aeschylus, Shakespeare, Goethe, Ibsen, all tell it you. The solution of the world, therefore, is what destroys its guilt. And nothing can destroy guilt but the very holiness that makes guilt guilt. And that destruction is the work of Christ upon His Cross, the Word of life eternal in your hands and in your souls. The relevancy of His Cross is not to a church, or a sect, or a creed, but to the total moral world in its actual radical case. The moral world, I say, is the real world, the ever modern world. And the supreme problem of the moral world is sin. Its one need is to be forgiven. And nothing but holiness can forgive. Love cannot. We are both forgiven and redeemed in Jesus Christ, and in Him as crucified unto the world for the holiness of God and the sin of men.

(Ibid., *pp. 227-28*.)

PERFECTION

It was I who, at my will's center, did that thing. It was
my will and self that was put into it. My act was not the
freak of some point on my circumference. It came from my
center. It was my unitary, indivisible self that was involved
and is infected. Faith is the attitude of that same self and
will of me to God. . . . Faith is not the faith of the sinless
but of the redeemed. . . . The very nature of faith is trust
of a Saviour, who is not the saviour of my past but of my
soul; and it is trust for forgiveness, for forgiveness not only
of the old life but of the new. . . . Penitence, faith, sanctification, always coexist; they do not destroy and succeed each
other; they are phases of the one process of God in the soul.

(*From* Christian Perfection, *pp. 6-8.*)

To treat a living person as an end, to seek him for himself,
has but one meaning. It is to love him, to have our desire
and energy rest in him, to have our personal finality in
him. . . . His great object with us is not our sinlessness but
our communion. "Give me thy heart." He does not offer us
communion to make us holy; He makes us holy for the sake
of communion. . . . The headlong sin is perhaps a safer thing
than the sinless security.

(Ibid., *p. 13.*)

The difference between the Christian and the world is not
that the world sins, and the Christian does not. It suits the
world to think that it is; because it offers a handy whip to
scourge the Church's consistency while resenting its demands.
. . . But the real difference (I must say often) is not in quantity but in quality. It is not in the number of sins, but in
the attitude towards sin and the things called sin. It is in the
man's sympathies, his affinities; it is in his conscience, his
verdict on sin, his treatment of it — whether the world's or his
own. . . . But with the Christian man there is a new spirit, a
new taste, bias, conscience, terror, and affection. His leading
attitude to sin is fear and hate. His interest, his passion, is
all for good and God. . . . The final judgment is not whether
we have at every moment stood, but whether having done all
we stand — stand at the end, stand as a whole. Perfection is

wholeness. In our perfection there is a permanent element of repentance. . . . God may forgive us, but we do not forgive ourselves. It is always a Saviour, and not merely an Ideal that we confess.

(Ibid., *pp. 31-37*.)

The sin dwelling in the man is a sinful will, sinful volitions. It is not as if he *had* sin, but did not *do* sin. Sin is essentially an act of the will. And our acts cannot be severed from our central will in the way that these extenuations suppose. There is nothing in a man deeper than his source of action. . . . There is nothing at the core which is unaffected by the act of sin. . . . In each act . . . it is the personality that is involved. . . . In the sinful act it is the personality that is involved at its center, but it need not be involved in a fatal and final way. It is very rarely that any single act embodies and exhausts the *entire* personality. . . . There may be sinful volitions in us, and yet the sinful principle does not really own us, but the good. . . . Sin captures certain volitions, but not the whole personality that exerts the volition. The sin comes from the center, but it has not its home in the center. Each sin comes from the central will, but not from the focus of the personality.

(Ibid., *pp. 40-43*.)

The coherent and continuous line in our Christian life is the line of faith. The sins make a certain series, but broken, scattered, irregular. They emerge but they do not make the continuity. . . . What is germane is Christ and faith. Our prevailing habit of soul and bent of will is Christ's. . . . The great justification does not dispense with the daily forgiveness. We walk in the Spirit, and escape the importunities of the flesh. It is only so that we are fair to both flesh and spirit. To treat life as a whole is the only justice to the parts of life.

(Ibid., *pp. 44-49*.)

The Pietist idea pursues perfection as mere quietist sinlessness with a tendency to ecstasy. . . . It is not the will of God that in this life we should be sinless, lest we should find perfection apart from forgiveness. . . . The true perfection is the perfection which is of God in *faith*. . . . Faith is in its nature obedience, but it is the will's obedience to Christ. . . . The error at the root of all false ideas of perfection is this: it is rating our behavior *before* God higher than our relation *to* God — putting conduct before faith, deeds before trust, work before worship. Now, I care comparatively little about what you do, but I care infinitely about whom you believe in. I know if you believe in Christ your conduct will be seen to; but I have no guarantee that if you behave well you will believe in Christ. . . . We are not saved by the love we exercise, but by the Love we trust. The whole Protestant issue lies in that.

(Ibid., *pp. 55-73*.)

The perfect, then, are those who by faith have settled into their divine place in the perfect Christ and become spiritually of age. . . . Faith is the condition of spiritual maturity in the sense of adultness, of entering on the real heritage of the soul. It is the soul coming to itself, coming of age, feeling its feet, entering on its native powers. Faith is perfection in this sense. It is not ceasing to grow, but entering on the real and normal region of growth. . . . Growth is then progress, not *to* Christ but *in* Christ. . . . To *believe* in Christ, to *be* in Christ, and to *abide* in Christ, are three stages of the same perfection — which you may call the Petrine, the Pauline, and the Johannine stages if you will. . . . It is a perfection which both is and *grows*. True perfection is not the power of unbroken growth, but of growing unto perfection, growing on the whole.

(Ibid., *pp. 104-114*.)

You are a perfect personality in the sense that you are distinct from all others, adult, complete in yourself, continuous in your history, and so far consistent with yourself that you are the same person now as long ago. Yet this perfection to which personality has come in you is quite compatible with a constant change and growth. So much so, indeed, that if you had ceased to change and grow it could only have been by dissolution of your personality itself. You only are because of your power to *become* what you are, to *grow*. Incessant growth is a condition of perfect living personality.

(Ibid., p. 119.)

FREEDOM AND RESPONSIBILITY

There is one qualification which has to be made, however, when we use the Pragmatism or Voluntarism of recent philosophy as a calculus for the specific action of Christianity. Action is indeed the material of truth (*Wesen=Actus*) — the organ, too, by which we reach it as well as spread it, and become true as well as see true. But we have to do with something more than the action either of nature, of men, or of mankind. To fall back thus on the will, energy, or resource of man is to make religion in the end impossible, except by a kind of moral positivism which leaves Humanity to worship but itself and its deed. What we have to realize is a spiritual world not simply in man but in which man is, a world that has to temper him and master him, that has to prevent him from taking his needs, passions and energies for charter or standard, a world that has to stand over him, test him, sift him, lift him, and end by setting him on a totally different base from the egotism in which he began. That is, we have to do, above all, not simply with an ideal world of process, but with a spiritual world of value.

And this spiritual world is not quiescent but active. It does not simply envelop us, it acts on us, and we react on it; and in that reaction we find ourselves, and we grow into spiritual persons with which we never set out. It does not swathe us and erase us, it besets us, it applies itself to us. It does not simply stand at the door, or pass and suck us into its wake; it knocks, enters, finds, and saves us — all in the way of creating our moral personality and giving us to ourselves by rescuing us from ourselves. It is an active not a static world. It moves, it works, it creates.

Its movement is not process, as so many today are seduced to construe it, in the wake of the great cosmic processionalist and marshal, Hegel, with his staff of subordinate evolutionists. This of Hegel's, indeed, is a conception which lifts us over much of the triviality and slavery of life; but only to substitute for petty bondage a vast tyranny, and to replace a prison by a despotism, with a first show of freedom but a final atmosphere of death. And especially it leaves us with a loss of moral liberty, and ethical dignity, and spiritual initiative and personal consummation. The actual course of history is not a process. And it is not through yielding to a process that history is created by its great actors. There are stagnations, too, degenerations, enmities which forbid us to call life a process, at the same time as they prevent us from treating its movement as our being rolled over and ground up in a greater process. Mere process ends in mechanism, coarse or fine, and extinguishes a soul. Behind everything that seems process on any large scale our active moral soul insists on placing an act, and an act from a new world — something ethical and personal in its kind.

If this spiritual world, so active, be one; if we are to escape pluralism, as well as monism; if we are not to escape being rolled over by a vast process only to be crushed by the active but awful collision of more spiritual worlds than one; then its action must be one infinite and unitary *concursus,* one compendious personal act, the *actus purus* of an infinite personality who is not only ethical but self-sufficient in his ethic. But what is an infinite moral self-sufficiency, an active, changeless, self-completeness, but *holiness?* The total action of the spiritual world both in us and around is holiness. We find ourselves before and within a holy God, a spiritually moral personality, self-determined and self-complete.

But no less, if this spiritual world and power be universal, it must assert itself supremely in the region of *history.* If its inmost nature be action we cannot think of it as secluded from that one region where action has real meaning and effect for man. It must assert, express, reveal and effect itself in history for the holy and mastering power it is.

Yet such a power cannot adequately reveal itself *dispersed through* history, or merely parallel with it, nor even in "mutual involution." For such a diffused revelation would not represent, and might even belie, a spiritual power whose nature was not only action but action of the sole kind which possesses moral unity, namely, the action of a moral person. If it reveal itself — I do not merely mean assert itself — in history it must surely do so in an act corresponding to its own total ethical nature in the spiritual world, in an act which gathers and commands cosmic history, as its nature is to focus and utter all spiritual being. A world of spiritual action with moral coherency can only be revealed in history by a supreme spiritual act, the supreme act of a person who both gathers up and controls human existence, and delivers it from that submersion in self and the world which in the long run is fatal to man's action as man. If spiritual existence be an infinite and eternal act, such must also be its revelation.

And this is the act of Christ in the *Cross,* the act of the gospel. It is the act of God's grace, met by the act of our faith — an act into which a whole divine life was put, and one that issues in a whole life on our part. This act is the gift of God; whose freedom we attain by no mere development of our own liberty, but by a free act which renounces our liberty for His, breaks with what is behind and beneath us, breaks with the old self, and, by accepting a new creation, exchanges an assertive individualism for a redeemed personality. The energy of such a spiritual world as we postulate in God can only act on us in the way of redemption and not more evolution from the world of our first stage. We cease to be self-made men, and we are men who let God make us, and make us by His grace and not His evolution. We achieve by this grace a personality we had not at the first. As we reach our freedom we acquire and attain ourselves; and we reach our freedom by surrendering it to God's. The best use we can make of our freedom is to forgo it, and to sign it away to one whose work and joy it is to create in us a freedom we can never acquire. We are but persons in the making, and we are not made till grace make us and faith is made. Our supreme ethical act is the faith that gives us at once our Saviour and ourselves. We exhaust our own exertions, and we deliver ourselves to a faithful Creator. And our perfecting God is a God of grace, because He not only finishes us, but finishes us as alone we can be perfected — by redemption, by a change of base, center, and affection. He is a gracious God and not simply a benevolent God, because He lets us exhaust, and even wreck, our private powers, instead of only guiding their education, so that with His free and creative act He may make of us what all our native force could never do.

(*From* Positive Preaching and the Modern Mind, *pp. 228-231.*)

PRAYER

The worst sin is prayerlessness. Overt sin, or crime, or the glaring inconsistencies which often surprise us in Christian people are the effect of this, or its punishment. We are left by God for lack of seeking Him. The history of the saints shows often that their lapses were the fruit and nemesis of slackness or neglect in prayer. Their life, at seasons, also tended to become inhuman by their spiritual solitude. They left men, and were left by men, because they did not in their contemplation find God; they found but the thought or the atmosphere of God. Only living prayer keeps loneliness humane. It is the great producer of sympathy. Trusting the God of Christ, and transacting with Him, we come into tune with men. Our egoism retires before the coming of God, and into the clearance there comes with our Father our brother. We realize man as he is in God and for God, his Lover. When God fills our heart He makes more room for man than the humanist heart can find. Prayer is an act, indeed *the* act, of fellowship. We cannot truly pray even for ourselves without passing beyond ourselves and our individual experience. If we should begin with these the nature of prayer carries us beyond them, both to God and to man. Even private prayer is common prayer — the more so, possibly, as it retires from being public prayer.

Not to want to pray, then, is the sin behind sin. And it ends in not being able to pray. That is its punishment — spiritual dumbness, or at least aphasia, and starvation. We do not take our spiritual food, and so we falter, dwindle, and die. "In the sweat of your brow ye shall eat your bread." That has been said to be true both of physical and spiritual labor. It is true both of the life of bread and of the bread of life.

Prayer brings with it, as food does, a new sense of power and health. We are driven to it by hunger, and, having eaten, we are refreshed and strengthened for the battle which even our physical life involves. For heart and *flesh* cry out for the living God. God's gift is free; it is, therefore, a gift to our freedom, i.e. renewal to our moral strength, to what makes men of us. Without this gift always renewed, our very freedom can enslave us. The life of every organism is but the constant victory of a higher energy, constantly fed, over lower and more elementary forces. Prayer is the assimilation of a holy God's moral strength.

We must work for this living. To feed the soul we must toil at prayer. And what a labor it is! "He prayed in an agony." We must pray even to tears if need be. Our cooperation with God is our receptivity; but it is an active, a laborious receptivity, an importunity that drains our strength away if it does not tap the sources of the Strength eternal. We work, we slave, at receiving. To him that hath this laborious expectancy it shall be given. Prayer is the powerful appropriation of power, of divine power. It is therefore creative.

Prayer is not mere wishing. It is asking — with a will. Our will goes into it. It is energy. *Orare est laborare*. We turn to an active Giver; therefore we go into action. For we could not pray without knowing and meeting Him in kind. If God has a controversy with Israel, Israel must wrestle with God. Moreover, He is the Giver not only of the answer, but first of the prayer itself. His gift provokes ours. He beseeches us, which makes us beseech Him. And what we ask for chiefly is the power to ask more and to ask better. We pray for more prayer. The true "gift of prayer" is God's grace before it is our facility.

Thus prayer is, for us, paradoxically, both a gift and a conquest, a grace and a duty. But does that not mean, is it not a special case of the truth, that all duty is a gift, every call on us a blessing, and that the task we often find a burden is really a boon? When we look up from under it it is a load, but those who look down to it from God's side see it as a

blessing. It is like great wings — they increase the weight
but also the flight. If we have no duty to do God has shut
Himself up from us. To be denied duty is to be denied
God. No cross no Christ. "When pain ends gain ends too."

(*From* The Soul of Prayer, *pp. 11-13*.)

Prayer is turning our will on God either in the way of
resignation or of impetation. We yield to His Will or He
to ours. Hence religion is above all things prayer, according
as it is a religion of will and conscience, as it is an ethical
religion. It is will and Will. To be religious is to pray. Bad
prayer is false religion. Not to pray is to be irreligious. "The
battle for religion is the battle for prayer; the theory of
religion is the philosophy of prayer." In prayer we do not
think out God; we draw Him out. Prayer is where our
thought of God passes into action, and becomes more certain
than thought. In all thought which is not mere dreaming
or brooding there is an element of will; and in earnest (which
is intelligent) prayer we give this element the upper hand.
We do not simply spread our thought out before God, but
we *offer* it to Him, turn it on Him, bring it to bear on Him,
press it on Him. This is our great and first sacrifice, and it
becomes pressure on God. We can offer God nothing so
great and effective as our obedient acceptance of the mind
and purpose and work of Christ. It is not easy. It is harder
than any idealism. But then it is very mighty. And it is a
power that grows by exercise. At first it groans, at last it
glides. And it comes to this, that, as there are thoughts that
seem to think themselves in us, so there are prayers that
pray themselves in us. And, as those are the best thoughts,
these are the best prayers. For it is the Christ at prayer who
lives in us, and we are conduits of the eternal Intercession.

(Ibid., *pp. 15-16*.)

Do not allow your practice in prayer to be arrested by
scientific or philosophic considerations as to *how* answer is
possible. That is a valuable subject for discussion, but it is
not entitled to control our practice. Faith is at least as
essential to the soul as science, and it has a foundation more

independent. And prayer is not only a necessity of faith, it is faith itself in action.

If I must choose between Christ, who bids me pray for everything, and the savant, who tells me certain answers are physically and rationally impossible, must I not choose Christ? Because, while the savant knows much about nature and its action (and much more than Christ did), Christ knew everything about the God of nature and His reality. He knew more of what is possible to God than anybody has ever known about what is possible in nature. On such a subject as prayer, anyone is a greater authority who wholly knows the will of God than he who only knows God's methods, and knows them but in part. Prayer is not an act of knowledge but of faith. It is not a matter of calculation but of confidence — "that our faith should not stand in the wisdom of men, but in the power of God." Which means that in this region we are not to be regulated by science, but by God's self-revelation. Do not be so timid about praying wrongly if you pray humbly. If God is really the Father that Christ revealed, then the principle is — take everything to Him that exercises you. Apart from frivolity, such as praying to find the stud you lost, or the knife, or the umbrella, there is really no limitation in the New Testament on the contents of petition. Any regulation is as to the spirit of the prayer, the faith it springs from. In all distress which mars your peace, petition must be the form your faith takes — petition for rescue. Keep close to the New Testament Christ, and then ask for anything you desire in that contact. Ask for everything you can ask in Christ's name, i.e. everything desirable by a man who is in Christ's kingdom of God, by a man who lives for it at heart, everything in tune with the purpose and work of the kingdom in Christ. If you are in that kingdom, then pray freely for whatever you need or wish to keep you active and effective for it, from daily bread upwards and outwards. In all things make your requests known. It will not unhinge such faith if you do not obtain them. At least you have laid them on God's heart; and faith means confidences between you and not only favors. And there is not confidence if you keep back what is hot or heavy on your heart. If prayer is not a play of the religious fantasy, or a routine task, it must be the application of faith to a concrete actual and urgent situation. Only remember that prayer does not work by magic, and that stormy desire is not fervent, effectual prayer. You may be but exploiting a mighty power; whereas you must be in real contact with the real God. It is the man that most really has God that most really seeks God.

(Ibid., *pp. 64-66*.)

Prayer is for the religious life what original research is for science — by it we get direct contact with reality. The soul is brought into union with its own vaster nature — God. Therefore, also, we must use the Bible as an original; for, indeed, the Bible is the most copious spring of prayer, and of power, and of range. If we learn to pray from the Bible, and avoid a mere *cento* of its phrases, we shall cultivate in our prayer the large humane note of a universal gospel. Let us nurse our prayer on our *study* of our Bible; and let us, therefore, not be too afraid of *theological* prayer. True Christian prayer must have theology in it; no less than true theology must have prayer in it and must be capable of being prayed. "Your theology is too difficult," said Charles V to the Reformers; "it cannot be understood without much prayer." Yes, that is our arduous puritan way. Prayer and theology must interpenetrate to keep each other great, and wide, and mighty. The failure of the habit of prayer is at the root of much of our light distaste for theology. There is a conspiracy of influences round us whose effect is to belittle our great work. Earnest ministers suffer more from the smallness of their people than from their sins, and far more than from their unkindness. Our public may kill by its triviality a soul which could easily resist the assaults of opposition or wickedness. And our newspapers will greatly aid their work. Now, to resist this it is not enough to have recourse to prayer and to cultivate devotion. Unfortunately, there are signs in the religious world to show that prayer and piety alone do not save men from pettiness of interest, thinness of soul, spiritual volatility, the note of insincerity, or foolishness of judgment, or even vindictiveness. The remedy is not prayer alone, but prayer on the scale of the whole gospel and at the depth of searching faith. It is considered prayer — prayer which rises above the childish petitions that disfigure much of our public pietism, prayer which issues from the central affairs of the kingdom of God. It is prayer with the profound Bible as its book of devotion, and a true theology of faith for half of its power. It is the prayer of a mind that moves in Bible passion, and ranges with Bible scope, even when it eschews Bible speech and "the language of Canaan."

And yet, with all its range, it is prayer with *concentration*. It has not only thought but will in it. The great reason why so many will not decide for Christ is that Christ requires from the world concentration; not seclusion and not renunciation merely, but concentration. And we ministers have our special form of that need. I am speaking not of our share in the common troubles of life, but of those specially that arise from the ministerial office and care. No minister can live up to his work on the casual or interjectional kind of prayer that might be sufficient for many of his flock. He must think, of course, in his prayers — in his private prayers — and he must pray his faith's thought. But, still more, in his praying he must act. Prayer is not a frame of mind, but a great energy. He must rise to conceive his work as an active function of the work of Christ; and he must link his faith, therefore, with the intercession which covers the whole energy of Christ in His kingdom. In this, as in many ways, he must remember, to his great relief and comfort, that it is not he who is the real pastor of his church, but Christ, and that he is but Christ's curate. The final responsibility is not his, but Christ's, who bears the responsibility of all the sins and frets, both of the world and, especially, of the Church.

(Ibid., *pp. 78-79.*)

CHRISTIANITY AND ART

Christianity introduced the world to a new idea on the one hand, and to a new passion on the other — and within both to a new power. The new idea was the idea of the true Infinite. The new passion was the passion of that Infinite as Love. And the new power was the power of the Holy Ghost and the eternal life.

The lost soul was brought into an indestructible relation to the infinite, holy Love. It was both awed and stirred at the discovery that it had eternal relations and an infinite destiny. We cannot exaggerate the vast change which passed over the human spirit when it awoke to feel itself beyond the limitations of the ancient, pagan, and delinquescent world. It may, with truth, be said that all the progress of modern Europe is due to this idea of the possibility for the soul, through the grace of an infinite God, of a holy progress and destiny which were also infinite. Life received a horizon in the place of a boundary. It got impulse where it had before met only with rebuff. It felt a new right of property in this world because it had received the next in fee. There was a new power immanent in the sphere of the seen, supplied by faith's assurance of the infinite resources of the hoped-for and unseen.

This infinity which men were taught to take home to their trust was not a mathematical infinity of extension, nor a dynamical infinity of energy. It was neither the infinite of space, nor the infinite of force. It was the Infinite of spiritual thought, passion, and purpose, in a word, of personality, raised to heavenly quality, divine intensity, and universal scope. It was the infinitude of holy, redeeming Love. The awful load which was felt to hang over life, and which might at any moment drop, was swept away. Fate, with its inscrutable, and therefore incalculable, action, gave way to the trust of a God who was known to be holy Love, who was morally calculable, who might be eternally relied on to act without caprice, in the steady wisdom of His changeless nature and His redeeming will, and who could be absolutely trusted with the sinful soul, with the longing heart, with the lost and loved — with all that life held or promised of good and dear. Men could now love boldly. There was new security given, so to speak, for the investment of the heart's capital in life. The tenants of the world were no more at the mercy of a dubious, capricious, or self-ish owner. If I may continue the image, they would be at last compensated for whatever they put on the soil or into it, when it came to leaving it. The unexhausted improvements which they left in their holding of life would return to them again after many days. Their labor was not in vain in the Lord. The mobility and uncertainty of paganism passed away. In importing interest, color, and beauty into life, men came to feel they were painting in view of Eternity. For was not the eternal Love like a red, red rose, as Dante imaged heaven? Were we not the children of One who, in perfect justice and perfect love of men, was working world without end? And those of them who rose above considerations of mere justice, enhanced life's color and content by the ardor of the devotion with which they repaid in love that infinite Love which had made them sons of God. So that while the new sense of Infinity expanded the volume of life, raised its possibilities, and reared from the soil of faith the passion for progress in the soul, the new revelation of love and justice increased the color, warmth, intensity, and variety of life, and brought to fruit in a genial air those germs of longing which the idea of Infinity had quickened into life. The divine Infinity, made historic in Christ's incarnation, and actual in His resurrection, expanded life, as the divine Love enriched it, without bound.

From such an impulse the greatest psychological results must sooner or later flow. If the Lord was risen, men could no more live at a poor dying rate. The new feeling of triumph and security was sure to take outward shape in powerful ways. And it would have been very strange if one of these had not been the way of art. Love does not ignore beauty, but spiritualizes it. Love is spiritual beauty, love in mastery is spiritual power, and its influx into the world could not but issue again in a joyful birth as art. And it was art of a new and special kind. The classic art was not, indeed, utterly disjoined from love, but the difference between it and Christian art begins to appear when we ask what it was that was loved. The Greek loved Nature, and especially human nature: the object of Christian love, on the other hand, was not natural, but supernatural. It was spent on a spiritual object, the same in kind as the soul that loved. The Greek loved beneath him, the Christian above him. The Christian loved above his station. He loved at once his equal, whom he *could* love, and his superior, whom he had *no right* to love, the God-Man, the human God, whose grace offered Himself to love. He loved a spirit, a person, like himself, not a thing; but it was a divine and holy Spirit, in whom existed complete all the perfections which his guilt had flouted, and his salvation could but share. This love, therefore, was an entirely inward matter. It could easily dispense with an outward expression. The art which bodied it forth was but an appanage, a servant, a voice. The Greek's love, on the contrary, being the love of an external thing, was not thus independent and self-sufficing. The expression of it was much less indispensable, more of its essence. The art, as I have already said, became the religion, and the religion the art. They rose and they fell together at the last. Christianity, on the other hand, has outlived serveral developments of art, as it outlives many forms of society; and it is independent of them all. It is supernational in art as in grace. And this is further to be noticed, that even where Christian art ceases to be intensely spiritual, it does not become merely naturalistic. Between pure spirituality, or the love of the divine Spirit, and pure naturalism, or the love of the obvious beauty, there is Humanity, the love of the dear, near human heart and soul.

(*From* Christ on Parnassus, *pp. 75-79.*)

The Christian mind is the reconciliation of Jew and Greek. A stage has been reached, by help of the Jew, beyond the Greek balance of body and soul, and, by the help of the Greek, beyond speechless awe. Mind has exactly reversed its place in India, and has now been lifted to look down on the matter which once bruised it with its heel. But to look down only as the Jew did. This transcendence of matter by soul, is it no more than the Jew instinctively realized, and received naively as a gift from heaven? No, it is not the same. It is something richer, fuller, more precious

in every way. It is not transcendence, and it is not immanence. It is the immanence of the transcendent. We do not
singly have the benefit of God's transcendence of the world;
we share it and its immanence.

(Ibid., pp. 82-83.)

The Christian conception, then, differed from the Greek
in that it placed soul, not on a level with Nature, but clearly
and eternally above it. Yet it differed from the Jewish conception in that it interpenetrated Nature with spirit, refined
the connection between them, and made the relation a far
more intimate one than that of the craftsman and his handi-
craft. It reconciled the immanence and the eminence of God.
It lifted the visible to the dignity of reflecting and witnessing
the mind of the Invisible and Eternal. Both Spirit and
Nature, man and the world, were thus exalted together.
And though many phases of Christianity seek to enhance
the one at the other's expense, yet the large and general
tendency of this revelation has been otherwise. It has up-
lifted our thought together of the Creator and the work.
It has blessed both Him that gives and that which takes.
And we have here an illustration of the first principle of
true progress. Raise the conception of God, and the faith
in Him, and you will not only exalt the soul's power but
deepen its insight into Nature. The revelation of Christianity
had thus the twofold effect upon the human spirit. It
exalted and expanded its characteristic powers by a release
from the world, and, on the other hand, it gave it a new
interest and sympathy with the world. Man by redemption
became free *from* the world *for* the world. The very influence
that made the soul independent of Nature gave it in the
same act a power over Nature, and an understanding of it,
which the Greek relation of equality did not develop. It
gave it leisure from itself to sympathize. The soul *descended*
on Nature like a heavenly hero, and forced from her moods
of submission, works of service, and secrets of charm which
she will yield only to a mastery truly sympathetic and divine.

(Ibid., pp. 85-86.)

Nature and natural passion are in their place divine. True

there is something higher. But it is not higher in any sense which would destroy the innocency and divinity of that earlier natural stage. Art here is surely the handmaid of the true faith which delivers us from the curse laid by superstition upon the beauty and affection of nature, as if intense passion were lawless passion, and the love of the body were not more than the history of the flesh.

(Comment on Rossetti, from Religion in Recent Art, *p. 35.)*

It is most hard to get people to realize how truly the Christian regeneration permeates the whole of human nature, renews it in its total aspect like a fresh creation, and quickens to divine vitality every noble faculty that man owns.

(Comment on Burne Jones, ibid., pp. 54-55.)

The principle of art is the incarnation of God's eternal beauty; the principle of religion is the incarnation of God's eternal human heart.... The time is coming, I am sure, when the Christ that is to be shall fascinate the imagination as it was enthralled by the medieval Christ, and inspire a piety purer, because lovelier, than the one-sided purity of Puritanism.... The path of beauty is not *the* way, but it is a way to God; and the temple in the heavens, like the old temple on earth, has a Gate Beautiful. We shall not go far in a true sense of the beauty of holiness without gaining a deeper sense of the holiness of beauty.

(Comment on Burne Jones, ibid., pp. 105-107.)

IX: THE CHURCH

CHURCH, KINGDOM AND MISSION

In the opinion of many the Church has had its day, but it lingers on partly mischievous, as in the case of Rome, partly negligible, as with the evangelical Churches. We hear impatient questions whether religion cannot go on without a church. To which the answer is that religion might, but Christianity could not. Not only does Christianity need a church negatively, for protection against the world, but the gospel necessitates it positively, for the exercise of faith and growth of service. Christianity put into men a new power that compelled a church by its racial nature. If Christ had not founded a church, the thing He *did* found would have done so. He created the new life, the New Covenant which, by its nature, was bound to create the Church. So, if it is asked, "What is the security for investing our souls' sympathies and energies in this concern, the Church?" we answer, first, that the question is one that no Christian could ask and no worldling would; and, second, that no amount of subjective religion secures the Church, but the creating Word of *a positive gospel*.

A church building is the outward and visible sign of a

local society. The spiritual has there a local habitation and a name. It has a *positive and cognizable center*. And that is what religion must have spiritually also — a positive center of fact and reality, local in time, as it were. What these buildings are on the ground, that the great events and doctrines of salvation, its great historic facts and intelligible fabrics, are for the soul. They are creative points and lines of power. We gather to them by their own compulsion, and we go out from them with power to endow and command the world. Christ, the incarnation, the Cross, the atonement, the resurrection, the Spirit, the Church — what a vague, rambling, feckless religion we have without such things! A brotherhood dies out which never meets: it has no father, no focus, no force. And can it live without thinking? You cannot have Christian communion without the Christian community, nor the Christian community without its centers, its laws, and its truths. We cannot be organs of the religion of God's will without its organization in a Church and a doctrine.

A warm spirituality without the apostolic and evangelical substance may seem attractive to many — what is called undogmatic, or even unconscious, Christianity. It will specially appeal to the lay mind, in the pulpit and out. But it is death to a Church. With mere spirituality the Church has little to do. What it has to do with is far more positive. The Christian revelation is not "God is a Spirit"; and so the Christian religion is not spirituality. Nor is the Christian revelation simply "God is Love"; and so the Christian religion is not simply charity. There are many cases when charity submerges righteousness and betrays truth. The Christian revelation is that the spiritual, personal, and loving God is holy, and only therefore eternal; so that its answering religion is the religion of the Holy Spirit; it is *Holy Spirituality*. And the site and source of that revelation, that gift, is the Cross of Christ, as the crisis of God's righteous judgment, holy grace, and new creating conquest of the world. The supreme revelation of God is the holy; and the central meaning of the Cross is less God's love than the holiness of it. We have no guarantee for the supreme thing, *the* divine thing, the eternal thing in God, namely, His holiness, except the Cross, which alone enables us not only to love His love but to trust it absolutely and for ever.

(*From* The Church and the Sacraments, *pp. 3-5.*)

The Church's one foundation, and the trust of its ministry, is not simply Christ, but Christ crucified. It is not His Person as our spiritual superlative, or even as our spiritual home and clime, but His Person as our eternal Redeemer in His blood. It is evangelical. It is mystical, but with the mystic action working at the heart and height of moral things in a world morally wrong. The Church rests on the grace of God, the judging, atoning, regenerating grace of God, which is His holy love in the form it must take with human sin. Wherever that is heartily confessed, and goes on to rule, we have the true Church. The Church is not made by men. It is no creature either of humane sympathy or of voluntary association, even though these give it a local and practical form. It is not put together by consents, contract, or affinities. It is a new creation of God in the Holy Spirit, a spiritual organism, in which we find our soul. Men unite themselves with the Church because they are already united with Christ, and because they are, in that very act of union with Him, already in spirit and principle organized into the great Church He created, and whose life He is.

In so far as the Church is a creature, it is the creature of the preached gospel of God's grace forgiving, redeeming, and creating us anew by Christ's Cross. The Church was created by the preaching of that solidary gospel, and fortified by the sacraments of it, which are, indeed, but other ways of receiving, confessing, and preaching it. The Church is the social and practical response to that grace. Wherever that gospel is taken seriously, and duly, and statedly, there is the Church. It is the living organism (I avoid the word organization) of the worshippers of Christ, created by His redeeming gospel in Word and sacrament. There is therefore but one way of recovering the idea of the Church. It is by regaining, on a scale worthy of it, the evangelical faith which

made and makes the Church always. To lose that is often
too easy. But it is a very hard thing to regain.

(Ibid., *pp. 34-35.*)

All this is of great value when we come to ask what the
relation is between the kingdom and the Church. It is
certain that Christ founded the kingdom. He knew He
was founding the New Covenant, the kingdom as a relation.
He also founded, though not in just the same way, the
Church. How do they stand to each other? If the kingdom of God is only an ethical idea, then it is very different
from the Church. It may by some be thought to be higher,
it may be held to be the end for which the Church is but the
means. It may go on as the converted State when the
Church had ceased to exist. But we have seen that the
kingdom is more than ethical, that it is religious, holy
with an absolute ethic; that it is a moral gift, i.e. that it
is founded on the justifying grace which founds the Church,
on Christ's fulfilment and satisfaction of the Father's holiness; that the hope of all its coming is the reality of it as
come; that we can thus enter a heaven which has not yet
arrived. Its foundation is the soul's relation of sheer faith,
loving obedience, and close communion with God both in
piety and practice. It rests on that kind of morality which
regards the holy, and takes shape in forgiveness and eternal
life. That is to say, it is created by that which created the
Church — by the New Covenant. The real foundation of the
Church was the founding of the New Covenant — the gospel. Christ at the end was more engrossed with the founding of that Covenant than of the Church. That again is to
say that what founded the kingdom also founded the Church.
Therefore they are the same.

The Church is not a means to the kingdom, but the
kingdom in the making. It is the new relation, the kingship, in so far as that has become a distinct society. It is the
family hearth or focus of the children of God. Truly the
kingdom's action is wider than the Church, for the kingship of God works outside that in a luminous penumbra.
But in so far as the kingdom of God is not just a holy

relation but a holy society, the Church is the kingdom of God. The mystic nature of the kingdom is conserved in the Church, the moral nature of it conserves the Church itself. Inside the Church it works as holy love, outside it as holy righteousness. And the Church is made righteous by it as society is made holy. If the kingdom were left without the Church it would become a moral pedantry. If the Church were left without the kingdom, the moral, historic and social element would be lost from it in mystic spirituality of an individual kind, cumulative rather than creative. The Church would then fall to groups of people so minded, or clubs for mutual improvement of a religious kind. The public element, the element of righteousness, would be too otiose and pacific. The note of fraternal intimacy would submerge the world of public good, as the inferior Christianity tends so often to do.[1] The holiness would be lost in the love, and the love itself lost in society. But if the kingdom is as supernatural in its possession of a holy God as it is practical for social righteousness, if it is as spiritual as it is moral, and as present as it is futurist, then the active Church, as distinguished from the pious group, is the kingdom of God inchoate. And each several Church has its right as it partakes of this great Church.

The sin of man has not destroyed the power of God. It has only refused it; and, in refusing it, it has but changed its mode of action on man. It has not in the least weakened it. God is no less King because of man's sin. His kingship takes another shape. He has resources to deal even with that revolt. It is a delusion, even of religion, to think of the kingship of God at work in heaven only, and not on earth or in hell. He is Lord as absolute in all three as in one. His holy will is done not in heaven only but on earth. And the irresistible pressure of that holy will is as real in hell as in heaven, though it acts differently on His creatures' wills. His loving will is at work on earth without man's will, and in hell against man's will, as surely as it is in heaven with it.

---

[1] As, for instance, when a minister makes kindness criminal by recommending a needy brother to a pulpit regardless of what his record shows this will mean for the Church.

The kingship of God does not fail, and it is never weary. There is no doubt about its purpose, and none about its result.

There is no idea, no power, which it is so needful to carry home to either State or Church as the kingdom of God, if only because it is the only power that opens our eyes to the kingdom of evil and the course to take with it. It is with an organization, a conspiracy, of evil that we have to do, and not a mere bias. This kingdom of God is the grand International, if our eyes could see it, since it gauges the whole moral situation of man and has no illusions. Amid all international changes it is the shaping power, whether we have vision to see it or not. And the number of those who do not see it makes as great a danger as the number ranged against it. The chief charge against popular religion is that it has blinded that eye, and taken that *flair* away. With the decline of faith goes the discernment of spirits. The Church, which is there for the kingdom, which as I say is indeed the kingdom inchoate, has yet done much to debase the idea of God's kingdom into man's paradise, and simply to transfigure an egoism it ought to regenerate. It has made God's reign a mere auxiliary to man's glory or comfort.

Goodness is a realm; and there is a realm of evil. Each is spiritually against the other. If the other world has a king, there is also a prince of this world; and there can be no peace except in a complete victory, so that such a war shall never be again. Most people live in an armistice, and many only drag on with the war; but the High Command on both sides knows the only terms of the end. Yet we cannot sort men into their camps. As we cannot certainly decide in individual cases who is a subject of God, so we cannot say that so-and-so is naturalized under Satan. The two sides do not understand each other nor the campaign — only the heads do; for the good do not readily see into evil, nor do the evil understand the good. The victory must be left to Him whose holiness gives Him the true measure and meaning of evil as the evil can never take the measure of good. The light shines into the darkness, but the darkness

does not take it in; therefore it can neither escape nor defeat
it. Its trickery is good, but its strategy is poor, and its
diplomacy stupid at the last. And the power, which came in
gleams of light, goes on to flashes of lightning; which are
the judgments of God upon things civil and religious, on
State and Church, on culture and crudity, on the progress
and peace wherein the soul sinks and rots, and eternity is
banished from the concern of time.

(Ibid., *pp. 94-97*.)

The kingdom is more than a social idea, but as a social
idea it dominates the Synoptics. In the Epistles it retains its
social note as the ideal Church. In the Fourth Gospel it
appears more mystically, and therefore more individually,
as eternal life. To put it technically, the eschatology becomes
a transcendency, and the last things are not simply the end
things but the ground things, the dominants. As the Church
went on to grow more external and egoist this idea shared
in the fall. Both the kingdom and its eternal life became
debased by contact with the paganism they overcame. But
now we are returning to the larger and holier note. The
kingdom of God is the emergence into the life of history,
both by growth and crisis, of that saving sovereignty which
is the moral power and order of the spiritual world. The
coming of the kingdom is the growth of the inroad of God's
will on earth to be what it always is in peace and glory in
heaven. I am thinking of what we have in the very opening
of the Lord's Prayer, where the phrase "as in heaven so on
earth" belongs to each of the three first petitions, and not
only to its next neighbor. "Hallowed be Thy Name" as in
heaven so on earth; "Thy kingdom come" as in heaven so on
earth. As if it should say, "There is a realm at the heart of
things where all is already won and well, all is Yea and
Amen. And access to it is not barred to faith on earth. And
it is the real workshop of history." Our commerce with that
country alters much, the whole complexion of our social
discussion changes, when we seek to measure and adjust all
things by their obedience to this power and their movement
to this goal. All changes its note and method when we seek

first that kingdom. That is the new creation in which dwells immortality.

(*From* This Life and the Next, *pp. 84-87.*)

THE MINISTRY

The Church provided and provides the *personnel* for an institution already created for it by God's Spirit. And it modified its form. It did this as the need arose for filling a place that could strictly never be filled again — the place of the apostles, whose companying with Christ, and their gifts of normative revelation from Him, had been quite original, unique, and historically intransmissible. The strict successor of the apostle is the New Testament, as containing the precipitate of their standard preaching. It is not the ministry that is the successor of the apostolate, but the ministry *plus* the true apostolic legacy of the Bible — the ministry *of the Word.* The ministry is the successor of the apostles only as the prolongation of their Bible — as the nervous system spreads the brain. The ministry of the Word is, therefore, not a projection or creation of the Church. The authority of the ministry is not drawn from the Church — only its opportunity is — else the message of the Word would be no message to the Church but only its soliloquy, the Church calling to its own soul, "Bless the Lord, O my soul"; and not the Church receiving the call and Word of God. What does come from the Church is the recognition of an authority it cannot confer, and the provision of opportunity. The word authority is ambiguous. It may mean the ultimate equipment, commission, and *élan* by the Spirit, or it may mean the license given by the Church, and its call to exercise the gift in its midst — especially for life. In ordination the two things must meet — the man's call (not by religious sensibility but *by the gospel*) and the Church's seal of it — the authority of the Spirit in the man, and the recognition of it by the Church. There is the creative and sacramental authority, and there is the judicial and licensing authority.

The Protestant minister is a surrogate of the apostles rather than their successor. But it *is* in the wake of apostles that he stands, with their soul in his as the Bible is in his hand. His effectiveness is therefore apostolic in its kind. It lies in what made an apostle an apostle — in the gospel as an act and power of person on person. It is evangelical. He is a successor of such apostles functionally if not canonically, evangelically if not statutorily. The apostles appointed no canonical successors. They could not. They were unique. Through personal contact, they had been trained by the earthly Christ for witness, and endowed with a fontal power of interpreting Him. That was their prerogative. But the apostolate in that limited sense died with the last of them. It was by its nature incommunicable. Christ gave no canon for its perpetuation. The ministry was an ordinance of Christ rather than an institution, with the atmosphere of a gift rather than the regulations of a fiat. Christ ordained a ministry, the Church ordains ministers. And the expectation of a near *parousia* made a scrupulous provision for successors to the apostles seem unnecessary; the necessity only arose when that expectation died away, and some substitute had to be found for apostles now gone. The apostles could not send as they had been sent by Christ.

The ministry is, therefore, not the canonical prolongation of the apostolate any more than the Church is the prolongation of the incarnation. The Church is the product of the incarnation, and the ministry is a gift to the Church. It is not the prolongation of the apostolate but a substitute, with a like end, and on its base. The prolongation of the apostolate and the legatee of its unique authority (I have said) is the New Testament, as the precipitate of the apostolic preaching at first hand. This is the minister's charter. The apostolic continuity is in the function, not in the entail; in the eternal Word proclaimed, not in the unbroken chain prolonged. It is in the message,[1] not in the order of men. A hitch in the conveyancing therefore matters nothing. The apostles were not chosen by the Church, but when they

---

[1] The apostolic succession was at first a succession of truth rather than of persons, till in time the depositories became more than the deposit. The Church fell to a bureaucracy in the sense that the officers vouched for the matter more than the matter for the officers. The *charisma veritatis* was planted on the bishop.

died out a ministry arose which was; and which, under different conditions, performed the like function of preaching, spreading, and consolidating the gospel as interpreted by the apostles once for all. Christ chose the apostles directly, the ministers He chose and chooses through the Church. The Church does not always choose right; but then Judas was in the twelve. The apostolate was not perpetuated, and certainly not self-perpetuated; but it was replaced by another instrument for the same purpose at the motion of the same Spirit. It was replaced not by a prolongation but by a mandatory to administer its trust — by the minister of the Word. For that Word the apostles had authority by a unique call direct from Christ, the ministry had function by a call truly from Christ but mediated through the Church and repeated generation after generation — the function of being the living sacraments of a gospel the apostles gave.

What the ministry had was a functional continuity in preaching the Word revealed to the apostles, administering its sacraments, and applying its principles in a Christian ethic. The apostolic succession is the evangelical succession. Its continuity lies not in a due devolution but in a common inspiration, a common ministration of God's grace as mercy. It is (so to say) not a vertical continuity descending in a line, but a solidary, spreading through a mass; not a chain on which the Church is hung, but a nervous system pervading it and, by the Word, continually creating it. This ministry took the place of the apostolate in the second century. The Ignatian bishop is a congregational minister. The Church changed and corrected the form of the ministry then, as it did at the Reformation, as it has always power to do. The apostles had a commission from God by Christ's endowment. They descended on the Church, they did not rise from it. But the ministry had also a mandate from men, from a Church who, by spiritual discernment, recognized in certain of their number Christ's gift of gospelling in some form. It did arise from the Church — though the trust it ministered, the gospel that made it, did not. The apostolate was not instituted by the Churches, the ministry was. But the trust was in common, and the function was alike. It was to convey (not merely to announce but sacramentally to convey) the grace of God to men. And that is the nature of ministerial effectiveness, in various forms.

I deliberately avoid speaking of the effectiveness of the ministry in the sense in which the phrase would be most promptly understood, where people are ceasing to believe in the Church, and coming to believe in congregations, agencies, movements, fabrics, and funds. The effectiveness of the ministry is to be found in its sacramental quality as I have explained it, its conveying quality, its moral, life-giving, life-deepening quality. We can never sever that great impressive idea of a real sacrament from the idea of the ministry. Without that conveying power, in the end it is nothing. We hear much question raised whether our ministry is a *valid* ministry. It is absurd. God alone can really know if a ministry is valid. He alone can search the chief results. Only that gospel validates the ministry which created it. And if the work of the Free Churches for the gospel during three centuries in this country be invalid, we must revise the whole New Testament idea of apostolic value and the Spirit's work.

Sometimes, however, the word valid is deprecated, modified, and we are only *irregular*. Again, there is but one thing that regularizes the ministry. It is the gospel and a Church of the gospel. Christianity began in an irregular ministry. It was disowned by every religious authority of the day. It began as a sect. And it burst and broke the Church in which it arose. The ministry is valid or regular according as it is effective as a sacrament of the gospel to our experience in a church. It is what makes the gospel, and Christ as the gospel, a real presence for life. The great sacrament of Christianity is the sacrament of the living and preached Word of reconciliation, whether by speech, rite, or work. The elements may be anything; the Word is everything, the active Word of God's Act, Christ's personal Act met by His Church's.

That sacrament of the Word is what gives value to all other sacraments. They are not ends, they are but means to that grace. They are but visible, tangible modes of conveying the same gospel which is audible in the Word. In the sacrament of the Word the ministers are themselves the living elements in Christ's hands — broken and poured out in soul, even unto death; so that they may not only witness Christ, or symbolize Him, but by the sacrament of personality actually convey Him crucified and risen. This cannot be done officially. It cannot be done without travail. A Mother Church must die daily in bringing the gospel into the world — and especially in her ministry must she die. There is indeed a real change in these true elements. Their transubstantiation is a constantly renewed conversion. It is the passage of the preacher's soul from death to life incessantly. The apostles were greater sacraments than those they administered, as man is more than the Sabbath, Christ than the Temple.

For the true sacrament is holy personality. The body and blood of Christ is the heart and soul of Christ, the broken heart, the soul made a libation. A soul elect to the Cross of the gospel conveys Christ as bread, wine, or water cannot. In like manner we say that, in strictness, a book cannot be inspired, but only the soul that wrote it: and the apostles were more inspired than the Bible. A Church cannot, indeed, live without sacraments, which are "essential means"; but still less can it live without sacramental souls, which are also ends in themselves. There then lies the prime effectiveness of the ministry. It is its sacramental power, not to change elements but to change souls, to regenerate personality. Let us rise above the idea that the preached Word of God is a mere message warmly told. It is a creative sacrament by the medium of a consecrated personality. It is more than good news fervently spoken, it is a soul's life and power from God. Ardor is not life. And the Word's bearer is more than a herald; he is a hierophant from the holiest place. He is, as gospelling, more than a herald God sent, he is a living oracle of God.

(From The Church and the Sacraments, *pp. 137-142.)*

THE SACRAMENTS

The Word and the sacraments are the two great expres-

sions of the gospel in worship. The sacraments are the
acted Word — variants of the preached Word. They are
signs, but they are more than signs. They are the Word,
the gospel itself, visible, as in preaching the Word is audible.
But in either case it is an act. It is Christ in a real presence
giving us anew His redemption. The sacraments used to
be called seals. A seal is something distinctive of the person
who uses it, and of an act of his. Being dead he yet speaks.
It is not simply a sign or relic of him, which might be
unconscious, unmeant, like his footprint or the smoke of
his fire. It means an act in which he intends to convey
himself, his mind, his will, his act.

The sacraments are not only signs or symptoms, but
deliberate seals of the loving will and work of Christ for
us. They bring Him to the spot in His crucial significance.
They are love-tokens to the Church — but love-tokens different, for instance, from a ring. The same ring might
serve for a token between *any* lovers. It has nothing characteristic of either. But if it has a name and a motto on it,
or if a lover compose a poem or a piece of music to his
mistress, this conveys his inmost self, and is both a sign
of love and a seal. It is much more than a memorial. A
child again is not so much a sign of love as a seal of it, and
a means of deepening it. In this sense the sacraments are
Christ's love-tokens to His body, the Church. They not only
suggest Him, but they convey Him to the Church. They
deepen the relation between them. They have a positive
meaning which He intended. They are not accidental sug-
gestions. They are connected with Him by much more than
association. They are more than souvenirs, keepsakes. They
are bequests. They are conveyances. And what they mean
and bring is of the very essence of what He was and is and
willed to be to the Church — its Redeemer and Sanctifier.

These love-tokens, these heirlooms, the Church has to
guard and use. She has to keep them bright, and not by
care only but by use. She must so use them that they shine
with their message and not merely by a polish. Like rails,
they gleam with traffic which carries value to the soul.

Every member of a Church has a duty by these sacraments, apart from the personal religious profit they may bring him in a conscious way. To think always of that alone may be too egoist for Christian faith. We come together in Church not simply, nor indeed primarily, to get good from God, but to confess God, to aid the Church's worship, confession, and preaching of His grace. For each member the sacraments are part of the confession. They are one way of owning and declaring the Church's word. Each member has to do his part to give them effect. He has to do his share in the Church's sacramental act as a worshipper — in the energy of common worship, and not as a spectator.

These sacraments are not primarily *individual* acts. They are corporate acts, acts *of the Church*. It is the Church that does the sacramental act. Nay, more, they are the acts *of Christ* really present by His Holy Spirit in the Church. It is Christ doing something through the Church as His body. It is only after these two higher senses are met that they are the acts of an individual. In the Communion individual administration is against its nature. Baptism is not primarily an act of the parent nor of the child, but of the Church, and of Christ in the Church. It is our individualism that has done most to ruin the sacrament of Baptism among us. We get a wrong answer because we do not put the right question. We ask, What good does Baptism do me or that child? instead of, What is the active witness and service the Church renders to the active Word of Christ's gospel in the Baptism of young or old? Baptism is not there primarily for the individual, nor for the family, but for the Church, to confess before God and man the Word of regeneration. It is not a domestic occasion but an ecclesiastical. Like a great theology, or a great psalm, it belongs to the Church rather than to an individual. To claim private property in a hymn is to sell the Holy Spirit. Baptism, therefore, should not be private in the house but public in the Church.

And the next thing for the Christian, after taking his part in the act of his Church, after keeping its treasure intact and using it, is to see that it does not lose its meaning but remains rich for himself. If Baptism have no result for you who take part in it, is that not because you have somehow

lost sight or sense of the truth for which Baptism stands —
the cleansing of the soul not by a growth in purity simply
but by the regeneration of the Holy Ghost, the baptism not
into Christ merely but into Christ's death, not simply by
self-sacrifice but by the burial with Him, and the rising with
Him to newness of life?

(Ibid., *pp. 176-178.*)

So, if it is asked whether grace is medicine, food, life, or
mercy, we answer thus. There is no Christian who does not
set out by saying that for him everything must begin with
the gift of God. His God is his Giver. What then is this
gift? We may take it perhaps that we are outgrowing the
stage in which that question was answered by saying it was
truth about Himself. It was nothing else and nothing less
than Himself that was the gift. The grace of God was His
holy, gracious Self. But that does not come to quite close
enough quarters with the real issue. It is enough to meet
the Roman view of the sacrament, which interprets the
divine self as the divine substance, and sees in a sacrament a
greater gift than grace, namely, the communication of God's
essence. If the gift of God was not a theology, or truth
about Him, was it His person in the sense of His act or in
the sense of His essence? Was it something moral — redemption; or was it something material (however fine), something metaphysical, something ontological, something in
the nature of a substance, a tincture, a virtue? Was it interpenetration with His will or participation in His being?
Was it given to our conscience or to our nature? Was it
grace as bestowed mercy or grace as infused vitality? The
new life — did it grow outward from the new conscience,
or did it suffuse the whole soul and just include the conscience in its sweep? Was it moral regeneration or pneumatic reinforcement? The evangelical view is that the gift
was God, holy God, and that it was new and eternal life,
but also that it was still more positive and pointed — that it
was the holy God's mercy to guilt in His atoning self-
oblation at the moral center where men are made men or
marred; it was not the flooding of our enfeebled nature by a

spiritual vitality which floated up the conscience among other things of equal moment. The gift was moral mercy, it was not medicine (far less was it magic). The great gift was for the last need. Grace was mercy to guilt, it was not medicine for disease. More than disease ailed us. We are not responsible for disease, except in a secondary way. Somebody may be to blame for my typhoid, but I am not. And who is to blame for cancer? In my sin even, others may have had some share, but I made my own guilt. Grace is the moral, the holy treatment of that, the destruction of that. The great grace is not sacramental grace in any substantial sense, but evangelical grace, moral grace, the grace of holy love dealing with the conscience by a personality, and not of mere generous love repairing our nature by the body even of Christ. That grace is the soul of sacrament, and its right to be.

(Ibid., pp. 297-98.)

Grace is a matter of moral and personal relation between holy love and deadly guilt; it is not a matter of substantial continuity, nor of energetic vitality of a pneumatic kind. And our best analogies will come from the region not of occult process but of moral psychology. Christ is more even than our food, He is our life. He is more than what refreshes our life, He creates it. But creation has no real meaning to us except in the moral and experiential sphere of redemption. It is the action distinctive of the Holy One, i.e. of the absolutely moral, whose very love has "Thou *shalt* love" in it. Christian love is a matter of conscience, of a mystically moral imperative (I Tim. 1:5). And the Act which gave us our new life gives also the principle of its maintenance. The principle of a sacrament is the principle of the *holy* gospel. It is moral in its nature, as redemption must be. And we become immortal by a kiss rather than a medicine — righteousness and peace kiss each other. We live not on a sacramental substance, but on a divine person; nor only on a divine person of benign excellence, but on a holy Redeemer of regenerating love.

(Ibid., pp. 302-03.)

BAPTISM

I shall have to enlarge later on the fact that we have
originally, in the New Testament, only adult and believers'
Baptism. It became infant Baptism at a later stage. And
the huge mistake made was this — that things moral, things
possible and true only for the adult experience, were transferred to the unconscious child, and thus became magic.
The error was hurried on by the tendency which had grown
up in the interval to treat the sacramental gift as something
in the nature of an infused substance or stream or virtue.
This meant the materializing of grace. The water absorbed
and conveyed to the soul heavenly powers. Nature was
renovated by a finer nature. And we have then not the
supernatural but only the supernal, the preternatural. To
treat the gift in a sacrament as a commodity is to reproduce in that region the same fallacy which is costing us so
much in economics, the fallacy of treating labor as a commodity which can be detached from the personal relations
of employer and employed and from the moral nature of
their cooperation.

It was the essence of the Reformation to discard this
pagan idea of grace. Grace was not an infusion of vital
substance or supernal influence, but it was a relation of
active persons. It was a moral thing and not a physical.
It was mercy and not magic. It was not virtue going into
us; it was the gracious will of the God of love acting on
the soul, and (as He is the *holy* God) centrally on the moral
soul, acting, through the Church's faith, as a felt forgiveness
and a power for goodness. But the child could not experience grace as a conscious man could. He could not have
faith. So baptismal grace in any moral sense was impossible.
In Lutheranism, as in Anglicanism, there remained a sur-
vival of Catholicism, and Baptism became spiritual inocula-
tion, a transfusion, and not a regeneration by the Spirit.
There was postulated some refined physical action of God's
rare Spirit on the soul. Even the old Protestant theologians
spoke of a "heavenly material" in Baptism joined with water
in "sacramental union," and effective in, with, and under

the element. It was the same idea as in the consubstantia-
tion of the other sacrament. The desire was to bring both
under one sacramental idea. Children were supposed to
secure in Baptism the seed of the Spirit, as in the Eucharist
the adult received a spiritual food or an elixir of immortality. But, as this seed could strike and fructify only by
faith, a subconscious faith was postulated in the child, to
obviate the idea of a mere *opus operatum*. An inchoate
faith was supposed to be created by Baptism in the child.
The thing was, of course, inconceivable, but it was believed
in as a theological necessity. Besides, it ought to be there
in advance, to make the sacrament effectual on Protestant
principles. Even today Lutheranism (like some Anglicans)
talks so. Even Frank does. And the tendency was aided
by the romantic, mystic theosophy of Schelling.

The fallacy was that, as in the New Testament Baptism
meant the adult's regeneration (in a sense I shall describe
later), it did so also when transferred to the child. And
indeed, if in the New Testament the sacramental effect was
magical and unconscious (as the Catholic interpretation is)
and the moral man was passive, then it might act on the
child as on the man. Regeneration would then mean pro-
viding the soul with latent possibility instead of bringing
it into a new personal relation. The power, the seed, might
slumber in the soul till maturity; or it might come to
nothing, like many seeds. If a subconscious faith was too
much, it was thought that without that postulate, and by
the germ theory, the immediate value of Baptism for the
child might be saved.

Our clue in traversing such an obscure region is this. It
is the simplifying principle that the spiritual virtue of a
sacrament is not drawn from the ethereal action of the
Word made flesh for us, but from the moral action of the
Word made sin for us, and unto us righteousness, and from
the social action of the Word made Church. That is the
only body of Christ that concerns us much now, and that
rests on the moral miracle of all miracles — the Son made sin
for us, that we might be made righteousness in Him. The
miracle of the incarnation is not the Word made flesh but

the Holy made sin for us. The whole Logos theology has done much to injure a true doctrine of the Spirit, to remove the center of Christ's concern from a moral act to a spiritual process, and to interpret the spiritual as mind supremely reasonable or (as in the sacraments) matter supremely rarefied. This has kept the atonement as a moral power out of the hegemony of Christian doctrine in the Catholic tradition, and therefore the moral out of control of Christian life.

(Ibid., *pp. 194-196.*)

Think of it this way. Think of what is involved.

1. Baptism is something that *happens to* the man at the Church's hand, much as it owes to his own act of faith. The baptismal act in which he enters the Church, like the birth whereby he enters the world, is something done rather on him than by him. Here Baptism differs from the other sacrament. Even when the submission to Baptism is the believer's own act, this is so. Even if we say its chief value comes from the man's own faith, the Baptism is an act administered to him, in which he is but indirectly active. He is enveloped by the social body of grace (as by the water). It is the medium of faith and love in which grace is to have its way with him. Here Baptism differs also from conversion, in which the man is a more active subject as he is more alone with God. And it differs from conversion further in that conversion is only in exceptional cases a sudden, memorable thing, occupying a point of time.

2. Consider also, and it is more important, what a sacrament is. Next to its connection with the Word, it gets its meaning from the Church. I have already said that we are on the wrong tack, we ask the wrong question, when we seek an effect on the soul outside the psychological effect, the moral action, of the grace of the gospel Word. But we are also wrong when we stake everything on its value to the subject of it. That debases its currency. Its first value as a sacrament is not for the individual but for the Church and its gospel. We are not to measure the worth of any sacrament by the way we feel after it. For the individual alone we might say it has no value distinct from its effect as

a proclamation and function of the Word, as a *That-predigt,* an enacted sermon.

An undue subjectivity, by way of sectarian individualism, is the worst depreciation of Baptism. It depreciates the significance of a communal and social life for the development of faith. That life is a thing whose moral value can hardly be exaggerated. What Baptism first means is the incorporation of the baptized into the Church, to which the evangelical promise is chiefly made and the Spirit given. He is entered of the Church especially as it is the social body of Christ, as the spiritual organism of history, as the soul's moral home and nursery, where Christ Himself moves as the unseen Providence and shaping power of His own salvation. It is not reception into the Church as a mere kindly community, a mere variant of other sympathetic associations; nor into the Church as a mere institution for the canalizing of grace. It is Christ that receives you, not a friendly society. If you were brought up in a religious community of merely humane and helpful people, who took you by the hand, and comforted, cheered, or forwarded you in life, that would still not be the Church (though it is what a multitude of people think to be the Church's whole duty with its young). Such would not be the Church action on you which Baptism represents. All that might be done, yet nothing done with such distinctively Christian experiences as forgiveness in Christ's Cross, reconciliation with God, or regeneration by the Spirit. It might all be done without bringing the Christ of the redemption to bear on you, or making you even begin to realize that you were reborn into the new Humanity with all its obligations. You might get nothing really which would be a counterpoise to the solid stream and pressure of the world, the flesh, and the natural man.

Baptism is really the sacrament of the new birth, and so far it corresponds to the old circumcision on the threshold of the natural or racial life. It is the sacrament of regeneration; which, however, it does not produce, but richly conveys by our personal adoption into its home. Atmosphere is the most potent element in the education of a new life.

To belong really to a real community does matter much. It makes a vital change to pass upon our native egoism, nay, on the religious egoism which may be acting even in the form of our conversion. The converted are not really regenerate except as they become real members of a real Church. They easily relapse unless they yield to the unique moral powers and influences of the community of the Spirit. Of course if these are not there it is not a true Church. It is easy now to denounce baptismal regeneration; but do our Churches exert a regenerating influence on the religious egoism of their baptized members? Is it the gift of the Church that becomes the determining power on their character? I have certainly known cases where but for that influence the man would have been a bully or a rowdy. On the other hand, there are cases where men have bullied or grieved the Spirit out of the Church. Against the Sacramentarians we ask, Is it we, or only something in us we know nothing about, that responds to the action of the Spirit? And of their opponents we ask, Is the sacramental gift in the Church the chief power that is making us what we are growing to be? Is our membership of a Church a matter of mere education, or is it a constant regeneration, which makes us not only wise to compass our moral desires but quite different in the things we come to desire? Do we grow in sonship or only in religious culture? The Church is only our true mother as it gives us to the Father. Our rebirth is not merely a hope ripening, but a process of creation. What acts upon us is not an imaginative ideal but a shaping power.

All the baptized are not regenerated. Some regenerates have not been baptized. Our regeneration is not in the sacraments but in the Christ who gave the sacrament to the creature He had not merely influenced but remade. The Reformers said it was not the disuse of the sacraments that damned, but the contempt of them; but we cannot say that of Christ, His Cross, and His Word of gospel for which the sacraments exist. His grace called into being both salvation and sacraments; but not salvation through sacraments, which are for the saved but not to save. The great legacy is that which saves, and sacraments do not save. You cannot evangelize the world with a gospel of sacraments, but only with sacraments of the gospel, and of its Word-in-chief. We do not refer our new life to Baptism, but to God's grace which put Baptism there. It is baptismal grace, but it is not a grace that depends on Baptism. The main thing is not when and how we were reborn, but the fact that we are, that we have the reconciled regenerate life in Christ, that we have the life which new birth but began. It is no true faith that has its ground only in the past. It is the Spirit which makes the past present, it is the Spirit that quickens. The true nature of the regeneration at the beginning of the Christian life must be discerned by the true nature of its course.

(Ibid., *pp. 207-210.*)

THE LORD'S SUPPER

Let us at least get rid of the idea which has impoverished worship beyond measure, that the act is mainly commemoration. No Church can live on that. How can we have a mere memorial of one who is still alive, still our life, still present with us and acting in us? Symbol is a better word than memorial. Only that the modern sense of the word symbol differs from the ancient, and differs for the poorer and not the richer. The modern symbol is but aesthetic and not energetic. It shows us, it does not act on us. The ring does not marry, it only means marriage. The symbol does not convey the thing signified. It just depicts it or suggests it. It impresses, it does not change us. It is not associated with change. The modern symbol does not do justice to the significate, to the present reality of God's action as the cause within our act. It is for eye or ear. It is not action but only expression. It is emblem. And we do not mind emblem, but we are too afraid of ritual.

A sacrament is as much more than a symbol as a symbol is more than a memorial. It is quite inadequate to speak of the sacrament as an object-lesson — as if its purpose were to convey new truth instead of the living Redeemer. It is not an hour of instruction but of communion. It is an act, not a lesson; and it is not a spectacle nor a ceremony. It does something. It is an *opus operatum*. More, it is an act of the Church more than of the individual. Further still, it is an act created by the eternal Act of Christ which made and makes the Church. At the last it is the act of Christ present in the Church, which does not so much live as Christ lives in it. It is Christ's act offering Himself to men rather than the act of the Church offering Christ to God. Now, as at the first, it is Christ giving over to men the sacrifice He was making once for all to God. So that we may say this. The elements are symbolic only in the modern sense of the word symbol — only as signs. They convey nothing. They point to the significate but do not include it. But the action (of the Church and chiefly of Christ in the Church) is symbolic in the greater and older sense in which the symbol contains and conveys the significate, and is a really sacramental thing. Christ offers anew to us, as He did at the Supper, the finished offering which on the Cross He gave to God once for all.

But the phrase *opus operatum* has perhaps put someone on the alert. For the fundamental objection we take to the Roman doctrine of the sacraments is that they are supposed to be effectual in just being done by the Church, apart from the personal faith either of the priest or of the people. They are *opera operata,* spiritual operations performed on the patient over his head. The technical way of putting the Roman view is to say they are effectual *ex opere operato* and not *ex opere operantis,* by the deed and not the doer, by their statutory performance and not by the personal response, the spiritual life and experience, of the parties concerned. That is a sound protest we make. But there is a sense in which the Roman phrase is true. The fundamental value of the sacrament lies in a supreme and final Act. It lies in an Act accomplished already, and here delivered to our address. The reservoir, always full in heavenly hills, is laid on to our door. The value lies in something done to our hand, in a finished work of Christ before and outside of our faith, before our faith was there — indeed, it puts our faith there, it creates it. For faith is a gift of God, not vaguely and supplementarily to enable us to believe on the Cross, but through the gift of the Cross and its native action on us. It is our moral response to the Cross, and not our qualification. The sacraments get their whole meaning from an *opus operatum* never to be repeated. It is wrong to say they are but memorials; but it is equally wrong at the other end to say they are valuable and effective as conjurations, with their power acting in them in a magical way, as if the formula employed had a coercing effect on the spiritual world when done by a duly canonical person recognized there, as if they acted on the elements and not on the people. They are not magic, nor machinery.

But it is not wrong to say that they act only in virtue of the foregone and complete Act of God's will in Christ's Cross which gave them their existence. They rest on an *opus operatum* there of the God whose grace so appointed them that the conduit is as much of grace as the stream. Only, God's *opus operatum* is not an act quite over our head, like baptismal regeneration, without action on the moral soul. As a moral act it creates moral action in response. Its nature is intelligible. Its effects cannot remain outside the conscious soul — though, as its scope is the whole world, the vast part of its range is beyond our conscious grasp or experience. This grace fills the sacraments always with the same power that gave them being. And they are useless without the reverberation of that foregone and incessant Act of Christ, which is the act of grace, and, as the Act of the Holy, is a moral act, and not one of mere power and fiat. So there is a certain place for the idea of an *opus operatum* in the sacraments.

(Ibid., *pp. 228-231.*)

We may thus illustrate. Think of three things — the spoken word, its letters (or its tone), and the meaning it conveys. A spoken word is the symbol or vehicle of a thought it conveys; but it is also the thought itself in action. The visible letters of the word only enable us to handle it. So think of these other things — the bread and wine, the act of the Supper, and the Act of the Cross. What the letters are to the word, that are the bread and wine to the act in the

Supper. And what the word actively spoken is to the active
thought which moves it, that is Christ's symbolic act here to
His real final Act of the Cross. The Supper was an under-
agent of the Cross — not the great Act to God but the
transfer of it to believers. The word is repeated often; but
the thought is there once for all. In music we repeat the
performance often by means of the score (the elements); but
the composer's finished work stands there ideally, eternally,
functioning in many generations. So Christ's redeeming Act
functioned in the Supper, conveying itself to its beneficiaries,
and it goes on doing so in the Church. We repeat the
ordinance often, and Christ acts as often in our midst, conveying *to us* His Act in chief. The work of Christ it sym-
bolizes is done to God once and for ever, it cannot be
repeated, but only given to us anew.

(Ibid., p. 236.)

Hence we must interpret "This is my body broken for
you" in some such way as thus. First, "This broken bread
represents my body as broken, not as substantial; not in the
substance, but in the act of being broken for you." So,
second, the essential thing was not His body but His will's
act of devoting it to be broken. We interpret, therefore,
"This visible breaking which I now do represents the
spiritual breaking and passion which I always inwardly
suffer, now begin outwardly to do, and shortly shall complete. This act of breaking and dispensing bread shows outwardly what I now inwardly begin to finish with God; and I
here consign that and its value to you as your very own salvation. This present deed is to give and assign to you the
great deed now in process and shortly to be finished. I here
give to you for your salvation what I have begun to give to
God as your atonement. This giving to you makes yours
my sacrifice to God. My spiritual, redeeming act of giving
my broken heart in atonement to a holy God, of giving to
Him my soul poured out unto death, is for you. This breaking of bread represents the breaking of my body and will.
This my act of giving to you, and giving it round, represents,
nay, carries home to you, all and sundry, the large inclusive

Act of giving myself to God for you which is now coming to a head. Now I give it expressly to you in advance; shortly I shall give it expressly to God with little thought of you. Your act of eating represents the way you must assimilate and live on me crucified and given to God. This bread, broken and eaten, represents the giving and the partaking of my person, which comes acutely, passionately, tragically to a head in the pouring of my blood, that I may be in you as the active life and kindling Redeemer." There is no suggestion of a higher gift than grace, of God's essence all-divine, being infused into the soul. But there is far more than a memorial of an event, or a mere symbol of an idea.

(Ibid., *pp. 237-38.*)

Apparently He took bread, broke, and gave to them, saying, "This is my body," and probably added some words more, indicating His life as given to God for them in His impending death. He took the cup of red wine, uttered the prayer of thanksgiving, and passed it around. "This is my covenant blood" (Exod. 24:8) "shed for many" (Isaiah). Jesus has both passages in His mind. He indicates that with His death a New Covenant was entered with God. He made over to His own the value of this covenant for man. Then followed an injunction to repeat the observance as carrying home the climax of His death to the Church and to the world, as pledging His indwelling presence, and offering to men His offering to God.

The essential thing, we must repeat, is the *bestowal.* Christ was not here doing His great work. He was presenting to man that offering to God. It is the *consignment* of a blessing. What was the blessing? With the words "shed for many" we have indicated the sacrificial, the atoning idea uppermost in His death. It was to be a sacrifice to God for His people. It was not an accident cutting short His career. And it is here made over to them by Himself proleptically, through an enacted symbol. He is not dying for them, but giving them His death as a sin offering, which should ransom the world from the condemnation of guilt to eternal life.

We then blend the covenant idea, the sacrificial idea, and the paschal or redemptive.

The act can hardly have been extemporized at this moment, but, like the parables, was prepared for the purpose I have named. And not only so, but it was a sacrificial meal renewing communion with God. Was this a pagan idea? No, it was Jewish also. I Corinthians 10:14-22 shows that it was a current idea, well understood, and going without the proof that a novelty would need. The act was more than a symbol or parable. It was more than emblematic. It was donative. It was *symbolic* in the great sense, and really sacramental. It does more than *mean*, it *conveys* what it means. "I make over to you my death in blood, which is *covenant* blood and atoning (for many)."

In the rite there are three centers of interest — the elements, His act, their act. But the ruling thing is not the elements but the act. And it is His act, not theirs, that is in the foreground. He did something, gave; they did something, and took. He did not just symbolize and they perceive. What He gave was the coming atonement; what they took was its new and eternal life.

(Ibid., *pp. 247-48.*)

RELIGIOUS LIBERTY AND INDEPENDENCY

Now I have already indicated what was meant by religious liberty among the sons of the Reformation. Its prime sense with Luther and all his train was not freedom among men but freedom before God. It was not freedom to hold any religion or none, but the freedom which was religious or nothing, the freedom which was identical with Christianity, freedom not of action or opinion but of soul. Forgive me if I repeat anything in trying to be explicit on a point so great.

There is a religious liberty which is the child of our Independency, and there is one which is its parent. There is our freedom among men for God begotten by our freedom in God for men. In a like way when we speak of political freedom we may mean one or both of two things. We may mean freedom in the State from an individual, or freedom

from the State for an individual. We may mean the freedom
of all the citizens from a ruler who is despotic, however
benevolent; so that each man has his responsible place and
right in the ordered State as a whole. Or we may mean freedom for each individual from the interference even of a free
and republican State in the region of his thought, conscience,
or faith. It is this latter — the laicity of the State — that is
the great product of the Reformation; and it goes on to
disestablish the Church everywhere. It goes on to secure the
State's ecclesiastical neutrality, and to place the establishment of Christianity in the ethicizing of its politics alone,
and the production of a Christian ethos as the national spirit.
All this was utterly foreign to medievalism, which knew but
of the *imperium,* or universal State, at the absolute service
of the Church. It is quite true that the Reformation in its
empirical beginnings had this inherited note. And it has not,
in England as elsewhere, succeeded in surmounting it entirely by its intrinsic principle. There are many remnants of
the theocratic idea still lingering in such venerable places as
the coronation service. It took English Nonconformity to give
to the Reformation its true self, and realize in practice what
it really meant by religious liberty.

The Reformation did not propose as an end religious
liberty in the political sense. It was not a battle for liberty
but for truth. It did not, and does not, care for liberty except
as a product of the truth and for its sake. Truth is the
Church's aim, liberty only the means thereto. And the truth
which concerned the Reformation was not the truth of the
intelligence or the reason but of the soul, of salvation. It
was saving truth and not scientific. It was the truth as it is
in religion, and not in the schools. The Reformation asked
(I have already said), What is truth — salvation by the
Church, or directly by God? And it answered — salvation
directly by God alone. This carried tremendous public consequences, which history was to unfold, and chiefly by
Independency. But these consequences were not the conscious
issue of the Reformation, which dealt with their gospel cause
or postulate, and not with themselves — as the way of the
Church must always be. When Luther spoke of Christian

freedom he had no idea of the rights of man or of classes. He and his friends did not in the least mean each man's liberty within the State to choose his own form of worship. He meant nothing so modern, so proleptic. That is liberty of conscience, and what preoccupied the Reformers was something higher and more fundamental — liberty of soul, religious liberty in the ultimate sense of the word. In the modern use religious liberty means the liberty of each citizen, as such, to be free even from God, to be an atheist without loss of rights. But in the strict Christian sense religious liberty means freedom before God, in God, "no condemnation," freedom of intercourse with God, unhampered by guilt and the demands of a law which God has now made His own charge and become responsible for in Christ. It is the sonship of faith, the being at home, not in society, but in the Father's house and kingdom.

There was another conception of religious liberty, which we have seen arose alongside of the Reformation though not from the same root, and which came into violent collision with it — the liberty claimed by the peasant movement and the Anabaptists. For these, in part, liberty meant freedom from the tyranny of the feudal lord, and in part it was a soul freedom based on an appeal to the newly opened Bible; and it insisted on the reorganization of society offhand according to the Sermon on the Mount. It demanded a radical reform of society apart from the deeper radicality of Luther's new creation by grace. It was urged by plain and pious men, who took the Bible as a code and charter of public right, and found it to counsel the subversion of all force and government. Freedom from the State was the ideal, not freedom in it. They were the Tolstoians (I have said) or pacific anarchists of their day, though pacific they could not remain. In a crude way they anticipated many of the ideas of religious liberty which only a later age realized. And they had a great and early influence upon the form of Independency (as has been shown), though they did not furnish its inspiration or its anchor. These came from a deeper source, by way of Geneva, and they were rooted and grounded on the Word rather than on the Spirit without the Word or above it.

It was the intimate liberty which *is* religion, and does not simply flow from it, that established Independency; it was a liberty conferred, not won; which in turn produced civil liberty. Spiritual release produced "religious liberty." And for us this must always be the case. We do not stand simply for civil liberty, but for civil liberty on a spiritual and evangelical base; not for a free State, but for a free State as the product of a free Church of men whom Christ has set free. That is the genius of our existence. We must always live *on* our cause, though we live *for* our product — on free grace for a free State. Our secret is in our inward and spiritual freedom, not in our outward and public. And the power in that secret, the power which as a historical fact produced civil liberty, was nothing else than the gospel of justifying and regenerating grace in Jesus Christ, our Lord and God. It can never be anything else at last. Nothing else exists which gives the guilty conscience experimental and practical freedom with God, and so makes him his own freeman with men. And what has been here said about civil liberty applies to theological also. It is a secondary, though inevitable, product. It is not our reason for existence.

(*From* Faith, Freedom, and the Future, *pp. 198-203.*)

The more spiritual any historic movement is, i.e. the more dependent on revelation, so much the more it must return always to its classic source to adjust its compass, and to realize its genius and its call. And the more spiritual it is the more also it will be found to have its classic and normative time at its source. Its principle is in its creation, like human freedom; which, being given by God, was given for God. The more spiritual it is the more it is of positive inspiration. And the inspiration of historic religions is chiefly with their founders or their foundation. It is at their creative head. The case is otherwise with movements which are but evolutionary. There the process works up from beneath instead of down from above. We have then to do with a mere development and not a revelation. So that we may find the law or principle in the finished product more clearly and powerfully than at the point of origin. And were Christianity but the index instead of the cause of man's spiritual evolution we should properly look for its normative principle in the latest developments of the Christian conscience — if we did not have to wait for it till the end of history. But it is not so that we learn Christ. He is not a great step in a greater process, not the hand at the sluice which releases a greater power than it possesses; but He is Himself the fountainhead of all that religion can ever be for man and his soul. He is our freedom who is our new Creator. It is to Him, therefore, and to the apostles He chose and inspired for His self-revelation, that the Church they created must always return for the standard, as for the power, whereby it is to go on and minister to each age as it arrives.

If it is so with the whole Church, it is so also with each great movement within the Church itself which recalls it to its true mission and genius. In developing such movements we must, in proportion as they are spiritual, profound, and regal for an age — we must return to their first spring, and to the apostolic men in whom they rose to power and effect. There we have the principle in its true purity and force. There it was most deeply and clearly grasped. It was bound to be so if it was to break through the frozen life, crusted prejudices, and iron orthodoxies round its source. The days of its creation are the days that contain the principle of its progress most richly, and mightily, and permanently. This was so in the Reformation. It is in the few first years of that renaissance of the new birth that we find its principle in its purity; when it flushed souls like a flame of fire in Luther, or a great smooth stream in Melanchthon; and before there resurged upon it the interests, the policies, and the scholasticisms which in a century had damped it to a smouldering mass, or clad it in a cumbrous mail.

And so it also is in the case of that Independency which, seizing and developing the core of the Reformation, seized and carried forward also, and still more purely, the principle of that gospel which the Reformation disentombed. It is to its messiahs and apostles, not its forerunners, that we must

recur for its true principle and gospel — not to its John
Baptist, Robert Browne, not to the Anabaptist and ultra-
spiritualistic tendencies which seethed with other elements
in the cauldron of our first flux. But we go to those who
disengaged the principle clearly and effectively from its
alloys (so useful at a stage), and made it not only face but
rule the hour in its true consciousness of itself. To Robinson,
to Cromwell, to Milton, to Goodwin, and their peers — it is
to such men, with a horizon and a lift in their thought, that
we must go — not to the dogmatists of a later time, who
burdened us with the debased Calvinism of the eighteenth
century, and who had lost the great sense of our place in the
whole Church and the whole history of the founded freedom
of the West. And when we so do, when we turn to these
classics, we shall find that our genius may perhaps be fitly
expressed in these two words that have just fallen from my
lips — FOUNDED FREEDOM. Not freedom alone is our
genius; for freedom alone is but caprice, atomism, and
anarchy in the end. But it is freedom created and founded
and reared by an authority which cannot be either evaded
or shaken; and which creates our emancipation, in the
very depth and crisis of our soul, by the eternal redemption
at the heart of all history in Christ's Cross. It is our genius
not simply to have set afloat on the practical world the re-
creative principle of freedom and self-rule, political, social,
and religious; but still more to have kept that principle in
the closest dependence on another, which is creative as God
is, and which is the principle of His new creation of us in
Jesus Christ. It is to have preached and practiced the foundation of all liberty of thought or action, public or private,
in the evangelical freedom with which Christ's Cross makes
free the world and the soul. That organic union of positivity
and liberty of Christian certainty and public freedom, in
Church and State, is our genius and our trust. We have
printed it on the free State; has our victory exhausted us of
our power to commend it to a free Church? Are we too
genial to be a power? more in love with liberty than sure
of the one last condition which creates it? Are we amateurs

of freedom rather than adepts of grace, a synagogue of the Libertines rather than a temple of the Holy Ghost?

We have a great tradition and a greater gospel. And the age has a great promise and a great need. It is a moral gospel and a moral need. They must meet in freedom. And we have much to do in the re-union.

(Ibid., *pp. 344-348.*)

CHURCH AND STATE

The Church, therefore, with such a gospel in trust, is not a private corporation but a public, not a club but an institution; and, with such a Spirit, holy and humane, for its life, it is not a group but a social personality, a greater *vis-à-vis* of the personality of the State. And as such it is entitled to recognition, both courteous, sympathetic, and practical, from the great organs of the public. The State is the Church's beneficiary, and to be thankless to it would be ignoble. It is entitled to privilege within the State, alien as it is to patronage. It can be honored if it cannot be controlled, and graced if it may not be endowed. It does not take special gifts carrying with them control, but it ought to have special consideration and room, corresponding to the unique nature of its work for society. That is no more than the recognition of its characteristic ethical genius and method, and its moral parity (to say no more) with the State in the matter of right. The State which guards rights should give special place and welcome to the society whose genius is the duty and service which found all right in the Cross. And it should concede such privileges as consist with the freedom of the Church's personality and the facility of its service. Gifts from the State do not in the long run make for these, since they are always accompanied with some conditions and controls; and also because it is impossible, with the modern number and arity of Churches, to give all round. For selection would mean a dogmatic judgment by the State. The great principle is the recognition by the State that the Church has intrinsic and autonomous rights at least equal in sanction, if superior in kind, to those of the State itself; and that there is due to it such scope as is required and such honor as is deserved by the nature of the Church's personality and the character of its work for mankind. For instance, in connection with the Church's absolute control of its own membership, the orderly and statutory proceedings of the Church, or its representatives, in the discussion of questions of moral character and conduct should be expressly recognized as privileged at law and not libellous. At present any case of discipline in a Free Church may involve an action for libel or slander. In respect of the Church's ownership and control of property, its representative officers for the time being should be its trustees, and the transfer of trusteeship should be simplified and cheapened accordingly. For those Churches that wish it their duly ordained ministers should be *ipso facto* empowered to perform marriage. And the moral judgment of the Church should be, if not a final plea, a very weighty factor indeed in the considerations that regulate divorce. The Church's income should be exempt from taxation in view of its vast public service; and its ministers, like doctors, exempted from certain public duties as on juries, as well as from magistracy. As theology proper is the monopoly of the Church, which is its expert as a culture, the Church's work in this department of civilization should be utilized by the State universities in the way which I hope in later pages to explain at more length. And some Nonconformists would not object to grants to efficient Sunday schools, not for religion, but for religious knowledge in so far as it was examinable, and reached a standard qualifying in other subjects of knowledge. If the Churches were united on such a creative dogma as I have named above, and a parliament of Churches sat in London or elsewhere, there does not seem to be anything in the freedom or autonomy of the Church that should decline the courtesy of a State visit from the Premier or even the Monarch, along with their congratulations, such as the assemblies of the several Churches at present receive and prize from the mayors of the cities where they meet.

It cannot be made too clear that the right of the Church (in its various Churches) is intrinsic and autochthonous. That is to say, its origin lay in no concession by the State.

That is not what makes a Church a public corporation with an autonomy. The validity of its right is independent of the State. It grew up within the State, beneath its pressure, and in spite of its weight. It lifted that weight, and even broke it, as a tender plant has been known to raise or split a flagstone. Its nature is quite different from law in the State. Its leadership is spiritual and not secular, and its last appeal is not to force but to conscience. Its right belongs to the class of public corporations and not private because it has no ends of its own, its parish is the world, its range international, and its beneficiary the whole of society as it is the whole of the soul. It is not by its nature a private corporation like a trading society. Nor is it a public corporation in the sense in which a municipality is. For in both these cases the right is a franchise conferred by the State; whereas in the case of the Church, public as its corporate life and right is, it is a right which the State cannot confer but must yet recognize. Or, as some jurists put it, there is a special region of right which it inhabits, outside what is known to jurisprudence as right private and public.

(*From* Theology in Church and State, *pp. 216-221.*)

The function of the Church to society is to lead it; it is certainly not neutral. Nor is it Byzantine; the Church is not to be dragged at the heels of the State. But we ought to be very clear that it is to lead in the sense of guidance and not in the sense of rule. Curialism and Ultramontanism are as foreign to the spirit of the gospel at one end as Byzantinism (which is the superlative of Erastianism) is at the other. The Church is to the State neither neutral, erastian, nor imperial. The ideal relation is not that of the old Nonconformity, nor that of Hooker, nor is it the coarse Byzantinism of Germany; nor is it at the other extreme a lordly popery toward the Empire. It is a case of moral guidance flowing from spiritual positivity, and welcome, kindly light burning in reciprocal freedom.

Within the Church also there is no hierarchy of prerogative. There may be an authority of function and convenience, where the bishop is the choice of those he rules. The first form of the Church was corporative — a pneumatic fraternity. Christ forbade gradation of rank; however, He recognized moral superiority and spiritual leadership among His disciples. The power of the keys He gave to all the apostles as representing the Church, and not to Peter only. The Holy Spirit He bestowed on all disciples. His own regenerating presence is the being of a Church; and He promised it to any two or three met in His eternal and reconciling name. That supposes that they are not met out of strife, and that they do not simply cultivate Him as their saint, but they meet to reflect His eternity, and so, with serious purpose, to serve in such a Church for life; which distinguishes them from a casual gathering that dissolves with the occasion. Nothing was known in the early days of a prince of the apostles, nor a vicar of Christ, nor of a monarchical bishop. And Christ did not found a Church here and a Church there, but *the* Church, which appeared here and there in facets of its vast polyhedral unity. To all these local but serious appearances of the one Church He promised equally His immediate presence, whether in Rome or in a desert; and it would be the possession of each remote Church none the less if Rome were swallowed by an earthquake, or the official succession broken for a hundred years. Whatever was given to Peter was given to his person, and not to his office, nor to his successors as such. It matters nothing whether he was ever in Rome or ever founded a Church there. Even had he passed the bishopric to Linus the legacy would have been quashed, and the succession extinguished, by the fact that succeeding bishops were chosen by the community of priests and laity, from, or through, whom the inspiration came. Indeed, there are no few spiritual and intellectual Catholics who say that the mechanical nature of the hierarchical headship, rising to autocracy, was the most powerful cause of the drop and the deadness which soon befell the Church.

All talk of a theocracy which should draw the secular power under the spiritual is foreign both to the gospel and to the true Catholicism. The Church has been at its best when it did not mix with political transactions in the way of

ruling prerogative or direct control. Its true influence is
that of its apostolic Word and its moral character. When it
sought first the righteousness of the kingdom it had all that
it needed of other things in tail. The chief example of
theocracy — the Mosaic — was one that ended by slaying its
Lord. To give either Church or State the rule over the
other, in one and the same imperial sense, means one or
another kind of despotism; their due independence of each
other is the condition of freedom. For conscience to bow
to a priest can be as slavish as to bow to a prince; but the
free prince and the free priest can do much for each other.

It is not easy to say which has done more mischief, the
State Church or the Church State. The original constitution of the Church, whatever it was, was not monarchical.
It was corporative: until Cyprianism; and until the black
years when first Constantine and then Charlemagne made it
a State Church, and turned its officers into civil servants, and
its government to a bureaucracy. And until, further, the
spiritual autonomy and monopolism of Rome asserted itself
in a form equally distorted and fatal, until a Roman bishop
of genius turned the State Church into a Church State,
whose officers not only refused service to the head of the
State but forced the State into its service. Such was the Church
of Hildebrand, Innocent, and Boniface. Its claims have not
abated; and all its troubles since then have been due to that
evil and unchristian principle.

No doubt the position had its advantages. It enabled the
court of Rome to discuss on equal terms with other imperial
courts. For it spoke the imperial language both in thought
and idea. It was a great advantage for the Church in large
affairs that its authority should be gathered into one point,
and when it could act f om that center as an Emperor can.
A court at Rome coulc deal with a like court at Aachen,
a cabinet of Cardinals at the Vatican with a cabinet of
Chancellors at Berlin, more easily than if the Foreign Office
of the Empire confronted a society cohering as a spiritual
organism only, with its powers scattered at centers all over
the world. But the result to the Church in the way of moral
debasement and spiritual declension has been unspeakable.

It is fatal to any bishop when he gathers up all power from his Churches and his clergy into one point in himself; how much more when he is the bishop of all bishops, the Pope! Yet that is what was done by the infallibility dogma of 1870, and what had been growing for centuries to the Church's demoralization. To what it has come we may mark in the attitude of the Roman see to this war[1], and its fatuous reply to sure proof of all the crimes and cruelties of the Germans in Belgium: "But then they deny it." The combination of the Christian bishop with the Pagan Pontifex Maximus began early, and it took long to ripen. For it wore several forms; and some of them were continued in Protestantism. It began with Constantine's State religion; and Luther placed the princes where Constantine or his successors had been. Little did he think that he was deposing the Pope only to produce a worse one in the Emperor, and exchanging the blight of Babylon for the blight of Berlin. Hence the moral paralysis of the German Church, as of the Roman, now that a call is made by the world-righteousness of the kingdom of God upon the prophetic office of the Church and its duty to beard kings in God's name. It is a Church which has lost in learned servility or pietist sentiment the sense of what a Church is morally for the kingdom of God. It has lost Christ and gone to Islam. God is on its Emperor's lips, like Allah, but never Christ. No doubt Luther meant to save the Church from the Church State, and restore it to its corporate freedom. But he has only succeeded in restoring the Byzantine State Church, with its religious parasitism. We had the like attempts with Luther's in the case of the Elizabethan Church, from which we were only saved by our Calvinist Puritans. It was the thorough Calvin that saved the Church from the State. Germany never had the blessing of regicide. It was only the Puritan execution of the king that saved us from what Germany became by the massacres of the Anabaptists (only now being expiated) and from what France became by the Bartholomew (expiated in the Revolution).

---

1 The First World War.

It grows clearer and clearer, as scholarship escapes from patristic prepossessions, that no form of constitution is sacrosanct; and none is undivine which gives scope to the word of the gospel and the prophetic freedom of its redemption. The only divine Lord of the world is He who does not wish to rule it, but to bless it by way of service. (It is the inner secularization of the Church to a polity that has been the chief cause of that outward secularization of its revenues which takes place in revolutions from its despotism.) No form is sacrosanct. But also to discard form is suicidal. If an imperial Church is mischievous, sporadic Churches are futile. For a Church to live anyhow is to die. To abandon all noble forms of worship and to potter at it in dressing-grown and slippers, at it were, and to do this as a principle, in the name of independence, is to subside into hugger-mugger at the end in spite of any mysticism. Free prayer by all means, if you can keep it up. But few can pray in public, and they need help. No public body can afford to live in its shirt-sleeves, and pick up its meals, to disregard its social ritual and live casually. Certainly no Church can go on doing so with its creative spiritual wealth. Here the form can never be independent of the content. To abjure entirely Church authority and the solemn tradition of the worshipping dead in worship or doctrine is to slip down into a heap of sand. No authority, no Church. Loose procedure means slack belief. And slack belief means loss of public influence for the kingdom of God. It is a mistake to think that a viscous belief appeals to the great public, or that mere mysticism is purer worship. Certainly no such sprawling and shambling type of Church can cope with the Catholicism of the day. That can only be done by a greater Catholicism, and not by a casual individualism. Without it the Church sinks either to be ruled by the world or to be eager to rule it; and in either case it is spiritual death. The Reformers found a Church dead one way; but they replaced it by a Church which, on the Lutheran side at least, was in another century dead in the other way. And it has never there regained, as a Church, spiritual life; while Calvin held the glorious West in fee.

(*From* The Church and the Sacraments, *pp. 77-81.*)

THE ECUMENICAL IDEAL

In our present connection we had to face the question why these elements, all of which had long been at work abroad before Independency became a power here, did not produce the same effect there; why there has been no Nonconformist Independency in the Protestantism of the Continent. And we had therefore to reckon in another and original factor, the special contribution of the English genius for liberty and self-government, which provided the one medium in which all these Reformation elements could combine fruitfully and firmly for the public and progressive liberty of the world, both in its promotion and its control.

But now let us continue our inquiry as to what our present position and prospects are in view of our original constituents, on the one hand, and of our public and historic service, on the other. Do we preserve these constituents? If we do not, are we therefore dispowered for continuing the work in the world which they enabled our fathers to do? Theirs has been a tremendous work when we measure it by the whole value of its fruit in civil and religious liberty — a work which chiefly enables the Church to claim the paternity of modern freedom. Does it exhaust our vocation? Is it our one work in the world? Were we raised up but for this, and, having done it, should we regard it as enough for any one section of the Church to have contributed to Humanity; and may we honorably retire, cultivate our own garden, and pass the great tasks of the future to other hands? Do we now linger on, as Judaism has long and not ignobly done since it produced the one Liberator of the Soul? Where we were once a world power, with effects indelible and inexhaustible in history, are we now to be but a little clan left with a great relic, a sect living on great memories with little ways, saying small things with a loud, insignificant voice, and repeating historic words as a class recites history? Are we going into dock only to be kept in good order and great honor, as the *Victory* lies in Portsmouth harbor, towed to her last berth — Nelson's deck now left by Nelson's power? Are we the pensioned remnant of a world conquest?

To that question it might first be answered thus. We might refer to the fact that even out of the eighteenth century a second world conquest was inaugurated by Independency, when its political and social victory was well afloat and able to go of itself. The Congregationalists and Baptists were again the pioneers of a world idea which was waiting in the Church for a fit organ to give it hands and feet. More than a century ago they were the founders of modern missions, and of all that these have come to mean and to promise since then. Truly it needed but the lead, the one word to let loose the gathered waters, and the other churches were quickly on the field. I only wish to trace the persistency in Independency of a certain world-mission, an evangelical imperialism, its service to that side of Christianity which has charge of its ecumenical freedom and progress on a firm and permanent base of gospel. The true ecumenical is the evangelical. I may also use the opportuntity in passing to recall the fact that the plantations of the Commonwealth were missionary enterprises in Cromwell's intention. And, further, that the Pilgrim Fathers went out not only to seek their own freedom of worship, but to spread into savage lands (alas, at points in a too savage way!) the power of the gospel. As it was said in a document of the time, they went "from an inward zeal and great hope of laying some foundation, or making way for propagating the kingdom of Christ, to the remote ends of the earth; though they should be but stepping-stones to others." The missionary passion, the passion for liberty, and the passion of the gospel, all go together; though in practice one may outrun the rest for a particular age.

(*From* Faith, Freedom, and the Future, *pp. 299-301.*)

In a word, the hope of the union of the Reformed churches is in no tradition of line or succession, but in the spiritual succession alone; not by apostolical succession, but by evangelical solidarity; not as sons of Abraham, but as sons of the promise. This means a church of one article. It is the gospel of grace and of faith in the salvation which is in Jesus Christ, the gospel not of personality but of personality redemptive and redeemed. The centrality and sufficiency of such a gospel is the one condition of church unity. And for this church of one article we have a legacy of facilities which the other churches have not; we have a mobility on that authoritative base which is not theirs, and which appeals to the swiftness of the democratic time. We are the flying squadron, the advance guard, the democratic side of the super-democratic Church. This is our *métier;* not freedom of thought, not theological freedom. Pure theology has fortunately never been our goal, as I have pointed out. We do not exist for pure doctrine. But we have been set, in our English way, for the quick translation of a fundamental theology, a theological gospel, into ethical and social life.

It is not the only service to the kingdom. Other churches other lots and other tasks. The churches are complementary. But it is a great and urgent service of the pioneer sort which has always been our ideal — often misleading us, but always keeping our faces to Jerusalem; sometimes inflating us, sometimes shooting up without deepness of earth, but on the whole making us the pathfinders of the public hour. Not indeed (as I have said) the pioneers of theological development. The development of doctrine is not the chief part of the work given us to do. It was not the work given to the English Reformation, which came in Independency to its true head and effect. We were delivered in great measure from that resurgence of scholasticism which made Lutheran orthodoxy in the seventeenth and eighteenth century a new Egypt for the new Israel. We were not supremely concerned with the determination of dogma, or the culture of pure doctrine; it was with the religious, social, and political application of dogma (and of one dogma in particular, the most mighty of all for personal faith — predestination). We were called for its application as the fundamental principle of religious and social life, for the constitution of the Church by it, and then for the moulding of all social life on the principle of that eternal society. We were not, as a people, or as a section of the Church, concerned with school questions, but with ques-

tions of life, public and private, on everlasting foundations.
In our day we were the Christian trustees of public progress
by popular power, and the stewards of the true social genius
of the Reformation, whereby Protestantism has become that
blessing to the modern world which the Roman Church
was to the world of the middle age. It was, I repeat, the
right we asserted for every local church freely to determine
and conduct its affairs that became the foundation of the
public principle so great and beneficent for the modern
world — the sovereignty of the people.

Upon English soil alone were the two great movements
of the Reformation age adjusted and consummated — Reformers and Anabaptists; the Evangelical and the Libertarian;
the Word and the Spirit; Fixity and Freedom; Faith and
Inspiration; Reformation and Renovation; and it was in
Independency that this most fruitful union took place. Such
is our hereditary genius — not liberty alone, but the combination of positivity and liberty, of authority and progress,
of security and freedom; wherein the liberty is secured by
the positivity, being the freedom that flows from a given
and historic Christ for every interest of mankind. We represent a free soul-faith on the base of a historic authority, with
an incorrigible bias to public affairs, and the resolve to
secure the establishment of the Church in the only real
way — its establishment not by law but in the laws, not as a
church favored by national preference, but as the Church's
Christianity glorified in national conduct.

(Ibid., pp. 308-311.)

The State, the nation, will not be christianized towards
God's kingdom by competitive sects, but only by a federate
Church of one gospel for one Humanity. And there is no
foundation, no secret, for this union but that we should
repair, with a new straitness, intensity, and power, to the
central gospel which gives us our right to be, and to be
free; that we should neglect everything else in comparison
with the confession and declaration of that gospel, in such
forms of expression, practical or theological, as may be
prescribed by the forces and necessities of the time; and that

our unity must lie in our confession of the mighty truth in our charge before it can take any effect as cooperation in the good works waiting to be done.

Our great positive task, therefore, is not social reform, political pressure, or philanthropic energy, but something which empowers and fertilizes all these. It is not even evangelization, in the current sense of the word. It is effective union of the federal, and not the imperial, kind, of the devolutionary kind, and not the centralized; convergent only on the common, but moralized, gospel of churches which are complementary in their action under that centripetal faith. It is only on such union that we can base a united moral effect on the world.

(Ibid., pp. 329-330.)

THE SOCIAL GOSPEL

Can it be that your moral standard, high and wide as it is, needs still to be truly universalized by theology of a practical kind? You have a high ideal, which you insist on laying upon all souls. Your motto is "Thorough." Do you not need (do forgive me if I am thorough too) one more high, more subtle, more comprehensive, more uncompromising, more holy, which will force its way into your whole soul, even to the rending of it, it may be? Your large moral world needs to rise heavenward in its ethical note till it break into a spiritual world whose height and depth and breadth are equal — a world as thorough in its spiritual penetration as it is in its moral exigence. Does your moral ideal pierce as much as it presses? Are its eyes as fiery as its wings? Would it not press much harder if it pierced much more? Does it search as powerfully as it urges? Has it power as it has weight and worth? Does your ideal of righteousness not need, ere it can master the soul, to become the ideal of a holiness before which you cannot stand? Is righteousness finally possible for society till holiness gets its own?

You are too engrossed with the soul's conduct instead of the soul's quality. Your society would be but a mosaic of souls instead of a body of Christ. You would change men without changing the inmost heart, change conduct and rela-

tions without changing life. You would increase men's power
of will without altering their style of will. But "the supreme
ethic," says Weinel, "is not, like other ideals, beyond our
power in its height, so much as it is beyond our own will in its
nature." You are working on the level of the self-respecting
moral gentleman, of the admirable English university product, who is in a position to live comfortably and finely on his
moral means, absorb spiritual ideas, and ignore spiritual
powers as if they were no nearer than London neighbors.
But the moral issue of the world is fought in a far more
inward region than that, and it turns on a far more inward
crisis. "There are no *rentiers* in the moral life." And the
battlefield of Christianity is not the clean and solvent soul
of the moral *rentier,* the moral gentleman, but it is the moral
bankrupt. There are far more of these than the refined
English gentleman or lady knows, far more than writers on
social subjects know, far more than is realized by those who
handle the final moral issue with no other equipment than
liberal thought and current culture. The moral crisis of
society is in a region which you may know little of. You are
bred, perhaps, in the sober, unbitten, and untragic atmosphere of intellectual West Ends, where evil is a study and not
a curse. You have never felt the botton drop out of your
own soul, the ground give way beneath your own moral
nature, while flying voices scream that Macbeth has mur-
dered sleep. You are masters of current ethic, but dilettanti
of the moral soul. You have never had the experience which
would give you intimate knowledge of the life that lies outside your ordered ways and kindly sets. You know no more
than to say that a tragic repentance is rare now, and the
sense of sin being outgrown, or that there are few people
who live in actual personal relation with Jesus Christ, or are
governed by His will. Why, there is not a section of the
Church, and certainly of the Free Churches, that could not
show them in thousands. You have not the experience of
the priest in the confessional, or the trusted pastor in his
intercourse with his flock. I would go a long way round to
avoid offending you, but how can any detour prevent me
from saying that, high, wide, and fine as your moral range

is, you lack some experience of men, and some moral sensibility at spiritual pitch? You respond to a supreme good, but you do not to the Holy of Holies. Your supreme good is but in the making. Your righteousness far exceeds Scribe or Pharisee, but you do not rise to thorough self-judgment; nor from that to the consciousness of the perfectly holy Self that judges even your judgment of yourself. A few even outdo my audacity with *you* in a kind of intellectual levity with *us*. They venture to lecture the theologians, with an ill-veiled contempt for their methods, if not always for their beliefs. They lecture them both on their spirit and *their subject,* without giving any indication that they have studied, in a scientific way, either a book of the New Testament or a single metaphysical master, or a single theological classic. Nay, they have been known to propound a theology publicly, giving clear indication that to them epistemology is a foreign country, moral philosophy an unknown region, and ethical ideas quite tractable with a cosmic calculus. But I willingly admit few have this confidence. And they cannot well be treated on my present line. They treat the problems of metaphysic with a mere hypophysic, and wield a calculus of the subliminal rather than the absolute, one more appropriate to the powers of an abyss than to the eternal and living God.

What lies incumbent on society for you (if I have your leave to return to you) is a law of righteousness. Yes, but what is it that lies incumbent, urgent, searching upon you for society, nay, for the sake of the power which is above society? Society is a collective and impersonal entity, and a law is all very well for that. But the soul is no mere impersonal entity. And the power that should rule it is no mere moral order, and no scheme of righteousness, and no Church nor society. It must be another soul, the righteous source of rights and home of duties, self-sufficing in its righteousness, a soul absolutely holy, and holy unto infinite love. Would it not be possible to gain the whole world for righteousness and lose our own soul? If you say that that is absurd, that to lose the soul in such altruism is to find it, I suggest that the supreme Teacher of that doctrine spoke only of losing the soul "for my sake and the gospel's." And might I further remind you that, by the most enlightened and modern interpretation, that peril was the essence of the temptation of Christ Himself? His tremendous sense of moral power presented to Him the possibility of conquering a social righteousness in man for God on lines which ignored the holy will of God in the Cross. What might He not have done for a reformed society, by a Cromwellian empire with an Ironside army, or by such service of man as made the regeneration of Faust? But where would His own soul have been then, in the face of *His* calling of God, whose grace to Him was to make Him taste death for every man? There are things which we may not sacrifice to the most promising and beneficent of social causes. Neither men nor women may unsex their soul for any dream or phase of the righteousness of God. But why should they not if social effect, as they see it, be all?

Over all your judgment of yourself or your society in righteousness is the judgment of your righteousness by the holiness of God. And practically that is the holiness[1] of God in Christ. But you present me, perhaps, with two difficulties. First, that you find the divine love in the mind of the Christ of the Gospels, but not the divine holiness; for He does not speak of it. And second, that criticism has so reduced our data that it is very little we can say about the consciousness of Christ. But are we, then, come to this, that we cannot speak with any force of conviction about Christ as the first moral figure of history? You will not go so far as that, perhaps. But if He be the first, is Humanity such a poor thing, in even its most eminent, that He has been unable to prevent His choicest followers for two thousand years from a moral blunder so great as that of finding in Him the very incarnation of the holiness of God, and in His Cross its supreme and complete assertion? They have not preached Him as the world prophet of social righteousness; they have persisted in finding Him the incarnation of God's holiness;

---

[1] Perhaps I ought to have been explicit before now that by holiness is not meant anything so abstract or subjective as mystical absorption, but the whole concrete righteousness of existence, self-sustained at white heat. For our God is a consuming fire.

and they have made His effect on social righteousness to depend on that. Have they made a tremendous moral mistake? Was idolatry of Himself the chief legacy of our greatest man to posterity?

I have in my venturous mind not the popular dilettanti of a social reformation upon ethical lines, but earnest and accomplished students of the matter. And yet I must make bold to say reluctantly, and with great respect, that their obsession by the theological antipathy has made them such victims of theology (by its negation), and has so narrowed their mind thereby, that they have never taken due measure of Christ as a moral fact, still less as a moral factor in history. They have indeed been interested in the historical Christ, and they have owned the spell of His character in the procession of prophets. Carlyle did, for instance. But they have not dealt as seriously with the moral meaning of the fact as with its moral effect, or its aesthetic or historical aspect. They have never integrated Him into the moral philosophy of history, into the grand moral psychology, into the spiritual organism of the race — as theology has at least tried to do. The historic or the ethical sense will carry a man far. But it will not carry him as far as the person of Christ takes him, if he give to that path a mind unstunted by scientific methods, or unstupefied by religious sentiment. You cannot treat Christ adequately by the historic sense, psychic research, cosmic emotion, the canons of natural ethic, or tender affection. The only adequate treatment of a fact so unique as Christ is the treatment proper to the moral nature of such a fact, the treatment it elicits and inspires, the treatment to which, in the first disciples, we owe anything that we know about Him, the treatment by faith. You must trust Him ere He seem worthy of your trust. He is really God only to the faith which has confessed Him as Saviour. His incarnation is an evangelical and not a logical, not a metaphysical, demand. The Church's views about His person were forced upon those whom He not only impressed but regenerated, forced on them by the logic of living faith poring on the new creation that had passed them from death into life. It was only the scientific forms of these views that were affected by the philosophy of the hour, which did not, and cannot, give the certainty of their substance. It was a real redemption that Athanasius sought to secure by the metaphysical Trinity. And the experienced verdict (and not merely the orthodox deposit) of His living Church in history is, that Christ is the incarnate holiness of the world and of eternity; that He is no mere part of past history, but of the race's total life; and no mere starting-point for the ideal, but the living object of each age's absolute faith. To trust Him is not a leap in the dark, but it is a venture none the less. It is a venture of courage and not of despair, of insight and not of bewilderment. In an age like this the greatest moral courage lies not in challenging faith, as the crude public believes, which believes in little more than pluck. That is cheap heroism now. But true courage lies in pursuing, amid the dullness of the public, the triviality of the pious, the desolations of criticism, the assaults of foes, and the treason of friends, such faith as places the precious soul, the wondrous age, and the cosmic world for ever and ever in those hands which twenty centuries ago were nailed for our advantage to the bitter Cross. To do that with open eyes today is a very great achievement of the soul, a very great venture of faith, and a very great exercise of moral courage of the silent and neglected sort. The world knows nothing of its debt to those who for the soul's sake are incessantly facing and laying the specters of the mind.

(From "The Insufficiency of Social Righteousness as a Moral Ideal,"
pp. 603-609.)

This ethical, cosmic, eternal estimate of Christ cannot be based on His biography alone, or chiefly, but upon His Cross, as we shall again find when we have surmounted the present fertile obsession by "the historical Jesus." Such an estimate is a judgment of value, a confession of faith, nay, a personal self-assignment. It is impossible to treat Christ adequately, except theologically and personally. Personally, for it is the theologian's hard and high fate to cast himself into the flame he tends, and be drawn into its consuming fire. And theologically, for we find the key of Christ's life in His work, find His work to be the Cross, and find the Cross to be God's atonement of Himself, and the world, and especially of our own soul, once for all. The spiritual interpretation of Christ centers in the Cross; and in the Cross as a sacrifice offered *by* God more than *to* God, but to God more than to men. It is offered to the holiness of God before it is offered to the service of men. To both, indeed, but in that order. It is certainly not simply the classic case of man's service of man. That gives us a broad Christian but not a full Christ. And nothing but the fullness of Christ can maintain our breadth or replenish empty churches. To banish the atonement from the creative center of Christianity is in the long run so to attenuate Christ as to dismiss Him from Christianity, and condemn Him to be outgrown. As it was the Cross that universalized Christianity, so also it is the Cross that is the permanent, creative, and extensive thing in it. All its faith, theology, and ethic are created and organized from the evangelical center there. And this divine atonement to infinite holiness through loving judgment is the only thing that can really appeal at last to the heart of the modern passion for righteousness when it is thorough with itself — a passion which is so much more deep than its own consciousness goes. We avoid this center only by our plentiful lack of moral wit, by the lack of evangelical experience, or of intellectual thoroughness, of moral sequacity. Can we really think of righteousness without judgment, of a universal righteousness without a universal judgment — whether you put it in the pictorial shape of a last great assize or not? Must that judgment not arraign every soul? You cannot think (unless you fall to thinking of justice as mere utilitarian arrangement) of a universal righteousness which is not founded upon righteousness eternal and absolute, i.e. upon divine holiness. Can you think, then, of universal judgment except as the relation to that holiness of every soul? And not only of every soul, but of the whole soul ranged before the whole God and the holy God? Could a personal soul be judged by a mere historic process? Does it not call for a personal God? And if there be any religious protagonist of the race — I own I tax you, and I am sorry, but it has taxed me more — must he not stand vicariously before the judgment of that God, and take home that love under the moral conditions of a righteousness so universal and a holiness so absolute? This is what (in the Church's faith) Christ did, and did once for all. It is the supreme service He rendered to social righteousness, and consequently to eternal — if we could but for an hour get far enough away from social problems to take their measure and proportion, feel their foregone solution, and so find rest and power for our souls. All this lifts Christ far above the level of a historic figure. A mere historic, stationary Christ is but a transitory Christ — which is a paradox. But you cannot tell the truth about the Cross without the lie of a paradox. A Christ who stood fixed only at a point in history would be, by this very fixture, a transitory Christ, because but a temporary, because He would be outgrown and passed by the moving race. A Christ merely ideal, stationed at a fixed point on earth but magnified to an ideal upon the clouds, would become a *Brocken-gespenst*. He would be a mirage whose very grandeur and purity would shame us far more than help us. And He would shimmer before us like an aurora, when we needed to be warmed and reared by a perennial sun.

The new passion for righteousness must end upward in a new sense of judgment; and especially among the religious, if their ethic is to grow more delicate and penetrating as well as more urgent. Social righteousness unaccompanied by moral delicacy and penetration could easily become another phase of Pharisaism. Love without holiness lends itself but too easily to dissimulation, to unreality. But to give God's judgment its due place in public righteousness is to raise ethic to religion, righteousness to holiness, and to make some kind of atonement inseparable from real faith on any social scale, and certainly on the social scale of a Church transcending and outstaying all the societies of men.

(Ibid., *pp. 611-613*.)

WAR

Public righteousness must be done even at the cost of war. To renounce that responsibility is to disown a national

morality when a great crisis of public righteousness comes.
. . . Yet a world of righteousness is the one purpose of Him
who in His Cross has a property in every soul, and a lien
on every conscience. The mightiest of the world forces is
the historic purpose of a righteous God.

(*From* The Christian Ethic of War, *pp. 35-36.*)

There is no suggestion that the New Testament has to
deal with something a world more than love as the instinctive
heart understands it, namely *holy love,* love as the moral
absolute, with a heart of grace and a method of judgment;
that the prime note of the Cross of Christ and of the love
there is the note of God's righteousness in a universal and
eternal kingdom, a righteousness that did not spare His
only Son.

(Ibid., *p. 38.*)

What holiness is to love in heaven that righteousness is to
love on earth. And the connection is much more than an
analogy; it is really a continuity — holiness continuing in
heavenly conditions the righteousness in earthly affairs, and
the same love being the bond of heaven as is the bond of
heaven and earth. Therefore we do not ramble when we
speak of the great atonement by holiness to the holiness
of God as being the foundation of all the ethic of righteousness on earth, and the principle of all judgment on men and
all justification of man before God.

(Ibid., *p. 164.*)

The effect of the present disaster to the world is that of
every judgment of God. It will sift and part. Many who
are but lightly persuaded Christians will drop out, as if
a man had leaned on a wall and a snake from it bit him.
It will make those who doubted and challenged to deny
and despair, especially if they shirked action and hung back
from the field; and it will make many of those who believed
but in progress, or trusted but on traditional grounds, and
were only comforted but never captured by their belief, try
to believe harder still on their old lines. While the elect,
renouncing a systematic apology, will take great words, and
say (with the supreme empiricist of grace), "Even so, Father,

so it hath seemed good in Thy sight." But what was within that word of sublime humility and victory? And what came from its heart to be the word of His very apostolate, who were the intimate trustees of His final world revelation? What is His message in those who have some right to speak from the *penetralia* of the Church and its Bible? How do they answer the very natural question of the public, whether we can still believe in God's government of the world and His destiny for it? It is a question so deeply natural that it is beyond nature (unless nature can explain itself). It can have no answer outside the grace that transcends nature. It has none for those whose religion is mercy without majesty and love without either power, sanctity, or judgment. What is God's own theodicy, His final theodicy, His Self-justification to the world? What is to be our final judgment about a final judgment by God upon all such things, and within them? How are we to be saved, amid the collapse, into a belief in salvation? It is the most extreme crisis for faith — how great we do not yet realize. And the serious people will not grudge that the answer should sound extreme, that it should not be as obvious as a journal, that it come from faith and from faith's inmost citadel, and that it should seem foreign to our untaxed thought and common hours. Only an extreme position can meet an extreme situation — so long as we can make it good.

And the attempt to make it good is worth while. It is confessed scepticism of both the Church and of the gospel, to sweep its ministry into the ranks of war. Those who are toiling in mind and suffering in spirit to provide from the gospel, by thought, comfort, or taxing prayer, some real and staying power in the face of all the facts of the hour are not outside the soldier host who so finely answer the public need and call. They are of the combatants and not of the drones. They are angels of the Lord of. Hosts, if not His captains. They are reservists against the hour when the trial of faith may become even more acute, when native courage begins to flag, and faith must be a song in the night that opens the prison gates. To speculate at such a time on the psychology of the Trinity might be but monastic. But to reinterrogate the Word of the historic gospel for its word to the historic time, to leave the theosophies which rule the mystic hour for a theodicy with a historic base, a moral genius, and a mystic power — that is to be a true chaplain to the Lord's host. To justify God is the best and deepest way to fortify men. It provides the moral resource and stay which is the one thing at last. With open face to see the glory of God in things as they are, to blink nothing of the terror and yet to be sure of the kingdom of God with all our heart — that is more for the courage of man than any nationalism or any patriotism when heart fails and grief benumbs. Since the civil wars there has been no such time in England. And we came through these only upon the puritan faith which a long peace and a thin culture have now drowned delicately as in a butt of Malmsey wine.

The solution of the great world juncture is at last a religious solution. And, being a historic juncture, it concerns the kingdom of God and God's provision for it in history. It taxes all the resources that faith has, but it settles us in a certainty which is very much in the world but not of it. The Church will come out of the present crisis both chastened and exalted if it takes itself seriously enough, and holds itself as morally greater than soul, family, or State. For it is the only society on earth whose one and direct object is the kingdom of God — if, indeed, it be not that kingdom in the making. There is much speculation about the situation after the war, and especially about the need for an effective international. And most of it leaves the Church out of the question, or any spiritual authority. Why? From the sand-blindness of those without, and the uncertainty of those within it.

(*From* The Justification of God, *pp. 13-15.*)

X: ETERNAL LIFE

LIFE AS SACRAMENT

As we follow up this line of reflection, I say, there is
borne in on us something more than the religious significance of life. There comes home to us not only its solemn but
its sacramental value. Life means more than even the
poets tell. It has more than an imaginative worth. It has
more than a supernatural. It has more than an everlasting.
It has a holy and eternal worth. I mean that not only is it
involved in the process or tragedy of the universe, but it is
partner in the solution of that tragedy in God. History is
not only reconciled, it is charged with the message and
power of reconciliation. Even art can embalm life in amber.
It can cast on it the aesthetic spell, and for a time transport
us to another world. It can make our noisy lives seem
moments in the energy of the eternal silence. But a greater
than art is here. There is a greater secret than even art
commands in the relation of the soul and the holy. The
action in time of the holy and eternal Spirit of our redemption is greater than that of genius. We are told indeed by
many a seer that "the momentary life of today is a factor in
the procession of all time and being." Philosophy can teach

us that, whether it get it home or not, whether there be much help in it or not. But we have to do with more than a procession of being, or a dance of ideas; and we have to do with getting that something more home to people. We have to do with an eternal providence, with a heart of love eternal, and with a will absolute over the hearts and in the wills of men; and we have to do with a public faith in it. I mean something more than dogmatics — certainly more than dogmatics as a sort of Palladium we carry about in an ark. I have in mind the riddle of the painful earth, for which theology must be some kind of solution. We have to connect up earth's tragedy with God's.

The tragedy of the plodding peasant, dragging a rheumatic existence from the soil, and dying alone and broken-hearted with his daughter's shame or his son's crime — we have to integrate that with an eternal tragedy, an immortal solution of it, and a final joy. We have to link it with God's disappointments in His son man, His grief and His joy and His victory in His Son Christ. Is there any experience possible to the soul, is there any power at work on it, any revelation, any redemption, whereby the very horrors of world-war and wickedness can be made sacramental of the fullness of joy? Can they be underagents for the last righteousness and angels of the last judgment which secures the last peace? Is it a delusion, or is it Time's sacramental secret, that a person, like Christ, of two thousand years ago is as near us all now as He was to men then? Have we with us a power of life by which these two millenniums do not divide us from Christ, like a world of mists and seas, but unite us — as commerce and invention make the ocean a bond and not a gulf? Is it a dream that the issue in His Cross is greater, and more creative, than all the issues of history? Why do the heathen rage but for the kingdom of God's Son? And have we a power by which ephemeral lives are not only absorbed in a stream universal but become revelations and energies from a person of absolute love? Can they become channels of the Holy Ghost, in the power of One who was more than a channel, and more than a revelation — who was the incarnation of God the Redeemer? That is what the Cross of Christ as the source of His Spirit proposes to do with them. The victory of an immortal Redeemer becomes the effective point and principle of life's most sacramental significance. It is the source of any worth life can have not only *to* God but among us *for* God, as the vehicle of the eternal Spirit, as a human priest to human kind. The power which makes life most deeply sacramental is its new creation by Christ. The eternal life that Christ's Cross won for us in the eternal Spirit acts on us so timelessly that it can give the meanest life the eloquence of the spiritual world. It makes it that it can be not only an object but a channel of supernatural blessing, and not only a channel but a medium. That miraculous power which turns the historic Christ from a memory to be the most real presence, and even constituent, of our life today, that power which makes Him who is so far off the most near, and changes the temporal to the eternal — that is what makes the true sacramental power in life, and transfigures it with the glow of something that lifts it and lights it for ever. Nothing makes the poor man's toil so full of worth and price as the work of Christ the Spirit. Nothing so lifts into eternal significance the loves, sorrows, drudgeries, tragedies of the poor men of the dull fields. It has done it in cases innumerable. Nothing so makes them know themselves, and seem to others, to be worlds more than mere atoms bubbling in a seething cauldron, or drifting in a desert dust, whirled in a universe of meaningless sound and fury. Such certainty as Christ can give, and does give, of a life beyond life by our partnership of it in Him fills the humblest soul with such power and price that the men of genius can neither fathom it (though they feel it) nor can they give, far less guarantee, that which they may divine of its wealth. The commonest life means worlds both Godward and manward. That is the sacramentality of life. The most Christian poets are those who, like Wordsworth, Burns, or Barnes, breathe that note from huts where poor men lie. And the warrant for it is its Creator, its new Creator — the power of the eternal Spirit by which that poor man Christ Himself won the endless victory over time, death, and the world. The simple have known that as they could know nothing else. And it made life for them, and for all who could read them aright, because they shared the same faith, full of staying power, mystic eloquence, and conclusive bliss.

"Grave in the sight of God is the death of His loyal and loving ones."

(From This Life and the Next, *pp. 78-83.)*

ON DEATH

We might grant that death teaches us much as to the value of life, and that life without death would become a very hard and coarse thing. With the abolition of death would vanish the uncertainty which educates faith, the mystery, the tragedy, which makes life so great, the sense of another world which gives such dignity and meaning to this, the range of sympathy that flows from believing that our affections are not for this world alone. Erase death, and Tithonus tells us life sinks at last into drab weariness. Its noblest, dearest interest ebbs and fades. Its tragedy and its chivalry both go. We should end by having no concern but feeding, drowsing, prancing and feeding again. Love, valor, pity, sacrifice; charm, music and all the nameless spell of nature and of personality; courtesy and reverence, all the sweet fine things of life that are tributes to soul, and that death seems to cut short most painfully — those are the things which would really die out if we succeeded in indefinitely averting death.

But, of course, it is not death that preserves these after all. It is the conviction that death is a crisis which opens a new phase of life. It is the conviction, latent or patent, of immortality and spiritual growth in it. How much more true is St. Paul: "Wherefore, my beloved brethren, be ye steadfast, immovable, ever abounding in the work of the Lord, for as much as ye know that your labour is not in vain in the Lord." The work is the Lord's. It is there not simply to meet man's need, but God's purpose. That purpose is a greater action-shaping power than our need is. It is not true to suggest, as this poem does, that death, understood as final, could have set afoot the new future of energy or desire, the eagerness of work, the strength of society, or the tenderness of affection. For men were already living in a city, "The City of Cain," before the accident took place or the stimulus of death came in. The enterprise of civilization had started well on its way. Did it need an accidental death to stir in the children of the first murderer the terrors that made life tragic, intense, and pathetic? It is not the poverty and brevity of life that draws out its resources; it is its sense of fullness and power. It is strength that is the root of action, not need. "Action-shaping need," yes, but not action-creating. Action-*shaping!* Yes, but what *inspires* action — moral *action* as distinct from mere energy, mere movement? What makes the good will which attends at all to the needs of others and does not just feed our own? A stream is not effective which just spreads out and flows into each hole it finds. It dies of diversion. That phrase was a piece of eggshell which clung to George Eliot from the hatching of her mind by George Henry Lewes, as anyone may see who reads his now forgotten books. Need may shape action, but it does not create action; which is the child of wealth not poverty, of the soul's fullness and not of its death. We were created by God not out of His poverty and His need of company, but one of His overflowing wealth of love and His passion to multiply joy.

(Ibid., *pp. 6-8.*)

ON IMMORTALITY

If the doctrine of immortality is held only on subjective grounds, it is quite likely to end in religious egoism. It is a fundamental principle of all I say on the subject that a sure belief in immortality does not rest where philosophy puts it, but where religion puts it. It is not founded on the nature of the psychic organism, but on its relation to Another. I mean that if it is based on the indestructible nature of the soul substance, or upon an untamed passion for adventure, or upon endless curiosity, or upon our instinct and thirst for personal perfection, or upon our native moral greatness, or upon any such stoic forms of self-esteem, or even self-respect, it is quite likely (if you go on far enough to give scope for its gravitation) to end downward in a supreme care for *my* immortality, whatever becomes of yours. And that ends in people elbowing each other out of the way to get at the elixir of life, or to dip in this Bethesda pool for eternity. But these are philosophic considerations, or aesthetic or egoistic concerns, which are not really religions. They detach man from God, the Lord and Giver of Life. At least they do not found on man's union with God. They set him, with his claims and presumptions, over against God, as the deadly way of Pharisaism was. Man may come thus to behave like a spoilt beauty, unschooled in duty, and craving for attentions without end. The Creator may even be reminded that He has made the soul immortal, that He cannot recall the initial gift of life, and that the soul bears stamped on it a signed concession of eternal rights. All that is egoist enough, or can become so. And I do not remember where we have Christian warrant for believing that man was created immortal.

But the case is quite altered if I am not thinking chiefly about *my* living for ever. I may be thinking of some dearer to me than life, for whose salvation beyond the grave I would risk my own. Or I may be thinking of the immortality of the race; which is a more potent influence on the present than a multitude of individual immortalities, because the efficiency of an organic group is greater than the sum total of the efficiencies of its units. A nation is great, a crowd is not. But still more is the case altered if I am thinking about our glorifying God for ever whether as a soul or as a race. All is different if I am thinking of what my soul means for others. Most of all when I am thinking of what it means for God and not of what it means for me, if I am not making Him to serve my egoism, if I am not thinking of the paradise of heaven but of the purpose of God and His righteousness. If my immortality is due to God's gift, it is due to His *incessant* gift and creation, and not to an infinite lease of life which He signed at the beginning. That is to say, it can go on only by communion with Him. But that is not the communion of love between equals, but of grace between unequals. And whatever we owe to God's grace glorifies Him far more than it glorifies us. What man tends to say, whether he do it naïvely or philosophically, is "Because I live I shall live." But what Christ says, and what faith hears, is, "Because I live ye shall live also." He alone has life in Himself, and we have it by His gift and by union with Him either here or hereafter. It makes a vast difference between the philosophic and the religious treatment of immortality when we re-member this — that in the Bible the supreme interest and the final ground of immortality was not the continuity of an organism, physical or psychical, but of a relation. The ground of the belief was not that such an organism must go on, but that a life in God, and especially in the risen Christ, could not die. The philosophic way is egoist, how-ever large and fine; it does justice to that excellent creature man. It is anthropocentric. The other way (of faith) is concerned with God, His stake in us, His purpose with us, and our service of His kingdom and honor. It is theocentric.

(Ibid., *pp. 20-23*.)

We cannot tarry to argue if there is an immortality await-ing us; we must obey the immortality urging and lifting us. We do not move to a possible mirage of a city of God; the citi-zenship is within us. Ask, am I living as immortal — not as one who will be immortal? Do not waste time asking if there is a coming eternity; ask, what must I do to give effect to my present eternity; how shall I be loyal to the eternal re-sponsibility in me and on me? Is my faith a life? It must make a great difference to life whether we treat our eternity as a present or a future, as a power or as a possibility, as a duty or as an ideal — whether our Christ is a Bystander or an Occupant of us. Our immortality is really our judgment and its joy of righteousness; it is not a mere condition of judgment, nor the region of it. It does not become a mere venue, a mere stage for judgment, a set scene. Nor does it provide a mere asbestos either for future flames, or for the happier incandescence. It has no existence apart from a content of weal or woe. And that content depends on us (under grace). Our immortality is not just the glory (or gloom) of going on and still to be. It is not mere duration.

There is no such thing, no such abstraction. Our eternity is something that remains when all its events have passed. It is the state of a soul, the content and quality of its life, when events in a sequence cease, when they have come and gone with the soul's verdict on them, and the reaction of such verdict on the soul. It is good or evil according to choice. It is a disparting to one of two great seas. It does not call chiefly for contemplation but decision. What Paul did in speaking to Felix was not to persuade him of immortality; it was to turn immortality from a curious interest to a crushing crisis, from a curious interest hovering about life, and discussible at the tables of roués, to a searching judgment on life's interior. It was preaching that Felix did not like with wine and walnuts. The salons shun it, and the reviews ignore it. Nor was it in the nature of popular preaching. It did not carry the accent either of culture, or of sentiment, or of mere urbane consideration. It did not humor the instincts of the heart, nor hallow the graces of the home. It did not agitate the questions that occupy the periodicals on the one hand, nor those that captivate the young on the other. But it was the kind of preaching which brings the other life into this, which shapes our behavior in time by the nature of an immanent eternity (whether we speak of public conduct or private), which transmutes time into eternity and does not simply prolong it. It translates a present, it does not discuss a future. It does more than educate, it converts. It does more than enlarge our moral horizon, or manipulate the themes of moral culture. It makes the new heaven and the new earth wherein dwelleth righteousness.

That is a sample of the way we must rescue the spiritual for the ethical, moralize our theology, and make creed practice. However much religion may be life, theology is deeper life. It rises deeper in God's life, it goes deeper into ours. It moralizes all by its origin in the holy. A theme like immortality, at least — we do it wrong, being so majestical, to explore it but as a cavern with our torches, instead of honoring it as our light and sun and showing it forth accordingly. It is much to live for eternity; to live eternity is more.

(Ibid., *pp. 60-63.*)

PRAYER FOR THE DEAD

How natural in this connection to turn to prayer for the dead. Prayer for the dead is healthier than tampering with them. Prayer is our supreme link with the unseen — with which otherwise we have no practical relations. We should resume prayer for the dead, were it only to realize the unity of the Church and our fellowship with its invisible part. In Christ we cannot be cut off from our dead nor they from us wherever they be. And the contact is in prayer.

No converse with the dead is so much of a Christian activity as prayer for them. There is no part of the practical Christian life which is so intimate and effectual as prayer. It colors and shapes us more than the obvious forms of action do. It is the work which chiefly influences the growth of faith and the quality of character. Life is affected from its foundation by whether we pray or not, and by how we pray. It is the main practical interest between this life and the life unseen. And we shall pray or not pray, we shall pray one way or another way, according as we believe in a future life, and hope for ourselves, or for those dearer than ourselves. Which is the better, to put them in God's hands and pray for them, or to bring strange devices to pass to conjure them up? If we believe in a continued life through spirits and not through Christ, if a medium means more than a Mediator for our contact with the unseen, the manner of our prayer will be accordingly. If we discard Christ's moral revelation, and say we get more if one seems to rise magically from the dead, we pass into another religion, and prayer sinks accordingly. If Christ's voice does not come to us from beyond the grave, if all we hear is but the dull sound and hard effort of a miner's pick trying to meet ours in a tunnel between the two worlds, the note of our prayer and of our life is going to be deeply affected. It will lose the infinite moral value of union with the intercession of Christ, crowning His moral and final victory of a *holy* Cross. Or if we go on to say that death ends all, it ends all prayer. It not only stops the soul that prays, but the thought of it paralyzes the soul and its prayer in life.

On the other hand, if death fixes and settles all, if the

tree lies for ever as it falls, prayer is much affected, and so life. One form of prayer is then excluded — prayer for the dead (though they need our prayer more if they are suffering yonder). Yet it would be easier to maintain a belief in immortality if we were encouraged so to pray. It would give us a practical relation with the other side, and to other immortality than our own. As it is, we have little direct and practical contact with immortality so far as the day's life goes. No act of that life brings us into direct and practical connection with the world of the dead. It is a dream; it is a world not realized. It does not belong to the strong and active side of our life. There is always about a life that works outward on another a certain note of distinction which is not made up for by any enthusiasm of Humanity. I knew an agnostic of a very fine kind who shortened his life by his devoted service to the very poor in a low part of London. There was to me a certain halo about him. And yet it is a different kind of spell that invests a life lived in the power of an endless life, a life that dwells with immortality daily.

I venture to say, then, that the instinct and custom of praying for our dearest dead, or our noblest (like many of the soldiers by whose pain and death we live), should be encouraged and sanctified as a new bond for practical life between the seen and the unseen, where we have bonds all too few. Nothing in our Christian belief is against it, and there is a good deal for it. It would never have been lost but for the abuses of purgatory, masses, and the commerce which the Church made of a magical influence on another world. But we threw away too much when we made a clean sweep. We are bidden to pray for everything that is not trival, *"In everything* making your requests known," and to cast every real care on God. There is nothing serious that we may not bring to the Father. A widow praying who does not know where her next shilling is to come from means more to the Father than a full choral service, and more engages His heart. And it is serious enough that half our heart, and all its treasure, should be snatched into the unseen. With that unseen our only sure link is the God to whom we pray. But He is as much the God of our dead as of us; and He is a God from whom they cannot be severed as they are from us. May our prayers to our common Father not put into petition what is always in our thoughts, and put into words what is always in our heart? If we name them before God, what are we doing in our way but what He does in His, and calling things that are not as though they were.

There are those who can quietly say, as their faith follows their love into the unseen, "I know that land. Some of my people live there. Some have gone abroad there on secret foreign service, which does not admit of communications. But I meet from time to time the Commanding Officer. And when I mention them to Him He assures me all is well."

(Ibid., *pp. 43-47*.)

THE POWER OF THE RESURRECTION

From the New Testament point of view the seat of chief power and authority in the universe is the Cross and resurrection of Jesus Christ. And there are many signs that we do not realize this, that we do not take such statements seriously, or in any other than in some figurative and moral way. For Paul the omnipotence of God was chiefly shown in raising Christ from the dead. But for the average modern Christian there is practically and experimentally more power in the processes of astronomy and evolution than he can by any effort feel to underlie either the death or the resurrection of Christ. The latter especially he associates with ease rather than effort, just as his conception of fatherhood has become joined with the affection rather than the judgments of God, with the child Jesus rather than with the Cross. We have largely lost the idea that there is a greater power at work even in the natural world than the might of cosmic process, glorious states, or brilliant genius. And that is the power of sin, which has it in it to bring all these things to dust with the alliance of time. We think that there are powers which meet us hourly today, of which Paul knew nothing — like the cosmic power of which I spoke. And we have a latent sense, that had he known of our modern forces, he would not have spoken so freely and with so little gratification

about the resurrection of Christ, as the supreme exhibition
of the power of God. And it is true that there are powers
familiar to us which were unknown to him. But there were
powers, and greater powers, familiar to him which are being
forgotten by us. And chief of these is the power of sin. In
these moral measurements of the universe which give us
final values, this is the ruling power unless it find its master.
The power which masters the world's sin is the real omnipotence of the universe. And the true sense of what power
is, comes home to us only in our sense of forgiveness and
redemption. And that sense issues for us from the twofold
act of the death and rising of Jesus Christ.

We have moved our faith's center of gravity, and we
have detached it too far from the experiences which gather
specially about the Cross and the resurrection. We cultivate
the pieties, and we are strange to the hells and heavens that
open about that historic moment, which was the crisis both
of our souls and of human destiny. We have a religion
whose keynote is evolution rather than crisis, education
rather than conversion, good form rather than great power.
Our preaching is ethical and aesthetic, and our piety is active
and tender. And we win much respect, we do not puzzle or
offend, and the papers praise us for being in tune with the
time. Only our place is to command the tune, and the Cross
should offend it. There are things we cannot do, which if
undone must undo us; and there are people we fail with, and
lose, who would be worth more than hundreds we gain.
And our lack is not a scheme but a life, not sympathy but
conviction, not union but communion. And it is communion, not with a vague spirit of piety or pity, but with
the spirit of our redemption, whose source and shrine is
indeed the person of our Saviour, but that person chiefly in
the act wherein He put forth His whole personal power — in
the Cross; and if we go behind that, and make two acts of
what was really one, it is in that other act wherein was
exerted the whole power of God for the world — the
resurrection of Christ from the dead. This resurrection was
chiefly the saving of His soul from the powers and pains of
death and their dominion over Him. The emergence from

the tomb was but the material expression of that first inner resurrection, which was the great victory, and whose nature and action are continued in our faith. For when we believed we were "quickened together with Him." We only believe by the power of His resurrection.

But if faith be no more than piety, it is not easy to associate it either with the resurrection or with power. And it is quite easy to work into sympathy and cooperation with many of the world powers and institutions that delude us with the promise of establishing the Church among men, or doing them good. My point is that what we lack in our faith and pay for in our effect is that element of power which makes faith the continued action in the Church of the greatest exertion of omnipotence ever known — the resurrection of Jesus Christ from the dead.

It is a point that will receive little attention. It will be treated as a piece of theology. And a leading minister told us last week that the Churches care nothing for theology. That may be bad, and even vulgar enough, but perhaps it is not the chief trouble; which is when they do not seem to know where theology begins, and are disposed to dismiss as theology the vital centers of saving and experienced faith.

(From "The Power of the Resurrection," The Examiner, April 11, 1901.)

ETERNITY WITHIN TIME

If during life we let the influences of eternity, of life in its simultaneity, play on us deliberately and in advance; if we court, by the culture of our spiritual life in Christ, the revelation of eternity in God, with whom is no after nor before; if we let it all act on our soul from there; should we not be doing much to anticipate the verdict of age, and to avert many of the regrets of eternity? The last judgment would then be always at work on us. We should live in it and its power and glory. We should in a short time fulfil a long time. By the eternal Spirit, we should so number our days that we turn our hearts to moral wisdom faster than we are changed by the mere lapse of the years. For the knowledge that we court with pains has a value that does not belong to what is forced on us, or what just sinks in subconsciously.

But this means for Christians placing ourselves in ever closer rapport with Christ's holy love, and especially with the holiness in it and the conquest that means. The real power of immortality is the eternity of the holy. It is, philosophically put, the invincibility of the moral absolute. Holiness, with its eternal moral conquest, is the eternal thing in love itself, it is the only guarantee of love's final victory. As we take home eternity from Christ, it is the holy we take home in love. It is the holy as what might be called the ingrain, the tissue, the physiognomy of eternal love, the content and quality of it, the gift and power it brings, the warp to its woof. It is to this supreme moral power that we expose ourselves for our cleansing, our shaping, nay, our new creation — which is something beyond love's power except as holy. And it is as moral persons that we do so, for the holy is a moral idea, it is a moral power. Therefore it is not the mere duration of the soul that concerns us, not the continuance of a *process* more or less natural by which we are swept in, but the immortality of the moral personality which is reared by our *action,* our personal action of response. And the influence of the holiness of God on that active personality is supreme, because the true eternity is His standing act, it is Himself in that pure holy action which is the native energy of His being. He is not a static being into whose kind love we sink, but He is the eternal Energy we join, which constitutes all being, and binds in holy action the coherent universe — the love which, as holy, moves the earth and all the stars. He is the most influential environment of the moral soul. For His holiness does not merely act on man as an object, as it does on the natural world; but it so acts on him that he returns the act as a subject; it is a case of reciprocal action in a rising scale. It is communion. And we know, not as science knows, but because we are first known by what we know, because His knowing us is the cause of our knowing Him. The object of our knowledge is the eternal Subject that knows. An eternity which begins by knowing us must have a very different effect on our life from an eternity which we but know, and to which we but look forward.

(From This Life and the Next, *pp. 54-56.)*

Another life — what is the other life *then* but that which is the other life *now?* What is it but the eternal life which is our true life here, only viewed as going on, viewed in amount rather than in kind, in extent rather than quality, as prolonged rather than intense, as expressed in terms of time, duration or quantity, instead of worth? We ask, how long, instead of how rich, how full, we live. Some will remember the Spinozist description of the two disparate aspects of the great reality. Spinoza spoke of these aspects as thought and extension. And there was only an empirical connection between them. Well, the two aspects of eternal life correspond. We may view it quantitatively, extensively, as everlasting, or qualitatively, *sub specie eternitatis,* as moral.

Now are these, like extension and thought, irrelevant to each other and disparate? Are we quite ignorant of what *has* these features, of that whose physiognomy they are? The life that goes on — is it not the life of moral personality? That is soul, that is reality. When we speak of another life we think of our life as enduring; but it is the continuance of the same eternal life which is our good as souls here — intense at each immeasurable moment, infinite in each particle, as it were, and royal in its quality, whatever its extent may be. It does not matter for the moment whether we think of its imperative as that of conscience or that of love. It is the great shaping and guiding power, whose influence is real out of all proportion to our sense of its range.

(Ibid., *pp. 67-68.*)

Eternity is thus beyond time only in the sense of being deep within it. "He hath set eternity in their hearts." It is within our interior, and beyond it — above it in that way. It is more interior. It inhabits our inner castle. "Religion is not the perception of the infinite; it is having the infinite within us." That makes the moral value of immortality for life. We are living now the life beyond. Time and space are rather distilling our eternity than preparing for it. Think of the automatic reaction on our soul of our resolves and deeds, so that what we have been makes us what we are. Think then, more deeply still, of the power, the eternity, moulding these wills and deeds. Our eternal life is not at the end of our days but at the heart of them, the source of them, the control of them. Time is there to reveal or to deposit eternity, not to qualify for it. Eternity does not lie at the other end of time, it pervades it.

(Ibid., *pp. 72-73*.)

We hear of many who are eating their heart out because circumstances do not allow them a fuller life. But it is not more life and fuller that we want. We need a different life, a life not simply with a new light on it but a new power in it and a new footing under it. We need a new center, not a transformation but a transposition. We need the completion not of the soul but of its radical change. The growing spiritual life, and not the natural, goes on beyond the greatest of its crises, in death, and goes on reversing its past all the time. That goes on into which we are being changed as personality grows by a constant revolution in our egoism. If life goes on for ever, it goes on coming round full circle, and reflecting an absolute change, an inversion of values which is presaged in the moral estimates of age compared with youth. If it is an absolute change, that means life going on for ever in an ascending spiral where looking back is looking down. For the eternal, in the qualitative sense of rich life and full, could not continue such if it did not include the quantitative also of long life, and time to work itself out. Grace would then simply be irrelevant to nature, and not related at all. Nothing can ensure to us indestructible being except a power which delivers us, by a higher way than mere persistence, from the mutations of time or space — which delivers us from their demoralization. Only what is eternal in the moral sense could ensure eternity in the temporal sense, for "morality is the nature of things." Eternity is time not simply prolonged, nor only sublimated, but hallowed, morally regenerated for the holy. That which protects us from time is that which delivers us from evil. So the kingdom of an endless heaven is the kingdom of a *holy* God. And it is the fruit not of *Christus Consummator* but of *Christus Redemptor*.

I dwell on this to point out that any discussion of Christian ethic which does not start with moral regeneration is by so much the less Christian. In the Christian faith "we die but once, but we are born twice." Immortality is precious as the continuance of that which has set life in quite another than the natural key, moved it into a new rhythm, and made its verdicts more than those of the natural judgment rarefied, or the rational just spiritualized. It is behavior in a new dimension. Have I not said that that is no true, and it is certainly no Christian, belief in immortality which hankers for a life after death just to give the old egoism supernatural opportunities, and to furnish the old desires with superior facilities for getting their head and their bread? Did not even the Pharisees likewise? They believed in a resurrection, but not in immortality as Christ understood it. For Him newness of life meant more than a return to life, for however long; it meant a new order of life and love. But for them it only meant a better chance for the old passion; it meant just making good the damage in earth's disappointments; it did not necessarily mean a higher stage of aspiration, or a change of quality in the desire. They need not be born again, as even their best, like Nicodemus or Hillel, must from Christ's point of view. Their divine future meant but the happier perpetuating of such national and social ambitions as filled the horizon of many a zealot in his public career. Christ thought of a new heaven and earth; they thought of a smooth-running repristination, the restoring of dominion to Israel. He thought of immortality as a worship; they thought of it as a reward, the return to them, repaired, of what death had taken away. For Christ the true resurrection and the true immortality meant a new ethic born of the spirit; for them it was worldliness reestablished and endowed, with security of tenure.

(Ibid., pp. 104-107.)

BIBLIOGRAPHY

Selected Works by P. T. Forsyth

Religion in Recent Art. Manchester, 1889.
"Revelation and the Person of Christ," *Faith and Criticism.* London, 1893.
"Mystics and Saints," *Expository Times*, V, 1894.
The Charter of the Church, London, 1896.
Intercessory Services for Aid in Public Worship. Manchester, 1896.
The Holy Father and the Living Christ. London, 1897.
The Happy Warrior. London, 1898.
Christian Perfection. London, 1899.
Rome, Reform and Reaction. London, 1899.
"The Slowness of God," *Expository Times*, XI, 1900.
The Atonement in Modern Religious Thought. London, 1900.
The Taste of Death and the Life of Grace. London, 1901.
"The Power of the Resurrection," *The Examiner*, April 11, 1901.
Holy Christian Empire. London, 1902.
"The Problem of Forgiveness in the Lord's Prayer," *The Sermon on the Mount. A Practical Exposition of the Lord's Prayer.* Manchester, 1903.
"The Reality of Grace," *Hibbert Journal*, IV, 1905.
"The Evangelical Churches and the Higher Criticism," *Contemporary Review*, LXXXVIII, 1905.
"Christian Aspects of Evolution," *London Quarterly Review*, October, 1905 (published separately, London, 1950).
"Authority and Theology," *Hibbert Journal*, IV, 1905.
"Revelation and the Bible," *Hibbert Journal*, IV, 1906.
"A Rallying Ground for the Free Churches," *Hibbert Journal*, IV, 1906.
"The Place of Spiritual Experience in the Making of Theology," *Christian World Pulpit*, March 21, 1906.
"Immanence and Incarnation," *The Old Faith and the New Theology* (ed. Charles H. Vine). London, 1907.

Socialism, the Church and the Poor. London, 1908.

Missions in State and Church. London, 1908.

"The Distinctive Thing in Christian Experience," *Hibbert Journal,* VI, 1908.

"What is Meant by the Blood of Christ?" *The Expositor,* VI, 7th Series, 1908.

Introduction to J. Monro Gibson, *The Inspiration and Authority of Holy Scripture.* London, 1908.

Positive Preaching and the Modern Mind. London, 1909; Grand Rapids, 1964 (pb.).

"The Insufficiency of Social Righteousness as a Moral Ideal," *Hibbert Journal,* VII, 1909.

"The Faith of Jesus," *Expository Times,* XXI, 1909-1910; comment on Adolf Schlatter, *New Testament Theology.*

The Cruciality of the Cross. London, 1948 (reprint of 1909 ed.); Grand Rapids, 1965 (pb.).

The Person and Place of Jesus Christ. London, 1955 (reprint of 1909 ed.); Grand Rapids, 1965 (pb.).

The Work of Christ. London, 1952 (reprint of 1910 ed.).

The Power of Prayer (with Dora Greenwell). London, 1910.

"Orthodoxy, Heterodoxy, Heresy, and Freedom," *Hibbert Journal,* VIII, 1910.

Christ on Parnassus. London, 1911; 1959.

"Christ and the Christian Principle," *London Theological Studies.* London, 1911.

Faith, Freedom, and the Future. London, 1912; 1955.

Marriage: Its Ethic and Religion. London, 1912.

"Self-denial and Self-committal," *The Expositor,* IV, 8th Series, 1912.

The Principle of Authority. London, 1913; rev. ed. London, 1952.

Theology in Church and State. London, 1915.

The Justification of God. London, 1916; rev. ed. London, 1948, with a foreword by D. R. Davies.

The Christian Ethic of War. London, 1916.

"Church, Ministry, and Sacraments," *The Validity of the Congregational Ministry* (with J. V. Bartlet and J. D. Jones). London, 1916.

The Soul of Prayer. London, 1916; Grand Rapids, 1965 (pb.).

"The Conversion of the 'Good,'" *Contemporary Review,* June, 1916.

The Church and the Sacraments. London, 1917; rev. ed. London, 1947; reprinted 1953, with a Note by Mrs. Jessie Forsyth Andrews and a Preface by Canon J. K. Mozley.

Congregationalism and Reunion. London, 1917; 1952.

The Roots of a World-Commonwealth. London, 1918.

This Life and the Next. London, 1918.

"Reconstruction and Religion," *Problems of Tomorrow* (ed. F. A. Rees). London, 1918.

"Unity and Theology," *Towards Reunion.* London, 1919.

"Religion and Reality," *Contemporary Review,* May, 1919.

"The Foolishness of Preaching," *Expository Times,* XXX, 1919.

God the Holy Father. London, 1957 (reissue).
Revelation Old and New (ed. John Huxtable). London, 1962.
The Church, the Gospel and Society. London, 1962.

WORKS ON P. T. FORSYTH

Andrews, Jessie Forsyth, "Memoir," published in the 1952 ed. of Forsyth's *The Work of Christ*.

Barth, Markus. "P. T. Forsyth: The Theologian for the Practical Man," *Congregational Quarterly*, October, 1939.

Bradley, W. R. *P. T. Forsyth, The Man and His Work*. London, 1952.

Brown, R. A. *P. T. Forsyth, Prophet for Today*. Philadelphia, 1952.

Escott, Harry. *Peter Taylor Forsyth*. London, 1948.

Glover, W. B. *Evangelical Non-Conformists and Higher Criticism in the Nineteenth Century*. London, 1954.

Griffith, G. O. *The Theology of P. T. Forsyth*. London, 1948.

Gummer, S. "Peter Taylor Forsyth: A Contemporary Theologian," *London Quarterly Review and Holborn Review*, October, 1948.

Hughes, P. E. "Forsyth: Theologian of the Cross," *Christianity Today*, December 23, 1957.

Hughes, T. H. "A Barthian Before Barth?" *Congregational Quarterly*, July, 1934.

———. "Dr. Forsyth's View of the Atonement," *Congressional Quarterly*, XVIII, January, 1940.

Leembruggen, W. H. "P. T. Forsyth: A Theologian of the Cross," *Reformed Theological Review*, Melbourne, 1945.

Mikolaski, Samuel J. "The Theology of P. T. Forsyth," *Evangelical Quarterly*, XXXVI, 1, 1964.

———. "P. T. Forsyth on the Atonement," *Evangelical Quarterly*, XXXVI, 2, 1964.

———. "P. T. Forsyth," *Creative Minds in Contemporary Theology* (ed. P. E. Hughes). Grand Rapids, 1966.

Rodgers, John H. *The Theology of P. T. Forsyth*. London, 1965.